North American
INDIANS
The Life and Culture of the Native American

North American
INDIANS
The Life and Culture of the Native American

Norman Bancroft Hunt

Illustrated by Michael Codd

Brian Trodd Publishing House Limited

ACKNOWLEDGEMENTS

The author wishes to extend his thanks to Ian West, Mike Johnson and Astrid Giese for their invaluable assistance.

Original artwork by Michael Codd

Maps by Norman Bancroft Hunt

American Museum of Natural History: 97; British Museum: 186; Denver Art Museum: 98, 100; Cambridge University Museum: 40; Feder/ Smithsonian: 109; Images 2–3; Museum of New Mexico: 68–69, 80–81; Museum of the Great Plains: 84, 141, 156, 164, 204–205; Peter Newark's Western Americana: 13, 29, 36, 42 left, 42 right, 44, 45, 108, 144, 148, 153 top, 172, 182, 184–185, 208, 218–219; Eric Spiegelhalter: 10; Werner Forman Archives: 6–7, 12, 14, 16 top, 17, 18, 21, 22, 26, 28, 32 top, 32 bottom, 33, 34, 38, 53 top, 53 bottom, 56, 57, 60, 61, 64, 65, 77, 82, 86, 89 below, 92 top, 92 bottom, 94, 101, 102, 110, 113, 117, 118, 120, 121, 122, 126, 129, 130, 132 top, 133, 134, 136, 138, 140, 145, 146, 150, 153 bottom, 154, 158, 161, 162, 165, 166, 168, 177, 180, 184, 188 bottom, 189, 190, 192, 193 top, 193 bottom, 194, 196, 197, 198, 202; Western History Collections, University of Oklahoma Library: 152.

Published in 1991 by
Brian Trodd Publishing House Limited
27 Swinton Street, London WC1X 9NW

ISBN 1 85361 225 1

Printed in Italy
by Offset Invicta Spa
Limena (Padova)

CONTENTS

Cliff Palace in Mesa Verde was built by the Anasazi ancestors of the Pueblo people. The remarkable number of large circular kivas, or ceremonial chambers, suggests that Cliff Palace was a centre of ritual significance for many small outlying groups of the region.

INTRODUCTION

The Indians of North America occupy a unique place in the imaginations of both young and old, and the image of the warrior mounted on his painted pony, feather headdress flying, gun held high is so popular and familiar that, for many, it epitomizes what American Indian life was about.

Such an image is, however, a misleading one. It is 'Indian' in a very restricted sense, since it applies only to the young men of particular Plains tribes from a relatively recent date and is dependent on two elements, the horse and the gun, that were introduced by Europeans. Furthermore, the lifestyle of this warrior of the popular myth excludes the majority of the population: the women, children and the elderly. The view that he sums up what Indian life was like results in a failure to see beyond the stereotype of the person behind the myth.

In reality the Indians of the United States and Canada possessed a remarkably rich and varied culture: from fishermen on the Northwest Coast to farmers in the Southeast; from the agriculturalists of the Southwest to subsistence hunters of the northern Subarctic; and, of course, including the nomadic buffalo hunters of the Plains. To these we may add the Eskimo and Aleut who, though not strictly American Indian, are nevertheless part of the indigenous peoples of the northern continent.

American Indian populations lived in areas that ranged from the permanently frozen snow-driven wastes of the central and northern Arctic to the desert reaches of the Plateau and Barren Grounds, and which also encompassed the rich, deep grasslands of the Prairies, the oak forests of the Atlantic coast, rain forests of British Columbia, and the tropical swamplands of southern Florida.

Within these diverse environments they built the first multi-storied apartment buildings, carved the largest Native wood carvings known to man, dug 25-kilometre (16-mile) long irrigation systems in desert areas that enabled them to produce two crops a year, constructed earthen mounds with ground plans larger than the Great Pyramid in Egypt, and developed social systems that were to become the basis for the Constitution of the United States.

In the process of establishing these cultures, they invented the toboggan, sledge and snow goggles, the barbed fishhook, birchbark canoe and laced snowshoes, and the toggle harpoon; they cultivated tobacco, potatoes, tomatoes and maize, all of which were unknown in the Old World; and they initiated such North American institutions as popcorn, maple syrup, and turkey Thanksgiving dinners. The early colonists were dependent on Native populations not only for provisions, to which they almost certainly owed their survival, but also for knowledge of the plants and herbs that would cure their sick. In this respect the American Indian shaman or medicine man was at least the equal of his European physician counterpart.

Coupled with their achievements in the material, social and healing arts, the Native Americans evolved a spiritual relationship to, and a sacred reverence for, the forces of nature and the powers inherent in the world about them. They had a deep concern for the animals and other resources they depended upon and an understanding of human responsibilities that are only now being recognized by the industrialists and politicians of the technological societies.

For many tribes, their history since the arrival of the white man has been a sad one. Much has been lost, and many books have been written delineating these losses and offering apologetic responses for what 'we' did to 'them'. This book is not one of those. The Indians are, and have always been, survivors. They have accepted and assimilated many new ideas throughout their long histories, without losing their own sense of being, and a consciousness of their place in a wider scheme of things. This characteristic, always central to Indian thinking in both individual and tribal senses, is becoming increasingly important in the Pan-Indian movements of contemporary societies. To write solely of the Indian of the past would be as misleading as to talk of the mythical warrior with which this introduction began. This book, therefore, is dedicated to the achievements of the Native Americans, and is written in honour of many Indian friends who carry these ancient beliefs and ideals forward into a modern world.

THE FIRST AMERICANS

Christopher Columbus discovered America in 1492, but it was not until 15 years later that Amerigo Vespucci named the continent *Mundus Novus* – the New World.

Both, however, were wrong. America had been discovered many thousands of years before Columbus glimpsed its shores, and for the people who lived there, the continent was very, very old indeed. Just how old is difficult to know with any certainty, since dating the arrival of the first people on the continent is far from straightforward, and often controversial.

The difficulty in determining a date and the reason for the controversy is that American archeology has until recently suffered from a kind of rigidity. A blind eye was turned to any suggestion which implied people had been on the continent for a long time. Many scholars put forward strong arguments for the view that the continent was totally unpopulated until about 8,000 years ago. Under different circumstances this might have been dismissed as far too recent; but it was supported by geological, physical and environmental

factors, and the lack of proof for a definitely earlier date meant that many academics were afraid to risk their reputations on what would have been considered wild supposition. Their reluctance is understandable. Powerful ultra-conservative elements, led by Ales Hrdlicka, ridiculed the more adventurous theories of some younger archeologists. That Hrdlicka and his adherents were often right in their attacks on obviously spurious claims was no consolation for those who proposed serious arguments in support of an earlier presence. To incur the wrath of these academic giants could easily damage a promising research career in the government service, or in the universities.

Hrdlicka had the First Americans coming from Asia in boats across the narrow strip of water between Siberia and Alaska which is now known as the Bering Strait. He dated this migration at not more than 8,000 years ago; but implied that it was more likely to have been as recent as 4,000 years ago. Serious doubt was first cast on his theories by the chance discovery, in the rather wonderful location of a curio shop in Ketchikan, of a spear

The Yukon River originates east of the Rocky Mountains and runs back to the Bering Sea. Its valley was unglaciated for much of the Pleistocene Ice Age and would have provided a relatively easy route of entry for the earliest migrants from Asia.

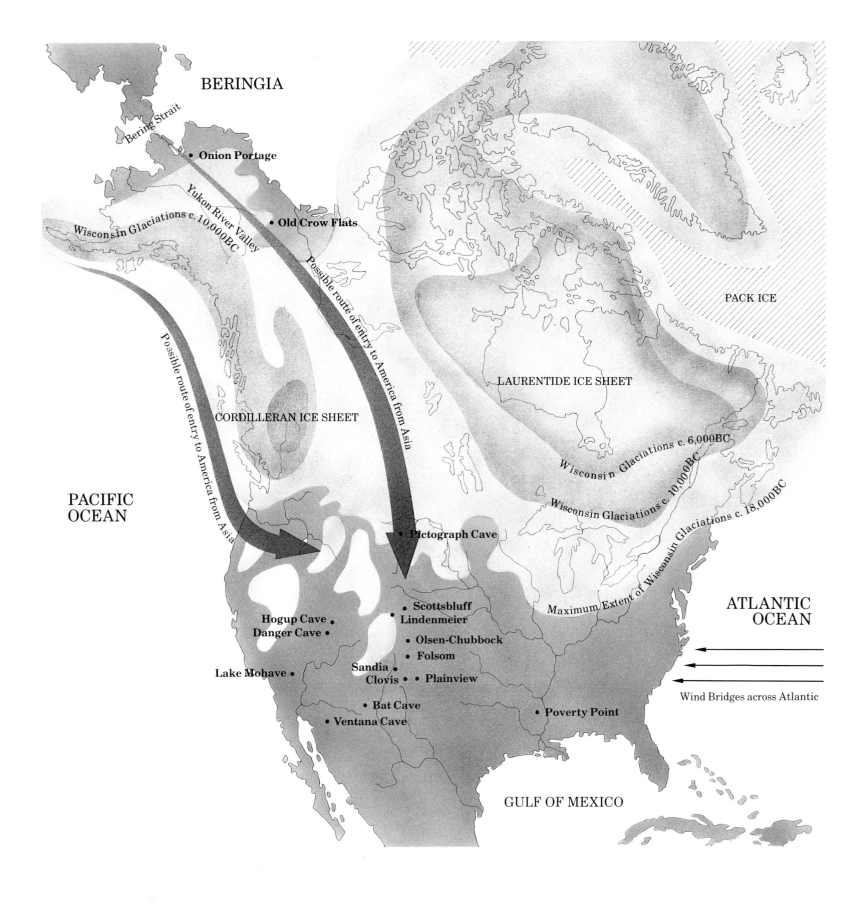

BERINGIA

Bering Strait

• **Onion Portage**

Yukon River Valley

Wisconsin Glaciations c. 10,000BC

• **Old Crow Flats**

Possible route of entry to America from Asia

Possible route of entry to America from Asia

PACK ICE

LAURENTIDE ICE SHEET

CORDILLERAN ICE SHEET

PACIFIC
OCEAN

Wisconsin Glaciations c. 6,000BC

Wisconsin Glaciations c. 10,000BC

Wisconsin Glaciations c. 18,000BC

• **Pictograph Cave**

Maximum Extent of Wisconsin Glaciations c. 18,000BC

ATLANTIC
OCEAN

• **Scottsbluff**
Lindenmeier

Hogup Cave •
Danger Cave •

• **Olsen-Chubbock**

• **Folsom**

Lake Mohave •

Sandia •
Clovis •

• **Plainview**

Wind Bridges across Atlantic

• **Bat Cave**
• **Ventana Cave**

• **Poverty Point**

GULF OF MEXICO

point that had been collected in Alaska and which was estimated to be about 10,000 to 12,000 years old. Then, in 1926, scientists from the Denver Museum excavating a site near Folsom, New Mexico, came upon a stone spear point embedded in the remains of an extinct species of Ice Age bison. The association of this point with the long-horned bison was proof that people had been in the

Americas at a considerably earlier date than the conservatives claimed; although Hrdlicka himself was to remain unconvinced and continued to argue for a recent presence until well into the 1940s.

A series of discoveries of similar Folsom-type points at other sites, and of an even older type known as Clovis, prompted archeologists to search

Map showing the maximum extent of the Wisconsin glaciations and indicating possible routes of entry to North America for early nomadic hunter-gatherers.

11

These Paleo-Indian chert blades from the Eastern Woodlands date to 7,000 BC and show superb technical skill in their manufacture. When in use they were bound to wooden spear shafts by narrow strips of hide or sinew. The largest blade shown here is approximately 10 cm (4 inches) in length.

for earlier possible migration routes. Glaciologists were only too happy to supply the necessary evidence. Their researches indicated that the Wisconsin glaciation, which marked the end of the Pleistocene Ice Age in America, locked sufficient water in the polar ice cap to lower sea level in the Bering Strait area considerably. Waters here are shallow, and the lowering of their level through the withdrawal of water to form the glaciers left a broad grass and tundra plain at least 320 km (200 miles) in width, connecting Asia and America. At the height of the glaciation, this plain extended to as much as 1,600 km (1,000 miles) wide, creating a land known as Beringia, in which Alaska was more properly part of the Asian than the American continent.

As far as the glaciologists were concerned, early man could simply have walked from one continent to the other. Massive ice sheets up to 3,000m (10,000 feet) high on the American side blocked passage to the north; but the Yukon River valley was ice free, and was believed to connect with another ice free passage east of the Rocky Mountains which then ran south right into the heartland of the continent. Access to the central areas would have been relatively easy for bands of pedestrian nomadic hunters.

Fortuitous circumstances – what we might more simply call luck – placed the estimated dates of the Folsom points and the Wisconsin glaciation close together, and the association with the bones of Ice Age animals proved conclusively that people were in the Americas before the extinction of these mammals. Archeologists had found what they were looking for: the advent of man in America was pushed back to the close of the Pleistocene, some 12,000–14,000 years ago. According to this scenario, the Paleo-Indians – the precursors of modern populations – were depicted as of Asian type, entering America accidentally in small hunting bands in pursuit of game, and bringing with them an already developed culture.

It was to prove a deceptively simple solution. In the 1950s there were significant improvements in radiocarbon dating techniques, which measure the amount of radioactive carbon lost at a constant rate from organic material once growth stops. Samples taken at a number of sites suggested that even 14,000 years was far too conservative. 37,000–38,000 years ago was indicated for sites in Texas and in Alberta, Canada. Another Texan site and one in the Canadian Yukon yielded dates of 27,000 years. Mexico gave 23,000 years; Peru 20,000 years.

Some scholars reject these dates, claiming they refer to a period for which we know radiocarbon methods can be unreliable. The most recent linguistic research does, however, confirm the general trend indicated by the radiocarbon samples. This research, which is based on the theory that diversification of language in a historic area is an indicator of the time that has elapsed since the area was first populated, suggests a human presence in the Americas of at least 35,000 years but probably for considerably longer.

A claim for far greater antiquity has been made as a result of the discovery of relics of obviously human origin beneath a Canadian glacial moraine that was laid down in excess of 80,000 years ago. It has proved impossible to verify this date by other means, and it is very likely that the relics are intrusive ones from a more recent period which have been relocated through earth movements. That people were in the Americas so early is an intriguing possibility; but it is nevertheless highly improbable, since if they had been there we should expect to find some indication for an archaic, or pre-modern, population, but there is no evidence for this. All the very early human occupants of the Americas appear to be *Homo sapiens sapiens*, a form we believe to have evolved about 50,000 years ago.

Amid this mass of dates and academic argument, there is general agreement that the First Americans came in large part from Asia and that they did so in the region of the Bering Strait. This is based on similarities in tool-making traditions, on physical type, and on cultural and linguistic affiliations, even though none of these would apply to our earliest American dates, which are so far back in antiquity that they remove the possibility of making such direct comparisons with a more recent culture. The Bering Strait is, however, the only obvious area which is geographically

suited to this kind of migration. While it is perhaps too much of an assumption to reconstruct early prehistoric movements from what we know of more recent times, since there are definite historic exchanges between Asia and America, agreement for the Bering Strait route as the most likely means of entry to the Americas is so strong that it is generally accepted.

Suggestions have been made for other possible routes of entry. The most popular among these are 'wind bridges' across the Mediterranean and the middle Atlantic, by which storm-blown vessels were driven off course and swept on to the American coast. Other people have asserted that the Polynesians were capable of making such voyages. Although these routes may sometimes have been used, the technology for extensive sea travel was unlikely to have been developed enough to explain the populating of the entire continent at the remote dates under consideration. A few pseudo-academic theories involving Vikings, Egyptians, the Irish and Welsh, or even the Ten Lost Tribes of Israel, can be readily dismissed, if only for the simple reason that the First Americans are clearly more ancient than any of these.

One thing we can be fairly confident of is that population movements more than 10,000 or 12,000 years ago probably took place on dry land or across ice. Glacial periods and the possibilities of land bridges connecting the continents can,

Deer effigy figures made from split twigs are occasionally found in remote caves in the Grand Canyon region. Their specific function is unknown, but they are likely to have featured in hunting rituals.

Far right: Hunting
mammoths required
cooperative skills, whereas
earlier hunting patterns had
depended on individual
abilities. The mammoth,
however, was too big an
animal for a single hunter to
overcome. This larger
quarry meant that a number
of hunters had to work
together, and with this came
an increased awareness of
leadership skills and the
development of more
complex patterns of social
organization. The hunters
shown here have chased the
mammoth into a swamp,
where it has become mired
and unable to escape.

therefore, be considered briefly to see whether they confirm any of the dates that have been reached by other means.

For most of the Pleistocene, passage into continental America was blocked by ice sheets in Alaska. Travel on these, though not easy, was possible, yet the absence of game animals or other means of sustenance rules them out as migration routes. There are, in fact, only three periods when conditions were suitable. The most recent is 14,000 years ago. The next earliest was between 25,000 and 28,000 years ago. If any earlier than this, it had to be longer than 33,000 years ago.

The bulk of the evidence increasingly suggests a first presence of between 35,000 and 40,000 years ago, with successive later migrations. Even if the earlier date is discounted, it is still apparent that there must have been a human presence in the Americas at least during the latter stages of the Pleistocene Ice Age. To put this into perspective, it means that the Paleo-Indians, from whom at least some historic American Indians can claim direct descent, were entering America so long ago that it was before *Homo sapiens sapiens* had diversified into the modern physical types we refer to as Mongoloid, Negroid and Caucasoid. It was a very early period indeed.

But who were these people, and what must their lives have been like? The term 'Ice Age' immediately conjures up visions of towering mountains of ice, driven snow, sleet blizzards, and bitter cold. We picture people wrapped in furs huddled in caves close to small fires in an attempt to keep warm, venturing outside only to spear some giant shaggy-haired animal that had become trapped in a snow drift. We are, nevertheless, giving our imaginations too free a rein. The conditions described above were true only of the polar ice cap, which was larger than today and where neither

people nor animals lived.

In the populated areas, although the landscapes would have been unrecognizable to the modern traveller, the environments were not inhospitable. Summers were a little cooler than today, but contrary to popular opinion, winters were warmer and shorter. All of southern central North America, together with parts of the west that are now desert, was deep grassland. Huge forests, mainly of oak in the south and conifers to the north, covered the eastern seaboard and extended across all the modern southern states. In the north, between the grasslands and forests and the southern limit of the glaciers, and thence extending southwards on the western slopes of the Rocky Mountains, there was either tundra or vast meadowlands that were rich in vegetation, brilliant with flowers, and teeming with wildlife.

Many of the Ice Age animals were ones we are familiar with; among them the pronghorn antelope, the ground squirrel, and the ubiquitous rabbit, as well as many smaller mammals, reptiles, birds, fishes and shellfish. Other animals would seem a little stranger, and generally a little bigger. Mammoths foraged in the grasslands, while their close cousins the mastodons, with tusks adapted for rooting in tangled undergrowth, maintained healthy numbers in the forest areas. Sabre-toothed tigers, larger and more powerful than any living feline, preyed on the forest giants. There were dire wolves, several species of Ice Age bison that dwarfed their modern counterparts, woolly rhinoceros, and four-horned antelopes that stood about as high as a man and which shared part of their range with various herds of prehistoric horses and camels.

Plant life, too, shows an astonishing variety, with great numbers of highly nutritious seeds, berries, nuts, fruits, roots and tubers. Far from being a barren waste, Ice Age America was an ideal environment for people who were hunters and gatherers. Small hunter-gatherer bands flourished and prospered. They formed no permanent settlements, nor did they remain in specific locations for extended periods.

Each of these hunting bands was probably a family group, numbering perhaps 8 to 12 people who were quite closely related either by blood or through some kind of marriage or other exchange. They formed a small and widely scattered population that was constantly on the move in pursuit of antelope, horse and camel; a diet which they supplemented with smaller animals, such as rabbits, and with insects, grubs and birds' eggs, as well as with the seeds, roots and berries they gathered near their camp sites.

It is unlikely that there was anything more than very occasional contact between these groups, and most of these meetings were probably friendly since we find no evidence to suggest these people were particularly aggressive. Sudden and profound changes or upheavals were not a feature of their lives. Each generation lived in much the same way as the generation before, or the generation before that; yet each of them made subtle alterations. They moved across the next hill and into another valley, discovered that holding a flint

This Folsom spear point is
10,000 years old and is
probably the finest example
of stone chipping known
from either the Old or New
Worlds. It is only 45 mm
(1¾ inches) in length, and is
made from banded chert
that may have been obtained
in trade. Fluting on the
blade meant the wounded
animal would bleed freely,
permitting easier tracking
and ensuring the quarry
would quickly tire from loss
of blood.

Bannerstones and birdstones were strapped to the flexible shafts of *atlatls*, or spear-throwers, to give added spring to the shaft; thereby improving accuracy and incrasing the velocity of the thrown spear. The examples shown here date to 1500 BC.

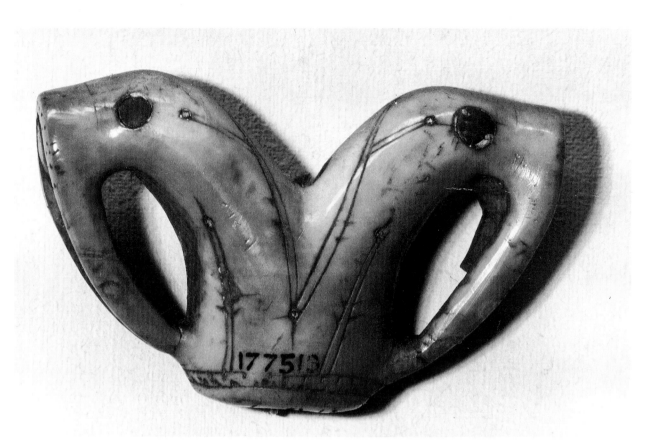

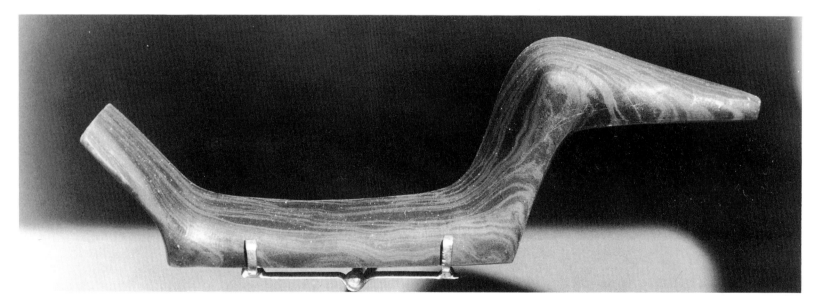

in a certain way made chipping a point a little easier, or found that the animals they depended upon had moved to a different watering place a few miles distant and followed their tracks to a new homeland. They were not engaged in conscious or wholescale migrations; even so, there was an almost imperceptible but inexorable movement forward. Over a period of thousands of years it was to result in the populating of the entire American continent.

By 12,000 years ago or earlier, the Paleo-Indian hunter-gatherer communities were well established in North America, with their greatest concentration in the central regions. It was still a sparse occupation involving relatively few people, all of whom had a purely nomadic existence. This

lifestyle was to continue for the next 4,000 or so years, but during this period significant material and social progress was made which marks the beginning of an evolutionary process that was to lead to the great diversification found among American Indians of more recent times.

Instead of constantly moving on to new areas, family groups began to return to favoured localities; perhaps places with an abundance of a particular resource that could be 'harvested' at certain times of the year. The change was slight, yet it is indicative that these people were no longer opportunistic hunter-gatherers. They were planners, able to predict a yearly sequence of events; who knew when they would find ripe berries available at one camp site, and that a certain species of

game animal would migrate past another camp at a different time of year.

Forward planning of this kind made life more secure by avoiding the threat to the opportunistic hunter of being in the right place at the wrong time. It was also a prerequisite for ritual activity that was intended to influence future outcomes. It is likely that some kind of predictive shamanic role was evolving, and that dances and celebratory events among the Paleo-Indians were being held to affect future results directly. Prehistoric rock art certainly depicts instances of hunters using ritual to ensure success, but these are notoriously difficult to date, and many of them may belong to later periods.

There is evidence that about this same time some of the small family groups were joining together during the spring and early summer migrations for the express purpose of hunting larger animals, such as the mammoth. Tackling an animal so big was beyond the resources of the smaller bands, which had an insufficient number of hunters. By cooperating with others they were able to overcome these giant creatures, and mammoth became an important food resource on the plains. Bands in the forests were developing similar skills in cooperative hunting of the mastodon; those in the west, where the larger animals were absent, continued their ancient tradition of small game hunting and gathering or in coastal areas, began to develop marine economies.

The question of why large game should be hunted when smaller animals were plentiful is easily answered. To survive on a diet of rabbits, a hunter would need to kill several each day to feed even a small family. A mammoth would suffice for several such families over a considerable period of time, until the meat spoiled. The larger the kill, the more efficient it was in terms of the time and energy expended in securing food. Small game and birds were still hunted, though less intensively, to vary the diet, and to maintain a supply of furs and feathers for clothing and other manufactured goods.

Large game hunting required extremely careful planning and coordinated action if it was to be successful. Organization of the bands therefore became more complicated, and certain individuals with an aptitude for planning and proven competence must have gained status as leaders of hunts. It is unlikely that these people enjoyed any particular authority at other times, their status was equated with their proven skills in specialized areas of activity.

As well as good planning, mammoth hunting created the need to process greater quantities of information accurately. To inform members of one's own family that bushes bearing abundant berries are to be found in the next valley is a relatively simple task. To convey to a number of disparate bands that mammoth have been located in the area, that they should gather at some specific place at a certain time, and to give detailed instructions to the individual participants as to the roles they should play and the strategy for the hunt is a far more complex process. Because of the need to process more detailed information, language skills improved. Vocabularies increased, and the languages themselves became more diverse – eventually to separate into an estimated 500 to 1,000 mutually unintelligible languages for the North American continent alone. With this diversification in language came the need for more advanced and complex forms of signalling and message-bearing devices.

The increase in efficiency and communications made the people's lives more comfortable. They were better fed and better clothed, more elaborate

Far right: This illustration shows a family group crossing the Bering Strait at the close of the Pleistocene Ice Age. Although they were not consciously migrating from one continent to another, small groups such as this wandered over the tundra and grass plain exposed in the Bering Strait area by the lowering of sea levels as water was taken up to form glaciers. They were opportunistic hunter-gatherers, who relied on catching small game and gathering whatever roots and berries they might find. Their possessions were few, and everything they owned was carried with them.

These winged bannerstones take their name from the shape in which they are carved, and from the fact that they were originally thought to have been erected on poles as banners, or emblems, of clan groups. Unlike the examples on page 16, many of those displayed here are pierced to facilitate fastening to the *atlatl* shaft.

social institutions were able to develop, and more leisure time was available to spend on things that were not immediately necessary for survival. This allowed exploration and experimentation through which technological skills were greatly refined. In addition to these improvements and probably the introduction of more complex and detailed types of ritual and ceremony, this period also shows that specialist occupations were being recognized, and that rudimentary forms of leadership were evolving. The beginnings of tribal structures, what we may think of as tribal prototypes, were therefore starting to emerge.

At the height of the Paleo-Indian period the Ice Age in America was drawing to a close. The people of the time would have noticed no immediate differences or rapid changes in climate or availability of game and other resources, but the environments were nonetheless altering quite radically.

Summers were becoming slowly warmer; winters cooler and longer. Higher temperatures in the central regions caused a gradual drying out, with the result that much of the deep grassland, particularly in the western parts, was replaced by shorter and tougher grasses, while that on the western periphery became desert. In the east the tree line moved north, following the retreat of the glaciers. As the conifers established themselves at higher latitudes, the areas they vacated were covered by deciduous forest and mixed tree

18

cover. Some of the former meadowlands became tundra, and a rise in sea level flooded coastal areas to alter the coastlines and create numerous small islands.

These climatic and environmental changes initially affected the larger browsing animals, whose foraging areas were both substantially altered and significantly reduced. Mammoth and mastodon suffered a decline, which was accelerated by longer, colder winters which meant an increase in infant mortality. Isolated pockets of these animals were to linger for several hundred years more, but the larger herds disappeared. With this loss, the survival of the carnivores that preyed on them also came under threat.

One by one the mammoth, mastodon, sabre-toothed tiger, woolly rhinoceros, prehistoric camel, giant ground sloth, dire wolf, cave bear, and several species of Ice Age bison found they were unable to survive in the new land that was being created. The prehistoric horse escaped extinction by migrating into Asia, where it may previously have been unknown, long before the final retreat of the glaciers closed the Bering Strait land bridge; but the remnants of the herds in America disappeared. When the Spanish reintroduced horses to America in the sixteenth century, they were, in effect, returning them to their original homeland.

Man was more adaptable than these animals, able to survive in environments as different as the Arctic and the Tropics, but by about 10,000 years ago the decline of the larger mammals had reached the point where they were no longer a viable food source for the Paleo-Indians. Mammoths had virtually vanished from the grasslands, and the hunters turned their attention to the bison instead. This was not the modern American bison, or buffalo, but a now extinct species, a larger and more formidable adversary whose horns spanned a width of 1.75m (6 feet).

In tackling this dangerous animal, they initially employed the same hunting techniques that had been used successfully against the mammoth. Bison were chased into bogs or swamps along the edges of the Ice Age lakes. Here they became mired and the thrusting spear and *atlatl*, or spear-thrower, could be used most effectively. This method was successful in providing for the needs of a few families; by the end of this period, however, the Ice Age bison was declining in numbers, to be superseded by massive herds of modern buffalo, and the bands were coalescing into much larger groups. Hunting methods changed accordingly.

Controlled stampedes were introduced, in which the hunters startled a herd into sudden flight. By placing people making loud noises and waving furs on the flanks of the herd, or even by setting fire to the prairie grasses so that the animals were driven before the blaze, the stampede could be directed towards an unavoidable natural obstacle, such as a cliff ledge, where the terrified animals, under pressure from the mass running behind them, plunged over the edge and to their deaths.

Buffalo jumps, as these cliff falls are popularly known, were ruthlessly efficient. In fact, their efficiency was such that the method was to remain virtually unchanged and in common use for hunting the modern buffalo in the plains area until the reintroduction of the horse. Later American Indians, working as large tribal units, utilized virtually the entire proceeds of such a hunt; but for the Paleo-Indians they resulted in a degree of overkill. The early hunters, though they knew how to preserve meat by smoking and drying, possessed no domesticated beasts of burden and were limited in the amount they could transport. As a consequence only the prime animals were skinned and butchered. The carcasses of the rest were left for the wolves, coyotes and jackdaws.

Artefacts associated with the remains of bison at these kill sites include finely worked jasper, flint and chert spearpoints, hide dressing tools of antler and bone, awls, engraving tools, incised bone fragments and small decorated stone tablets. Many of these still bear traces of red and yellow pigments. All the artefacts are very highly finished, and show a far higher level of workmanship and accomplishment than the flint points used by their predecessors against the mammoths. There is also an indication that the materials used in these manufactures, particularly for the spearpoints, were often obtained in trade, and that especially fine and rare stones – such as honey-coloured flint – were eagerly sought.

As bison hunting became firmly entrenched in the plains grassland areas, so changes in the bands' economy and way of life started to occur on the edges of the region where the environments were altering even more radically. 8,000 to 9,000 years ago, certain hunting bands in the western areas began returning so frequently to particular camp sites that they had, at the very least, a regular seasonal occupation. These people organized their year around moves from one camp site to another at fixed times, within a fairly well-defined band territory that was held more exclusively than the territorial ranges of the nomadic bison hunters.

At these sites, we find for the first time a number of milling stones, associated with villages scattered along the shores of a now dry lake, called Lake Cochise, in what is today New Mexico, Arizona and northern Mexico. These heavy stones could not be easily transported, so numbers of them were stored at each of the village locations where they were ready for use when the bands returned. In addition to maintaining a stock of milling stones, these people also began to store the excess part of their food resources and to place greater emphasis on the acquisition of other material goods, in the form of exotic stone and chert.

Soon after this (in terms of the very long time scales we have considered so far) there is evidence for settled occupation. These were the first farmers in America, who now turned their attention to conscious management of existing resources. That these farm sites were managed and not simply allowed to grow naturally is obvious from an analysis of seeds recovered from debris at the villages, which are larger than those from similar plants growing wild in the locality. According to

Eskimo hunters of 1,500 years ago carved and decorated these ivory points. The lightness and delicacy of the points suggests they were probably attached to bird spears rather than being used for hunting larger game.

botanists, this is a clear indication that selective planting was being practised.

From selective planting to the actual cultivation of crops, and early forms of agriculture, is only a short step. Indications soon appear for planted fields of pumpkins, beans and melons, followed at a slightly later date by corn, or maize, which, curiously enough, has no known wild ancestor. Even the earliest specimen of corn in North America, from Bat Cave in New Mexico, although primitive, is a hybrid. This has a radiocarbon date of 5,600 years ago; but it must be the product of a long period of experimentation and growing that stretches back many centuries before, to the ancestral form that we believe originated far to the south.

Lacking any form of native species that could be domesticated as a draught animal, North American agriculture developed around the hoe rather than the plough. Fields were small, mostly garden plots, and crops were mingled: even in the historic period, mixed plantings were made in which bean vines were supported by the stalks of corn. Such a method had one major advantage: the leafy growth of crops grown close together in this way shields the ground, and prevents weeds and soil disease, thus eliminating the need to tend the crop after planting. Initial clearing of the ground could be done by hand, planting could be done using a simple digging stick. The bands could then move to their other villages and engage in different activities while the crops were left to mature, returning to their fields in time for the harvest.

This suited the semi-nomadic existence of the

Far right: Climatic changes at the end of the Pleistocene resulted in the demise of the mammoth, and hunters turned their attention instead to the buffalo. Here, a herd of Ice Age buffalo have been deliberately stampeded towards a cliff, where the rush of animals at the rear has forced the leaders over the edge. Such buffalo jumps were an extremely efficient method of hunting, and provided sufficient food to enable family groups to merge together as tribes.

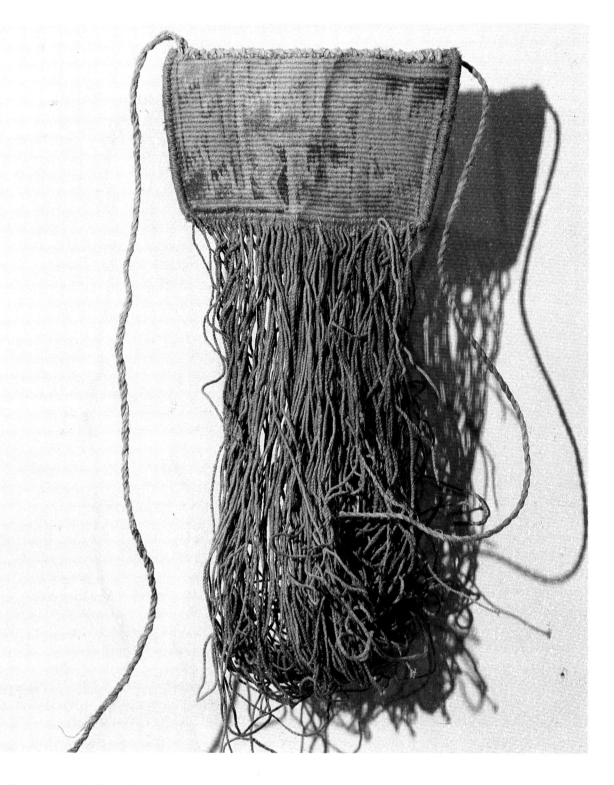

Early occupants of the Southwest region excelled in making products from rush and fibre. Most of these artefacts have long since perished, but a few, such as this fibre apron which would have been worn as a pubic covering by a Basketmaker woman from Mesa Verde, have been preserved in dry caves.

early farmers, and allowed time for the development of other skills. Fragments of basketry, textiles and paintings indicate that skilful artisans were at work, often embellishing their products with decorative designs and patterns that served no utilitarian purpose, and leaving us evidence for the very high level of material culture achieved during the Paleo-Indian period.

Among the artefacts are remains of baskets which had pitch painted on the inside surface, or which had been lined with clay. These can only have been intended to hold liquids. Such baskets would burn if placed over an open fire, but the presence of small pebbles near the hearths – and in some areas where pebbles were rare, the manu-

facture of clay balls – suggests that stone-boiling had been developed. In this process, stones are placed in a fire until they become red-hot, and are then dropped into the liquid. By alternately removing cooling stones and replacing them with hot ones, the contents can quite rapidly be brought to the boil.

The advent of stone-boiling and the significance this had for Paleo-Indian cultures is rarely given the attention it deserves. In some ways, it can be placed on a par with other cultural milestones like the introduction of agriculture, since its implications are far wider than the obvious fact of adding variety to the diet. Certain food products, the starchy grains for example, can only be prepared

by boiling them. This requires not only the technological skill to make watertight containers, but also a knowledge of plants, and the ability to cultivate specific species that can be used in this manner. Hot water was made available by stone boiling, which led to advances in dyeing techniques and the use of steam in the making of bent wood artefacts. It also made it possible to leach the poisonous tannins from crops such as acorns, which were to become a staple in some areas. Acorn meal bread was baked, which carries with it the implication that some form of oven must have been in use. Food could be prepared in advance and, in the case of soups and stews, was constantly available. This in turn, facilitated the practice of food-sharing as a means of ensuring greater social interaction and stability within the groups. This latter point was of particular importance to the later Paleo-Indians, since populations were expanding and the demands made on relatively limited resources led to increased competition. The larger, stable groups were better placed to exploit, and if necessary defend, the resources within their areas, and to maintain the integrity of their bands.

As a by-product, it was discovered that the clay linings of the baskets could be lifted free when dry, and used as containers in their own right. They were fragile, but the addition of binding material like grass or straw added strength. When these early populations started to replace the binding material with a non-burning substance, usually mica or shell, and began heating the trays to harden them they had invented rudimentary forms of fired pottery.

Similar developments were occurring elsewhere on the continent, as the people adjusted to their new environments. The expansion of the forests in the east attracted animals further north, and the hunters followed and established new communities around the Great Lakes, which had hitherto been buried beneath glacial ice. Here they found a readily available food source – the wild rice that grew abundantly in the shallow waters of the lake perimeters – and they also utilized the numerous fish species found in the lakes. Twisted fibre nets and specialized fishing gear, together with complex systems of lines and fish traps, water craft, and intricate hunting decoys characterize the cultural achievements of these people. Other forest groups started to build extensive trade networks, and the goods obtained through these often found their way, sometimes in enormous quantity, into elaborate burials that were frequently associated with massive earth mound constructions. Not everyone was accorded the same recognition at burial, if the quantity and rarity of the grave goods interred with the body can be used as an indicator. It is fairly certain that these societies were becoming highly stratified, with a clear hierarchy of individuals within the group.

Another centre of marine economy established itself along the British Columbia coast, with expressions of this culture extending into southern Alaska and also influencing the groups in the northern parts of California. Fish, particularly the salmon, formed a major part of these people's diet;

yet there was a strong dependence too on the use of sea mammals, which led to an ocean-going capability and the manufacture of dug-out canoes. Their culture was undoubtedly influenced by the presence of huge cedar trees, the primary constituent of what was becoming a typical rain forest environment. It is not surprising that the major cultural achievement in this area was to be the development of a very strong wood carving tradition that is perhaps unequalled anywhere else in the world.

By 3,500 years ago, at a fairly conservative estimate, the climatic shifts resulting from the cessation of the Pleistocene had settled into a stable pattern and the occupants of the North American continent had begun adapting to a variety of new environmental conditions, ranging from arctic to desert. This meant developing cultural patterns that cover virtually the entire range of human activity: there were fishermen and farmers, hunters, gatherers who survived on a meagre subsistence diet, and people who were laying the foundations for vast highly-organized city-states and confederacies. We do not know if these diversified societies came only from the early populations of perhaps 40,000 or more years ago, or whether the tremendous differences they cover are the result of successive migrations at later dates. Probably it is a little of both.

What we do know is that the New World Paleo-Indians were very distinct from their contemporaries in the Old World. They had independently invented skills in weaving, basketwork and pottery; their abilities in stone-working techniques and in the preparation of flaked arrow and spear points were certainly superior; they had cultivated several plant species that were unique, and can probably be credited with the development of the most ancient hybrid food plant. They were the first people to discover the use of leaching to remove poisons and make foods palatable, and their development of agricultural techniques is contemporary with the earliest Old World examples from Mesopotamia.

We can say with certainty that the Paleo-Indians were not primitive Stone Age men, as they are sometimes depicted; instead they were skilled, competent, closely attuned to the environments in which they lived, extremely varied, and already expressing the multi-faceted talents of the New World that the European colonists were to encounter at a later date.

THE EASTERN WOODLANDS

The Eastern Woodlands is a vast area defined by the Gulf of Mexico, the Atlantic coast, the St. Lawrence River and the Great Lakes, and an imaginary line running west of the Mississippi River. Its only true characteristic is that it is almost entirely forested; but the forest is far from constant in either type or density of tree. Severe winters and relatively low summer temperatures in the north combine with acidic soils to give mainly pines, although some hardwoods are found in localized areas. Oaks dominate in the central and southern regions, but there are also significant numbers of chestnuts, yellow poplars and hickories. In the southeast, where summers are very hot and winters mild, the tree cover consists of cypresses, tupelos, cottonwoods and red gum trees.

Such forest lands evoke a sense of permanence. The trees are deeply rooted and change takes place imperceptibly. They offer shade and protection, not only for plant and animal life but also for human populations, plus an abundance of resources. Even in the most severe circumstances, the Woodlands have an enveloping character that tends to shut out danger and uncertainty. In some

ways this creates a narrow perspective, because it is impossible to know what lies beyond nearby limits of vision; yet it also has a quality that encourages stability.

In keeping with the nature of the land, there is a long history of human occupation in the Woodlands that shows gradual rather than sudden change. A continuous line can be drawn from the early hunter-gatherers through the cultures of the Red Paint and Old Copper peoples of 4,000–5,000 years ago, who lived around the Great Lakes and in New England and the Maritime Provinces of Canada, down to the historic peoples of the region. At no point is there any clear demarcation between the end of one phase and the start of another. This does not mean that no change occurred, since each group built on and elaborated the social and cultural institutions of its predecessors; but it does mean that any division into culture periods is an arbitrary one that is convenient for archeologists, rather than a true reflection of Indian life in the area.

With time, this stability was to give rise to complex social systems, and large city-states and confederacies of tribes. The foundation for these was

This 33 cm (13 inch) wide snake was cut from a single sheet of mica by a Hopewell craftsman between 200 AD and 500 AD. The snake, or serpent, was a widely used symbol throughout the Americas, but the exact function and significance of these mica cut-outs is not known.

already being established by the Red Paint peoples, who had amalgamated into large groups with permanent villages, and among whom there are indications of sub-groups, or clans, claiming a common ancestry. Certain individuals, possibly clan leaders, were accorded particular respect, and at death their bodies were placed in log-lined tombs that had been painted with brilliant red hematite – an iron oxide that is the colour of blood. As populations increased, the power of the clans grew. Their influence spread into other areas, hastened by climatic changes around the Great Lakes, and their tombs became larger and more elaborate. 3,000 years ago, in southern Ohio and parts of West Virginia, Pennsylvania, Kentucky and Indiana, the people began piling earth on the tombs to form low mounds that were a more permanent marker for the deceased, gradually increasing these in extent until the mounds were surrounded by great earth embankments and ditches. To honour their dead still further, they imported native copper from Michigan and hammered this into bracelets, rings and gorgets which were intended as grave goods to accompany the deceased. At the same time they were developing skills in pottery and weaving, and starting to become dependent on cultivated crops of sunflowers, squash and maize.

The culture of these peoples, which for convenience we refer to as Adena, reached its height about 100BC; but all its traits were carried to further extremes in a later phase, called Hopewell, which lasted until about 800AD.

Hopewell mounds were bigger than anything that had been erected previously. Often 12m (39 ft) or more high and 30m (98 ft) across at the base, they were surrounded by earth embankments as much as 500m (1,600 ft) long, which were built in complicated arrangements of circles, squares, rectangles and octagons. The labour involved in building these must have been immense, since all the earth was carried in by the basket-load. Even today it is still possible to discern the faint imprint of a basket on the side of an embankment, where it is sheltered from the elements. Only a people who had a highly organized and co-operative society could have undertaken such a stupendous task.

Eventually the mounds began to take on new shapes, as naturalistic figures that may have served a function as clan markers. The most famous of these is the Great Serpent Mound in Ohio, where an earthen snake twists and coils sinuously along an exposed hilltop for a length of 400m (975 ft). Visible from a great distance, it is a majestic and impressive figure in which the earth itself becomes the representation of the clan, and reaffirms the people's link with their environment.

It was not only in mound and effigy building that the Hopewell peoples excelled, for their industriousness was applied to everything they did. Migrating populations established village communities in areas as distant from each other as the lower Mississippi, Kansas and upper New York State, although Ohio continued to be the main focus of the culture. The earlier Adena exchange routes were expanded into a vast trade network that covered virtually the entire North American continent. Obsidian came from the foothills of the Rocky Mountains, grizzly bear teeth from Wyoming, shells and shark and barracuda teeth from the Gulf Coast, and silver from Ontario.

All these materials were worked into exquisitely beautiful objects that were often made purely for show or as grave goods. Nuggets of silver were beaten out to a thin foil which could be applied to objects as diverse as axes and ear spools. Sheets of copper were embossed and painted as breastplates, or cut into sections which might be reassembled with fine copper wire to make masks and headdresses. Shell and bone was carved and incised, and sheets of mica, imported from the Appalachians, were used to make cut-outs of serpents and human hands.

Among the most beautiful objects they made are tubular stone pipes carved with animal effigies. On these a hawk swoops down with outstretched talons to catch its prey, or a jaguar crouches warily. Playful animals, such as the squirrel, scamper along the stems. A beaver squats on its tail, its paws raised up while it stares out at the world with an expression of extreme curiosity and interest. All these animals have a life and energy that denies the fact they are carved from stone, but reflects the perfect understanding their carvers had of animal behaviour, and the importance of tobacco and smoking rituals.

Tobacco was never smoked for pleasure. The plant was sacred, nurtured carefully and grown under ceremonial conditions; when the pipe was lit, its smoke carried upwards, thus uniting the powers of Sky and Earth. In this way it created a

bond of harmony between the physical and spiritual, acting as a symbol of peace and friendship. Hopewell traders always carried a pipe with them, which guaranteed their safety and was smoked before any trade took place to bring the parties together in peace and fair dealing.

So important was the pipe that its use, reinforced by the Hopewell trade links, became universal in North America. All tribes used native tobacco as an agent for purification and to seal bonds of friendship and alliance. Highly elaborate smoking rituals were often central to the performance of any act intended to promote well-being and security. Once the pipe had been smoked, the smoker was ritually bound by a sacred oath to refrain from acts of violence; even an enemy tribe respected these constraints, and a pipe-bearer could enter any village unmolested.

A gradual change started to occur in Woodlands' cultures about 400AD to 600AD. The Hopewell trade network declined and their influence, which had been ideological rather than expansionist, slowly gave way to a new expression that was not only expansionist but aggressive to the point where subjugated peoples came under the rule of colonizing groups. These people were concentrated along the rich river bottomlands in the southern part of the region, where a favourable climate and the introduction of a new strain of maize which would mature rapidly gave them a prosperity that could not be equalled further north.

Although this new development – which we know as Mississippian – owes its origins to the Adena-Hopewell people, it embodied beliefs that were unlike anything that had been expressed in the area before and which may be due to an influx of immigrant groups of Siouan-speaking peoples.

Under the Mississippians, towns grew to massive proportions – functioning essentially as city-states – to become administrative, political and religious centres. The town of Cahokia in Illinois, for example, contained over 100 mounds in an area exceeding 13 km^2 (5 sq miles). In spite of its great size, Cahokia is dominated by one feature: the immense Monk's Mound, with a base area exceeding that of the Great Pyramid in Egypt. Monk's Mound, like other mounds in the Mississippian context, was a flat-topped platform which supported a wooden temple. The town complex was surrounded by a palisaded wall with a defensive purpose, since not all other groups submitted readily to colonial intrusions. Beyond this were fields of cultivated crops with small hamlets and numerous scattered homesteads.

The rapid expansion of these aggressive groups was facilitated by the new strains of maize which were capable of supporting much larger populations. At the height of the Mississippian period population density had increased at least fivefold in comparison with that of Adena-Hopewell. It is significant that in the southern part of the Mississippian domains, where two harvests a year could be made and where population increase was

Although smoking rituals
were highly developed
throughout North America,
the carving of naturalistic
animal effigy pipes, such as
the one of a frog shown here,
was epitomized by the
Hopewell. This pipe is
unusual in that the animal
looks towards the smoker, as
in most carvings of this type
the animal faces in the
opposite direction.

Above: Map showing the
approximate locations of the
Eastern Woodlands tribes
when first encountered by
Europeans.

Far right: The Great Sun
was the undisputed leader of
the Natchez villages, and
was venerated as a demi-god
who was the human
incarnation of the life-giving
celestial Sun. He was able to
exert a despotic rule over his
people and could command
whatever he wished.

at its most intense, particularly aggressive forms
of expansionism took root.

The Southern Death Cult, a hierarchical
politico-religious movement, originated here. Cult
members wore distinctive regalia, and are often
depicted on items such as shell gorgets carrying
trophy heads from their slain victims. Temples
became surrounded by spiked poles on which the
heads of enemies could be displayed. Although
warfare may not have been continual, it was
certainly far from being infrequent.

Although the heyday of the Southern Death
Cult was over when the Spanish military expedi-

tion led by De Soto marched from Florida towards
the Mississippi in 1540AD, many of its beliefs
were still being practised by powerful tribes such
as the Natchez and Taensa. The Natchez, in particular, had gained a deadly reputation; yet they
halted De Soto's advance more by strategy than
force of arms.

Having heard that they worshipped the Sun, De
Soto felt he could make his presence immediately
felt by claiming to be the Sun's younger brother.
He had guessed rightly that stories of these
strange, bearded white men had preceded them to
the Indian villages, and that some tribes felt these

These shell gorgets were worn suspended on the breast by members of the Mississippian Southern Death Cult. The top gorget depicts the crested woodpecker, symbol of the warrior, protecting the four directions that surround a central sun. The spider on the other gorget bears a cross on its thorax, which represents the Mississippian sacred fire.

were reviled and that anyone who suffered at their hands provided an excuse for the Natchez to wage war. To this end they erected poles painted red and hung with red-dyed feathers in each of their towns. At the slightest provocation, warriors would rub red paint on to their arrows and clubs and strike the pole to indicate willingness to strike their foes in the same way. At the back of each Natchez man's mind was the constant thought that sooner or later he could deal the death blow to a hated Chickasaw.

The Chickasaws undoubtedly harboured similar feelings for the Natchez. They were about numerically equal, and had also driven De Soto from their territories. Neither the Natchez nor Chickasaw was inclined to give in easily to the other, and this characterizes the nature of warfare in the area. Both sides could field large armies, although pitched battles rarely took place and a decisive victory was only obtained by ambuscade. War nearly always took place between groups who could be thought of as equals, despite the rhetoric that each side employed.

As a direct consequence of their involvement in the Southern Death Cult, the Natchez had developed a complex social hierarchy. At the top of the social ladder was the Great Sun who, although human, was considered to be a demi-god. To ensure his constant elevation he was carried everywhere by a group of prominent warriors, supported aloft in a great litter with a state bed of goose-down, buffalo hides, and bear skins. He wore a swan feather headdress with scarlet tassels, and only respected older men could waken him in the mornings, by bowing low and whispering softly in his ear.

Once awake, he stepped to the door of his cabin to greet the Sun in the sky, of whom he was the personification on earth, before issuing a series of proclamations and orders covering any matters of note that would arise during the day. His was an absolute rule. He could demand whatever he wished and it would be immediately granted. So great was the respect he instilled in his people, that it is said a man who had spoken out of turn would willingly offer himself for execution and prostrate himself at the Great Sun's feet with a plea to be put out of the misery he suffered for having caused offence.

The Great Sun always lived in the principal village, residing in a large cabin atop a long mound. Close by was another mound bearing a second cabin, which had carved and painted wooden birds fastened to its roof, and the walls were hung with feathers. Entrance was forbidden to anyone other than the elder priests of the temple, and the Great Sun, who held the office of high priest. Inside, the priests tended a sacred fire of oak bark which burned continuously. Should the fire be extinguished, the Natchez would cease to exist, since the fire contained the spirit and warmth of the Sun from which the people drew breath. Only once a year, at the summer renewal ceremonies, was the fire put out and then rekindled so the annual cycle could begin again.

At the back of the temple, separated from the rest of the building by a partition screen, was the

must be a race of super-beings. Legend predicted the gods would return to the earth as white men who walked across the waters, and this was one thing the Spaniards had unwittingly managed to achieve. The Natchez were shrewder than De Soto imagined. After a short council they decided to test these strangers: if they were gods, then it would surely be a simple task for them to dry up the mighty Mississippi River. The Spaniards failed this test of their ingenuity, and the Natchez, under the leadership of Quigualtam, drove them from the area.

When De Soto met the Natchez they were living in several fortified towns in the lower Mississippi Valley. These towns consisted of a number of mud-plastered rectangular houses with curved roofs of bent saplings covered with thatch or bark. The whole town was surrounded by a palisaded fence of thick posts set vertically in the ground. At least two other townships were under their protection, as refugees from Chickasaw aggression. This was not an indication of Natchez benevolence; merely a reflection on the fact that the Chickasaw tribes

This deer mask, which may have been used by a shaman, comes from Mound Spiro in Oklahoma where the Mississippian Southern Cult reached its western limit.

The hairstyle and facial decoration of a Southern Cult participant are depicted on this Mississippian copper plaque, dating to 1,000 AD.

inner sanctum where the bones of previous Great Suns and other relics were kept in perpetual veneration. They belonged to the Sky, and could not be returned to the Earth by burial.

Even though the position of Great Sun was that of a king, Natchez social position actually ran through the female line, with the children of women of high status gaining rank above those of men of similar status. At the top of the hierarchy were the Great Sun and his immediate female relatives, who were classed as Suns. Next came the Nobles, a position usually inherited from the status of their mothers, and then Honoured People, who might achieve status through war or piety. Beneath them were the Commoners or Stinkards, people who were considered of inferior rank and importance, yet who must nevertheless have formed the larger part of the population. The only classification beneath that of the Stinkard was to be a slave, since the Natchez, in common with other groups of the area, adopted women and children from other tribes or captured them in war but gave them no status. Slaves were put to work in the fields but they were rarely treated harshly, and, in some communities, it is likely that they outnumbered the Natchez themselves.

The Great Sun and his female relative Suns were enforced by custom to marry Stinkards – a term so low in abuse that it was never mentioned to the Stinkards themselves for fear of causing grave offence. Yet, in this matriarchal system, the offspring from a female Sun and a male Stinkard would become Suns, and it was from among the children of the Great Sun's sisters that the heir to his throne would be chosen; whereas the children of a male Sun could never hope to rise beyond the status of Nobles.

In keeping with their ancestral links to the Southern Death Cult, there was an excessive concern with mourning ritual among the Natchez and other tribes of the region. This is perhaps best illustrated by the mortuary rites attending the death of a Great Sun, since it is here they were at their most extreme.

The rites began with a dance of death, accompanied by a great deal of weeping and wailing; hysteria appropriate to the loss of a god was shown by the women, who would cut off their hair and gash their arms and legs deeply. Some women, inconsolable in their grief, committed suicide; whereas others were driven by desperation to vent their sorrow on their families and to strangle their children. Such extremes can be understood, in the context that the Great Sun was the embodiment of the Natchez themselves, since it was through him that the Sun gave the people life. He was not considered to be a person, but was a link with a higher principle that governed and controlled every aspect of Natchez society. By strangling her children in an act of piety and remorse, the mother gave a personal sacrifice from which everyone would benefit; her children would accompany the Great Sun and continue to shower blessings on the people. In recognition of her personal loss she would later rise in status, and by this means a Stinkard mother could acquire the rank of a Noble.

Members of the Great Sun's family were destined to accompany him to the grave. Twice a day they were led out to form two lines in front of the temple, where they acted out the scene of their execution, accompanied by eight relatives who would be the executioners; and who, again because of the gravity of their action and the personal trauma involved, would thereby rise in status and exempt themselves from dying at the death of any future Great Sun.

Care of the Great Sun's children was handed over to others by his wives on the day of interment, and as the litter bearing his corpse was carried three times round his cabin and then brought to the temple, the bodies of sacrificed children were thrown to the ground at the feet of the corpse bearers. This procession was led by a priest wearing a red feather crown and a skirt of red and white feathers. His upper body was painted red, and he carried a red staff to which were attached strings of black feathers. Accompanying him was the oldest warrior of the tribe, bearing a war pipe. When the procession reached the temple, the priest carried the body of the Great Sun into the inner chamber and placed it beside the remains of former Great Suns; though it is probable that the body was then buried in the temple and the bones exhumed at a later date. His wives and other members of his household were drugged prior to being strangled by their relatives, and the ceremony was concluded by burning the Great Sun's cabin to the ground.

John White illustrated this tattooed chief from North Carolina in 1585. The tattoos depict tribal and clan affiliation, and were made by cutting incisions in the skin and then rubbing in a mixture of ash and berry juices.

The funeral of a Great Sun was, of course, a relatively rare occasion and the funerary rites for other individuals were scaled down according to the status they had enjoyed. Generally, the lower the status, the fewer the people who became directly involved and the smaller the number who would make any personal sacrifice on behalf of the deceased. At the end of the scale, the death of a slave was a matter of little consequence, and frequently did not even require the burial of the body.

This obsession with the twin themes of death and status is the most characteristic aspect of the southeastern tribes; but in order for it to be expressed there had to be a strong economic base to support it. Farming was of major importance, with huge fields of maize, millet, sunflowers, pumpkins, melons and tobacco stretching out beyond the palisades of the townships. Their skills in the material arts were also highly developed, to the extent that the Natchez were renowned for the softness of their dressed deerskins, the beauty of their turkey feather cloaks, and the exquisite quality and fineness of their bark and nettle weaving. Their pottery, too, was acclaimed as being the best in the region.

They were a tall, strong and impressive people, and the Nobles and Honoured People adopted a haughty manner that echoed their belief in their superiority over lowlier members of their own tribe and over all other tribes of the area. The men in particular presented a striking spectacle, with elaborate tattoos and mitred foreheads, the consequence of their mothers flattening the front of their skulls with a padded board when they were newly born, while the bones of the skull were still soft and malleable.

From the time of De Soto's visit until the arrival of the French in the early eighteenth century, the Natchez remained a powerful force in the area. In 1713 the French settled nearby, and a small trading post was established. Relationships were cordial. The French undoubtedly enjoyed the attention of Natchez girls who, contrary to European ideals, were encouraged to be sexually promiscuous before marriage, usually demanding payment from those on whom their favours were bestowed.

This cordiality was quickly to turn sour. From 1716 friction between the Natchez and French increased, until in 1729 – with the appointment of a new French commandant named Chépart who demanded the site of the Great Village itself for his plantation – there was a Natchez uprising. Over 200 Frenchmen were killed, and several hundred French women and children, and their Negro slaves, taken prisoner. As a sign of their utter contempt for Chépart, the Natchez warriors refused to raise their weapons against him and it was left to a Stinkard to beat him to death with a stick.

Within two years, however, French retaliation had destroyed the Natchez. 400 were sold into slavery in the West Indies in 1731. Their towns were razed and their warriors killed by French troops, who enlisted the help of the Natchez' Indian enemies – especially that of the Choctaw, who played a double game by agreeing to assist the Natchez and then suddenly turning against them. The remnants of the tribe scattered as small refugee bands to seek protection from other tribes wherever they might find it. Some even settled among their former enemies, the Chickasaw. Today, the name of the Natchez exists only as a place-name on the American map.

A similar fate befell other tribes of the southeastern area who came into early contact with the self-styled 'discoverers' of their lands. The Spaniard Ponce de Leon arrived off the coast of Florida in the spring of 1513, only to have his landing prevented by a fleet of 80 war canoes manned by Calusa Indians. He tells us nothing about these people, except to marvel at their bravery and the hostility with which he was greeted.

The Calusa, in the south, shared Florida with two other strong tribes: the Timucua in the central areas, and the Apalachee in the north. Of these the Timucua earned what we must consider a compliment as being the tallest, most muscular, and the most spectacularly tattooed; though whether they dominated neighbouring groups to the same extent as did the Calusa is not recorded. It is nevertheless clear that fighting was a way of life with them; early reports tell us that the men habitually grew their fingernails long and filed away the sides for the express purpose of wounding and blinding their enemies.

The Florida tribes were river dwellers and seafarers, with a propensity for undertaking long sea voyages in dug-out canoes for trade purposes. When Europeans first met them, they had established a regular trade with the inhabitants of Havana, where they were resisting the attempts of the Spanish to convert them, just as they had successfully prevented any Mississippian incursions into their territory. Many of the goods obtained through this trade were destined to become offerings at shrines erected near the villages, in order to placate or to seek favour from the various deities that were considered to control the weather or the seas.

Such offerings were placed at the order of the chief, on the advice of a council of elder men who had abilities as seers and prophets. He could, if he chose, ignore the advice he was given, and in this sense he had powers of leadership as an absolute ruler similar to those of the Natchez. Whether the Florida chiefs were as despotic is unlikely; but they were able to exert their authority with often cruel punishments. The arms of a Timucuan who had been negligent in carrying out his or her duties would be broken if the chief so decreed; and the French adventurer, Laudonnière, claimed to have been present on two occasions when watchmen who had fallen asleep were clubbed to death. Such punishments were undoubtedly harsh; yet anyone who did not do his or her share of the work threatened the stability of the group, and for a watchman to fall asleep could easily result in the burning of the village, and the massacre of its inhabitants by one of the warring groups in the vicinity.

There is no indication of sacrifices and suicides on the death of the chief, but there is a rather curious custom by which a group of women were

This deer head effigy comes
from Key Marco in Florida.
It dates to between 800 AD
and 1400 AD, and is one of
few wooden artefacts to have
survived from this region.

selected, and possibly paid in some form, to be official mourners. Their task was to lament and wail
for the departed at dawn, midday and twilight for
a period of six months, during which they kept
their hair cut short and wore no ornaments.

At other times, the Floridians dressed with an
elegance stunning for its simplicity. Men wore only
a palm leaf breechclout and tied their hair up in a
top-knot, but they supplemented this with quantities of bone and shell ornaments, and with
brightly coloured feathers of tropical birds that
glowed against the blue-black colour of their
tattoos. Women, too, had a profusion of ornaments
of shell and feather, and also wore through their
ears tiny fish bladders, which were inflated and
painted bright red. Their aprons, woven from tree
moss, had the delicacy of lace and the subtle
blue-green colour of the tropical forests and
swamplands, and often had long flowing fringes
interwoven with bright shell beads.

Villages were sited on rivers and ocean inlets,
where fish and shellfish could be caught from
canoes or trapped in weirs. Although these formed
the major part of their diet, they also planted
small fields within the village enclosures, and
hunted deer, birds and reptiles of various kinds.

Even the alligator was hunted for food. For the
alligator hunt, a stout branch was sharpened to a
point at one end. When the reptile opened its jaws
to attack, this pole was thrust into its throat so it
could be flipped onto its back, exposing the soft
and vulnerable underbelly. Food-obtaining activities generally produced a surplus which was
smoke-dried and placed in store-houses for future
needs.

The French, taking advantage of the Spanish
failure to establish themselves, started to build
forts here between 1562 and 1565. They received a
very different welcome from that of Ponce De
Leon, being cordially met by a Timucuan chief who
supplied them with provisions from the store-
houses in return for their promise to help him
wage war against a rival chief. So impressed were
the French with the abundance to be found in this
new country that they named it Terra Florida, the
Flourishing Land.

The French made no attempt to interfere with
the lives of the Timucuans, being intent only on securing a passage to the north where, so rumour
had it, gold and silver could simply be picked up off
the ground. To this end they made pacts of friendship with several rival chiefdoms, thereby earning

These Huron moccasins are made from smoked deerskin to give them a dark colour, and are elaborately decorated with moosehair embroidery in typical Woodland patterns.

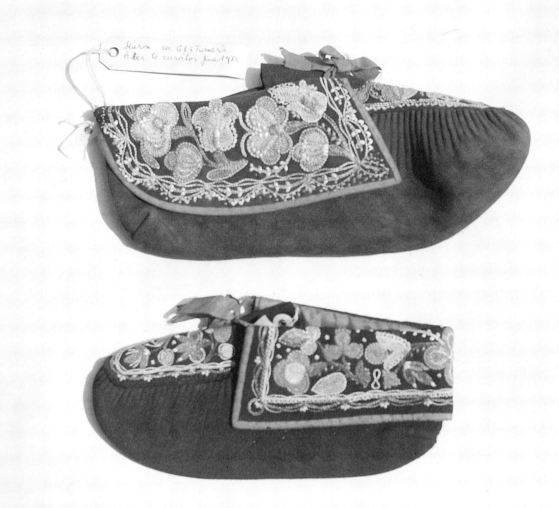

the distrust of all. Meanwhile the Spanish, who considered the French incursion a violation of their rights, decided to send a war fleet to Florida. On arrival they found the French in an impoverished condition and, through cunning, intrigue, and vicious cruelty, massacred them.

Determined to consolidate Florida as a Spanish base, they set about converting and proselytizing the tribes. The Florida Indians were defiant and for a long time the Missions met little success. Some tribes went so far as to claim that the only way their gods could be placated at the annual renewal ceremonies was by the sacrificial offer of a Spaniard, although it is probable that these claims were made for the benefit of the Spanish and not from any belief held by the Indians. Finally, provoked by the Spanish insistence that the traditional ways were wrong, the Timucua and Apalachee formed an alliance in 1656 to drive these strangers from their country; but the tribes had been weakened by introduced diseases and their rebellion failed. Weakened further by losses sustained in the rebellion, the Timucua and Apalachee were susceptible to incursions by Creek and Yuchi Indians from the north. With English encouragement and assistance, they had destroyed or enslaved the Apalachee by 1704. The Timucua, in turn, disappear from history in 1736.

Only the Calusa still held out, having fled to the Florida Keys; but they vanish from the records in 1763 when the British took control of Florida and deported the remnant of the tribe to Havana. They numbered only 350 people, of a population which in 1612 was said to occupy 70 towns, and to control many others who paid them tribute.

Although relatively little is known about the Florida tribes – the main French and Spanish contributions to Indian history being the introduction of syphilis and smallpox – we do know a great deal more about the Creek Indians who helped bring about their demise.

European contact with these tribes began in the Carolinas during the 1500s, when they were living as local tribal leagues with little influence on their neighbours, and sometimes subjugated to them. The Creek Nation as such was not then in existence. Even the name we know them by is an arbitrary coinage, attached to a small group who lived along the banks of Ocheese Creek, now the Okmulgee River, and whom the English called 'The Indians of the Creek'.

Although these tribes were small, they were not without pride and, in the case of the men, were taller and of better build than many of their neighbours. Strangely, the women, even though they are usually described as being among the most beautiful and handsomely proportioned of the area, are also noted for the slightness of their stature. Some reports, perhaps with a degree of exaggeration, add that when a Creek man and his wife stood side by side she gave the appearance of being not much more than half his height.

The influence exerted by these tribal groups changed in the late 17th and early 18th centuries, when the Creeks began to confederate, ultimately controlling about 50 townships with a population that may have exceeded 30,000 and speaking at least six different languages. They were organized into two separate divisions. The Upper Towns, also known as the White or Peace Towns, were responsible for civil ceremonies, and it was from these that the principal chief was elected and from which most of the Creek government was administered. The Lower, Red or War Towns had responsibility for ceremonies of warfare. A council of elder men, known as the Beloved Men, chose the war chief, or Great Warrior, from one of the War Towns.

Creek towns were built around a public plaza formed by four buildings placed in a square. These housed the chief and priests and can be thought of as the administrative centre of the tribe, since it was here that council deliberations were held and decisions affecting the group were made. The general populace lived along streets that radiated from the square in regularly spaced rows, in rectangular frame buildings covered with split cane matting. A single family, dependent on both status and need, might occupy a number of these house sites.

Status was acquired in a number of ways. To some extent it was hereditary, and a man born into a leading family was always a prominent member of the community. But it could also be gained through personal achievement in war and hunting, through the acquisition of wealth, or by the demonstration of particular skills. It might even be achieved by becoming a prominent player in the ball game, a form of lacrosse which they shared with other tribes of the area such as the Choctaw.

European visitors to the ball games describe them as stunning spectacles. The object of the game is deceptively simple: to catch a leather ball in a netted stick and to carry this down the field and place it between two posts marking the opposing team's goal. The first team to score won. But to refer to them merely as team games would be an underestimation. Each side might field several hundred players, their bodies painted in team colours and wearing long, trailing horsehair bustles. There were no rules, and few players ever actually saw the ball.

As soon as the game started the whole mass of players surged into action: a dizzying rush of colour and paint, of hair, and of game sticks raised more as weapons against an opponent than to catch the ball. Songs and shouts of encouragement were roared by the spectators as they urged their favourites on, and the trampling of hundreds of feet raised great clouds of dust that hung over the pitch. Such a game could last all day, with the advantage shifting constantly from one team to the other but with no decisive result. When one team came too close to the other's goal, spectators might invade the pitch to prevent a score. Every so often a player would emerge from the mass of bodies, perhaps bleeding profusely from a head wound or simply to rest for a while before leaping back into the fray.

At the end of the game, the player who had finally managed to score was treated as a hero and given prestige equivalent to that of a leading warrior. Dances and feasts were given in his honour and he was fêted wherever he went. His status was undoubtedly well earned.

The Creeks were primarily farmers, planting crops similar to those of other tribes of the southeast but with a greater degree of personal ownership. Any Creek man could claim unused territory for his exclusive use as long as it lay within the town's boundaries. Even so, individual ownership meant that certain families owned greater resources than others and this gave rise to a moneyed aristocracy in which a few people were able to exert disproportionate influence in the deliberations of the tribal councils.

Not everyone was happy with this and, as we might expect from a confederation containing diverse elements, Creek history is full of reports of factionalism. Groups disagreed with the government, dispersed, formed new alliances, returned, then departed again. When the Apalachee towns were overrun, many Creek Indians decided to leave the confederacy and stay in Florida, adopting some of the dispossessed Apalachee and forming a community with its own distinctive traits that was to be the basis for the tribe now known as the Seminole. Even the roles of the White and Red Towns were never adhered to strictly, and often appear to be more of a theoretical construct than a practical application; yet, in spite of this apparent

Corn, or maize, was the staple crop throughout the Eastern Woodlands, and had a ritual importance that was recognized by the Iroquois in their corn husk masks. This modern example is only 6 cm (2½ inches) high, but it has the characteristic form of the larger masks that were formerly made.

Right: Porcupine quills were flattened and dyed, before being sewn to hide in decorative and symbolic patterns. This Ottawa back ornament has motifs depicting the Thunderbird, and was worn so that the large shell rested on the wearer's breast while leather thongs passed over his shoulders to support the backpiece.

Far right: Cunne-Shote, or Stalking Turkey, was a Cherokee chief who visited London in 1762 where F. Parson painted this portrait of him.

Opposite: The modern game of lacrosse derives from the ball game of the Southeast. Unlike its modern counterpart, the Choctaw game shown here had few rules and an unlimited number of contestants. Team members wore distinctive costumes and body paint, and the object of the game was to pass a ball between two upright posts. The first team to score was declared the winner, but the game might last for several hours before a goal was made, and injuries were frequent in what was essentially a free-for-all. Spectators would often invade the pitch to give active support to the team they favoured.

instability, the confederacy held together surprisingly well.

It was, initially at least, able to withstand the pressures brought to bear by White intruders: many Creeks became wealthy through trade with the Whites, owing to a Creek law which stated that a man owned personally all that he achieved by his own labour and industry. Creek ascendancy may actually be linked with the fact that so many of their laws and customs were similar to those of the Europeans who were encroaching upon their lands. The principle of private ownership and personal wealth left few ideological reasons for conflicts to occur. During the eighteenth century the English married into their leading families, and Alexander McGillivray, the son of a Scottish trader and a half-French Creek mother, became the undisputed Creek leader. When McGillivray died in 1793 he was one of the wealthiest men in the entire southeast.

Because of the late formation of the confederacy, at a time when European influences were being felt, Creek culture has a peculiarly hybrid Indian-European character. Individual wealth was only one aspect of this. Clothing, other than that worn for ceremonies, was manufactured from cloth obtained in trade, and the men quickly adopted the custom of wearing turbans instead of the more familiar Indian featherwork or going bareheaded. Even in some ceremonial contexts items of European manufacture made an appearance, as in the custom for Creek women at a Busk – dances held for both social and religious reasons – to tie

lengths of brightly coloured silk ribbon in their hair; a custom that has persisted to the present day.

Hunting continued; but pigs, cattle and sheep were taken over and raised, and farming intensified. So successful were the Creek in these endeavours that it was later to lead to their removal to Oklahoma under the protests of White farmers that the Creek offered unfair competition! Similar trends were taking place socially. Strict formal laws were declared and upheld by a council of elders in an Indian court, although the basis for the judgements they handed down was strongly influenced by the older system of personal vengeance and restitution. Negro slaves, who were often adopted into Creek families, were set to work on farmlands that were starting to become typical southern plantations.

Warfare with other tribes continued, yet even this was strongly influenced by European needs. Consistently pro-British, the Creek became a buffer between the British and more hostile tribes, and the bastion against both French and Spanish expansion, which explains their involvement in the war prosecuted against the Apalachee by the British. They fought valiantly for the British against the Americans in the war of 1812-1815 until they were finally defeated by the forces of General Andrew Jackson, who was later to become President of the United States.

By 1815 most Creeks had accepted American dominance, but an anti-American group holding strongly to the formerly prevailing mood emerged. They were known as the Red-Sticks, and to demonstrate their authority they massacred 350 pro-American Creeks at Fort Mims. In retaliation the pro-Americans, mainly from the Lower Creek towns, and aided by militiamen from the surrounding states, volunteer frontiersmen, some

Yuchi Indians and 600 Cherokee warriors, killed 200 of the Red-Sticks.

In the Creek civil war that ensued, the Red-Sticks were beaten and fled south to join their relatives in Florida, where they tripled the Seminole population overnight and where their descendants still live.

The final blow to Creek autonomy came between 1821 and 1825, when the leading chief, William McIntosh, ceded 25 million acres of Creek land to the state of Georgia. This was illegal under both state and native laws, since it was opposed by nine-tenths of the Creek population. McIntosh was executed by a tribal court and the treaty annulled the following year; but it had set in motion a determined campaign of harassment and fraudulent land claims, led by the Governor of Georgia – McIntosh's brother – which had the stated intention of removing the Indians from the area. Mobs invaded Creek country, their fields and houses were burned, and their children sold into slavery.

Appeals to the Federal government were refused, resulting in the arrests of anti-Georgia Indians and the forced march, in manacles, of the tribe to Indian Territory, now the state of Oklahoma. 3,500 Creek Indians died on this 'Trail of Tears', and on arrival in Oklahoma the tribe was destitute. Other tribes from the Carolinas, Tennessee, Kentucky, Alabama and Georgia have a similar history to that of the Creeks and suffered the same fate of removal to Indian Territory. These were the Choctaw, Cherokee and Chickasaw, who, with some Seminole Indians and the Creek are known collectively as the Five Civilized Tribes. All of them had successfully tried to adopt the new ideas being introduced by Europeans and lived amicably with their White neighbours, intermarrying with them and leading lifestyles that were

Warfare was commonplace in the Eastern Woodlands, and the Iroquois needed to exert their presence forcibly to exist as viable tribes. This Huron ball-headed war club was made in the late 18th century.

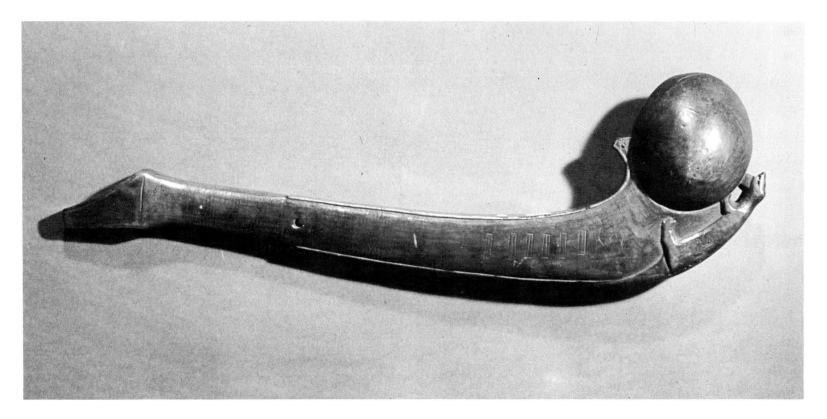

not so very different from theirs; yet each of them fell foul of the European need for land. In Indian Territory they resolutely started to rebuild their lives in an alien country, erecting new courts and schools and attempting to re-establish the farming and stock-raising base of their economies. It could never be as productive as it had been in the south, since the climate of Indian Territory was unsuited for large-scale farming; yet it did enable the tribes to make a rapid recovery.

One notable achievement was that of the Cherokee. A young half-breed Cherokee named Sequoyah, who had been working with the missionaries assigned to the tribe, decided that a major advantage the Whites had over the Indians was their ability to read and write. In 1821 Sequoyah devised a set of symbols, called the Cherokee Syllabary, which represented the major sounds of their language. By 1824 he had printed parts of the Bible and a song book in Cherokee, and by 1828 the Cherokee Phoenix, a bi-lingual weekly newspaper, was being read regularly by about 75 per cent of the tribe. Sequoyah's 'alphabet' was not the first attempt to write an Indian language, but it is remarkable in that the system was so simple it could be learned within a few days. The Cherokee Nation changed from being totally non-literate to fully literate in just seven years.

The story is a different one in the coastal forests of the Atlantic and through the eastern part of the region. Much of New York State was occupied by the warlike Iroquois tribes. They were ancient inhabitants of the Woodlands who had moved north from their original homelands and forced the Algonkin-speaking tribes of New York further to the east and on to the coasts. Like most other Woodland peoples, they were maize farmers and lived in permanent villages; but they quickly gained an unparalleled reputation for ruthlessness. As a consequence of continual warfare with neighbouring tribes and among themselves they began fortifying their villages with such massive palisades that the first Europeans in the area referred to them as 'castles'.

Within these fortifications they constructed characteristic longhouses covered with elm bark and up to 18m (60 ft) long, which served as shelters for matriarchal clan groups. Each of the houses was owned and administered by women, and ruled by a Clan Mother. In any activity a man undertook, he reported back and was responsible to the Clan Mother of his wife's longhouse. Even chiefs, who had a role as spokesmen rather than leaders, were elected by a council of women known as the 'Mothers' of the tribe.

The ferocity of the Iroquois turned eastern and central New York State, and the Valley of the Mohawk especially, into a battleground. War parties were constantly away from the villages, and their activities began to weaken the groups to such an extent that during the late 1400s or early 1500s a reformer known as Hiawatha, immortalized in Longfellow's Song of Hiawatha – although he made the mistake of attributing this tale to the Chippewa on Lake Superior – began to travel from village to village pleading the case for a confeder-

The Mohawk chief Thayendanegea was a supporter of the British. who knew him by the name of Joseph Brant, and personal friend of the Duke of Northumberland who presented him before the House of Lords in London, where Thayendanegea made an impassioned plea for the Mohawk cause. This portrait of him was painted by Ezra Ames in 1806.

acy of Iroquois tribes and the cessation of hostilities. Hiawatha, an idealist, was supported by two other influential people: Daganawe da, a famed organizer and law-giver; and Jogan sasay, a wise and highly respected old woman who was a member of the Neutral tribe. Even so, he met with considerable resistance. His own tribe banished him, in spite of the fact that he claimed to have supernatural sanction from Atotarho, the medusa-headed spiritual leader of the Onondaga Iroquois, and he was forced to seek residence elsewhere; but he eventually persuaded five of the tribes to join together, in the League of Five Nations.

These tribes were the Seneca, Cayuga, Onondaga, Oneida, and Mohawk, going by their geographical position in a line from west to east, who were located to the south of the Great Lakes. The Seneca were the guardians of the western door; the Mohawk, guardians of the eastern door and the receivers of tribute; and the Onondaga in the centre were the keepers of the council fire and of the beaded wampum belts which recorded tribal treaties. These belts, made from white and purple seed beads, were used by both the Iroquois and their Algonkin neighbours and constituted a form of tribal 'history'. The Huron tribes, who had already formed a league of their own, refused to join the Five Nations; the Neutrals chose to remain independent from either group.

The vision of Hiawatha was of a peaceful union of Iroquoian tribes with an unwritten constitution authorizing the election of a representative body. This would be called into session when any matter affecting the group was to be discussed, and each member tribe would have a single vote, canvassed from among its own population, which would be

cast at a meeting of the Onondaga council. For war to be declared the vote of the Onondaga council had to be unanimous.

In reality, the establishment of the League resulted in the cooperation of several tribes in subjugating their neighbours. In 1650 the Five Nations decided to punish the Huron for refusing to join. For some time the Huron held them off; but the Five Nations were receiving guns in trade whereas the Huron, far away from European population centres, fought back with bows and arrows. Eventually they were forced to flee to the Neutrals for protection. When the Neutrals refused to give them up, taunting the Five Nations to come and get them if they were strong enough, they, in their turn, were annihilated.

Although the constitution of the Five Nations may, in retrospect, seem to have encouraged the notion of gain for a unified group, it was nevertheless held in high esteem by the White colonists. Through its voting system it enabled everyone to have a say in the decisions of the group; it embodied the ideal of freedom in a democratic state; and it allowed the individual to bear arms and to resist any intrusion upon his or her personal space, so long as this had no adverse effect on the broader ideals of the community.

In 1744, when Connecticut and Pennsylvania negotiated with the Iroquois to adjust land claims, the constitution of the Five Nations (now the Six Nations, since the Tuscarora had joined in 1722, though they never enjoyed the full freedom to vote and had their interests represented by the Oneida) was written into the state laws. Later, when Alexander Hamilton and John Adams established the Federalist Party in 1789, the constitution of the Five Nations became enshrined in the Constitution of the United States.

To be fair to the Iroquois, the Algonkin territories they had entered were not renowned for peace and tranquillity. Much of the reputation the

Iroquois acquired may be attributed to the fact that they fought harder than most (if they had not done so, they would have been unable to survive) and also that they were organized efficiently enough to consolidate their gains. Stories of the tortures they inflicted on captives are legion, and such would probably have been the case for the Huron who had been so openly defiant; yet many prisoners, usually women and children, were adopted into the tribes and not enslaved.

It is worth bearing in mind that the Colonists of the time were themselves regularly burning 'heathens' alive, as was also the punishment for witchcraft; that they practised execution by quartering in which the victim's body was hacked to pieces and then scattered; and that rather than adopt an Indian woman captive, her fate would have been rape, mutilation, and an agonizing death. Even Indian children were regularly killed, and sometimes scalped alive, by White bounty hunters. Such practices can be considered no less barbaric than those of the Iroquois.

Within their own households, the Iroquois showed a much kinder face. Any disputes were dealt with by arbitration, and children were rarely punished for their transgressions. The idea of whipping or hitting a child for some minor fault was abhorrent to them. Slaves were generally treated kindly; the only difference in their lives was that they had no vote in the councils. They worked no harder than anyone else, and shared the same benefits as the rest of the household.

Although the Iroquois were relentless towards their enemies, they were honourable and trustworthy to their friends, and much of their life was run on the basis of communal sharing. When the corn fields were planted, even though they were owned individually, groups of women would work together, planting each other's fields in turn. When the crop started to ripen, the entire group joined in celebratory ceremonies. Similar coopera-

Huron tribes of the Great
Lakes resisted the efforts of
the Five Nations to bring
them into an Iroquois
confederacy, and vigorously
defended their villages
against Five Nations
raiding. In spite of their
undoubted courage and
valour, the numerical
superiority of their
opponents finally forced the
Huron to disband and to flee
as refugees to other tribes in
the area.

The pipe tomahawk is a curious blend of war and peace emblems, since the pipe sealed bonds of friendship whereas the tomahawk is clearly aggressive. This contradiction can be understood when it is realized that the pipe tomahawk was introduced as a trade item by Europeans. The metal axe heads were required for use against Indian opponents, whereas the pipe confirmed friendship with the traders. To facilitate smoking, a hole was burned or drilled through the shaft of the tomahawk.

tion was shown in planting and harvesting the tobacco fields owned by the old men of the tribe, and the longhouse itself was a symbol of community sharing since it housed several families who worked together in the preparation of meals and in caring for children.

A similar idea appears in their beliefs, based on the struggles between elements such as light and dark, and good and misfortune, but with no conception of any force that was truly evil. All the forces of the world were thought to live and cooperate with each other in some kind of perpetual harmony, maintained by equality between the various dualities. It was only when something happened to disturb this that things went wrong, and ceremonies had to be performed to restore order. Many of these ceremonies were known only to members of the secret societies, of which the Iroquois had many. It was their responsibility to ensure that the correct rituals were enacted for the benefit of the group. Perhaps the most famous society was the False Faces, who carved grotesque faces into living trees and then carefully removed the carved portion to be worn as a mask. The grimaces of the faces represented various characters of the other world who were inclined to cause mischief; but by imitating them the negative aspects of the other world could be safely harnessed.

Much of the False Face Society's activity was intended to keep the 'Flying Heads' at bay, since they brought disease or famine to the tribe. Even so, illness was not always thought of as being delivered by a malign spirit; often it was felt to result simply from an unfulfilled dream. In all their endeavours the Iroquois sought to maintain the qualities they held most important: truth, goodwill, well being, peace and plenty. These, of course, were qualities they applied to themselves

and to the tribes with whom they were intermittently friendly. The Delaware, for instance, who lived to the south, were referred to by the respect term 'Grandfathers', although they belonged to a different language group.

Even though the Iroquois managed to establish themselves as the dominant force in New York, the Algonkin tribes who had been forced out by their original incursions were far from being a disappearing race. They had formed their own alliances which were strong enough to resist Iroquois aggression and which prevented the Five Nations expanding from their territory to the eastern seaboard. The entire coastal region, from North Carolina through Virginia, Maryland, Delaware, New Jersey, New England, and into Maine, was controlled by Algonkin-speaking tribes, who were far from being meek and submissive.

Initially, they consisted of perhaps a hundred or more small groups, which slowly began to consolidate into larger alliances; but they never formed a permanent league, and there was always a feeling that each tribe could act independently. In some respects this was the reason that the more centrally organized Iroquois could invade their territories; yet there was a strong sense of an Algonkin identity, which enabled particular individuals to gather groups together as cooperative units.

Such was the case with Chief Powhatan, who was able to demand the allegiance of some 200 villages belonging to 30 different tribes. Powhatan's confederacy was unusual in that he held a rigid leadership much like those of the Natchez and Timucuans; but looser alliances had always been a feature of Algonkin societies and these were almost invariably organized under charismatic leaders. Powhatan's leadership was simply an extension of this, the alliance holding together longer than most because of the iron rule with which he governed it.

For most of the Algonkin tribes, petty feuds and squabbles were characteristic. These were usually family rivalries or village fights, prosecuted through ambushes in which one or two people might be killed, or the deliberate burning down of a village and the destruction of its crops. Vengeance and revenge seem to be the prime reasons that the Algonkins went to war, and even though casualties were never very great, this pattern of warfare made it impossible to form permanent alliances, since there would always be one family group who held a grudge against another.

As a result villages remained small, quite unlike those of allied or colonial tribes characteristic of other parts of the Woodlands. Crops of maize, beans and squash were planted in garden plots rather than fields, and these were located close to villages where individual family houses were made of oval pole frameworks covered with rush. The massive cities of other groups, the communal houses of the Iroquois, and the organized towns of the Creeks, were all alien to Algonkin thinking. The only major trait that Algonkin villages shared with those of other Woodland peoples was the respect shown for their chiefs, or Werowances, whose bones were preserved in a building apart from the others and tended by a special caste of priests.

Even though many of these tribes lived on or near the coast, they seem to have made little use of maritime resources other than shellfish. They looked to the interior instead, manoeuvring their graceful birchbark canoes skilfully along the streams and small rivers that served as highways. A portage around a waterfall or some other obstacle presented no problem, since the birchbark canoe was light enough to be carried by a single man. It was a society in which the individual was free to act according to his or her own conscience, tempered only by the overiding concern that all actions should ultimately be for the benefit of the group.

Algonkin life was never marked by an excessively warlike temperament, and when the English colonists arrived here they found them to be amiable and exceptionally friendly; so friendly in fact that the settlements only survived their first few years through Algonkin assistance. The Indians brought them supplies, taught them how to live in the forests, and even treated their sick with the herbal remedies for which their shamans, or medicine men, were famed.

The colonists were welcome onlookers at their summer councils, called 'pow wows' – a term which has come to be applied generally to any dance gathering of modern Native Americans – where they were feasted and gifts were exchanged. There were displays of singing and dancing, and of lacrosse. Contests of skill were held, with wagers being made in articles considered of great value because of their beauty. Popular among these were 'friendship bags': shoulder pouches exquisitely decorated with twined patterns of thread from the inner bark of the swamp ash, or similar bags, made from deerskin and embroidered with dyed porcupine quills. When a man went on a visit he often carried several of these bags with him; packed with dried meat and other presents, they were gift bags to be solemnly presented as a gesture of friendship and goodwill.

The Powhatan Confederacy was the first to come into contact with the British when the settle-

Ribbons introduced by Europeans were widely used in the Woodlands to decorate clothing and other goods. The Fox ribbonwork moccasins shown here were made about 1880.

Bags and pouches were important items in the Woodlands, where they were used for transporting and storing a variety of goods. A visitor to another tribe carried several such pouches; filled with manufactured items and dried food, these were given as goodwill presents to his hosts. The bandolier bag in this photograph was made by the Fox.

ment of Jamestown was established in 1607. Peace was maintained by the marriage, in 1609, of Powhatan's daughter, Pocahontas, with John Rolfe. It ran into difficulty, however, when Pocahontas introduced the settlers to tobacco farming, which resulted in their demanding Powhatan lands for their fields. Ownership of land was something the Powhatans could neither understand nor even consider; the Earth was sacred, created by Manibozho for the use of all men and animals equally. The concept of ownership was totally alien to Algonkin thinking. The settlers, considering this an indication of Powhatan intran-

sigence, responded by digging up part of the traditional hunting grounds of the confederacy. This caused a general uprising in 1622, which was quickly suppressed. The quelling of the revolt did not prevent a second uprising in 1641 when more than 500 British settlers were killed; but by 1644 the Powhatan Confederacy had been decimated and the remnants of the tribes placed on reservations. In 1676 the now-peaceful Powhatans were massacred by Virginia settlers.

None of the the Indian tribes along the frontier escaped unscathed. They were pushed into the foreground by the English-French conflict: the extent of their involvement is reflected by the fact that these wars are known collectively as the French and Indian Wars. Indian allegiances followed traditional tribal enmities; the Iroquois sided with the British, whereas most of the Algonkins and other tribes who had suffered from Iroquois aggression were pro-French.

For the next hundred years there was continual conflict, and the Indian simply became a pawn used in a power play between conflicting European nations, and later between the British and Americans in the Revolutionary War. The Indian tribes fought bravely, often defeating large European or American armies, and leaders such as Little Turtle of the Miami tribe, Pontiac of the Ottawa, and Blue Jacket and Tecumseh of the Shawnee, gained the admiration and respect both of their own people and of their opponents. Yet ultimately it was the Indians who lost their homelands.

Hardly any of the Algonkins of the central regions now exist as tribal entities. They have either been annihilated in the wars inflicted on them, or they have become refugees in other tribes. A few groups, pushed into the northern parts of the Woodlands, had to make radical changes in their ways of living. Those who retained some farming traditions and found fertile areas were soon under pressure to move as White competition for their fields increased. Virtually all the Indian lands east of the Mississippi had been ceded to the United States government by the early part of the 19th century, and their original inhabitants removed to Indian Territory. Even those who crossed the border into Canada found themselves becoming increasingly dependent on White manufactures, through the fur trade. Some tribes, such as the Cheyenne and Dakota, fled the area entirely; crossing the Mississippi and becoming fully immersed in the culture of the Plains Indians.

The only tribes to escape the brunt of the conflicts were those such as the Chippewa living around the Great Lakes; too far north for successful agriculture, they occupied country that the White man did not covet. They were involved to some extent in the French and English wars, when they supported the French, but there were no cries for their removal and many of their descendants still occupy the lands of their ancestors.

They had a lifestyle similar to that of the other Algonkins of the region, except for a dependence on wild rice as a staple food instead of corn. The shallow waters around the edges of the lakes were ideal environments for rice, and also attracted

The Iroquois believed that sickness and misfortune originated in the spirit world through the actions of malign forces. Prominent among these were the False Faces. To combat these malignant influences, dancers in secret societies impersonated the spirits and thereby turned their power back. The False Face dancer in this illustration wears a mask that has been carved from a living tree, and carries antlers and a tortoiseshell rattle that are imbued with ritual significance.

huge numbers of migratory birds which the Chippewa caught by using realistic decoys they made from wood and rush. With the aid of duck calls made from hollow reeds they were able to trap and net more than sufficient to meet their needs. Life was comfortable, yet these northern forests with their unpredictable mists and sudden changes always contained elements to be feared and respected. To guard against negative influences, their villages were surrounded with carved wooden posts bearing ancestral and spiritual figures. Many of these were carvings of the supernatural animals from which families claimed descent. So central were these to Chippewa thinking that their name for these powers, ototeman, meaning 'relatives', has passed into modern anthropological terminology as the word 'totem'.

Chippewa belief placed an animate soul in every aspect of their world, and they moved through it showing a reverence for all things about them. Everything had an identity that could be related back to that of the people, since all things were created simultaneously and none took precedence. The fish they took from the lakes gave themselves up in a gesture of support, and should be treated courteously and respectfully. Even the bark with which they covered their conical houses, called wigwams, was blessed and thanked before being stripped from the trees.

When hunting, they never went back to the same area for a second year but always moved on to new hunting grounds. The animals in the first area had already given their lives willingly, and deserved to be left in peace to recover and to regain their strength. The same held true for the maple forests, which they tapped to make maple sugar, and for the lakes in which they fished for sturgeon, where they alternated their fishing between Lake Michigan and Lake Huron.

These inoffensive people initiated a great ceremonial institution called the Midéwiwin, in which all the powers of nature were called into the service of mankind. The Midé ceremonies were recorded on strips of birchbark incised with mnemonic devices, enabling the priests accurately to recite long and complex ritual incantations. These strips are unique in North America and provide the only evidence for any kind of aboriginal written record.

In the Midéwiwin, initiates were 'shot' with shells containing the secrets of the 'mystic society of animals': an initiation into that mysterious world where people and animals could talk together in a common tongue and share the secrets of existence and of the purposes for which they had been created. It was an all-encompassing institution by which the Chippewa – and their allied tribes in the Three Fires Confederacy, the Ottawa and Potawatomi – could continually reinforce their belief in the close links between man and the natural world.

Unfortunately it is only with some of the scattered Chippewa bands and a few Iroqois groups that any of the old beliefs have been retained. Many of the attitudes expressed in these forest lands today are very different from those which prevailed in earlier times.

It is still possible to walk in the mountains and enjoy the thunder of uncontrolled waterfalls, or to relish the quiet of a woodland glade. One can stroll peacefully along the banks of a brook which bears an ancient Indian name, or sit beside a lake that bears testimony of Indian encampments. The entire area contains echoes of its Indian past: Saugatuck, Lakes Winona and Winnepesaukee, Massachusetts, and Connecticut are all Indian names. Even Manhattan is a memorial to the Manhatte Indians who sold this land to the Dutchman Peter Minuit for a handful of glass beads.

There are many places where stone arrowheads can be picked up by the observant. But the laughter of Algonkin and Iroquois celebrations has been stilled, the hunter and warrior no longer negotiate its waterways in their birchbark canoes, and the great villages with their extensive fields are gone.

The Indians of the region were brutally and ruthlessly repressed. Today, an Indian presence of any significance in the Eastern Woodlands is nearly always of only historical concern. Few people recognize the fragments of tribes that remain, and fewer still realize that they are the last remnants of once strong nations.

The Chippewa Midéwiwin Society had complex rituals whose precise order was known only to shamans with a priestly function. As aids to memory, since the correct performance of the ceremony was essential, the shamans used birchbark scrolls incised with mnemonic symbols. The top scroll pictured here shows the order of a sacred song; the bottom one depicts the seating plan of a Midé ceremony.

BIRCHBARK PICTURE RECORD OF SACRED SONG

THE SOUTHWEST

The Grand Canyon, Canyon de Chelly, Shiprock, Enchanted Mesa, Sky City – Acoma, Spider Rock, Corn Mountain, the Painted Desert and the Petrified Forest – evocative names for a country of deep canyons and high mesas, created by the action of wind and the turbulent waters of powerful rivers such as the Colorado and Rio Grande. It is a country of wild flowers which spring into bloom only after sudden rainfall, of curious and majestic rock formations, and of vast desert tracts of cacti, creosote bushes and yuccas. This is the Southwest: the desert lands of New Mexico and Arizona, extending into parts of Utah and Colorado.

It is a land of spectacular differences between ground and sky, of awe-inspiring grandeur but also of minutely beautiful detail, of brilliant colour and dense shadow where line and form is either sharply delineated or totally obscured. It is a country of contrasts, in which one constantly expects to find the unexpected.

It is not an environment that lends itself easily to cultivation, since it is generally arid and hot; yet at least 5,000 years ago people planted corn at Bat Cave, in New Mexico. The Bat Cave occupants were descendants of early gatherers who had lived in this area. Like them, they followed a seasonal existence; once their corn had been planted they moved on and utilized the other resources of the Southwest, before returning to their fields for the harvest.

About 2,000 years ago this lifestyle changed and settlements became more permanent. Small agricultural villages were established in the high ground of the Mogollon Mountains, in eastern Arizona and southern New Mexico. At the same time, the Hohokam ancestors of the modern Pima and Papago (the name is a Pima word meaning 'Those-who-departed-long-ago') cultivated crops along the Gila and Salt Rivers by means of flash irrigation. Another group, ancestral to the Pueblos but known by the Navajo name Anasazi, the 'Ancient Ones', was eking out a subsistence living without the benefit of extensive agriculture, in much the same manner as their Bat Cave predecessors.

The Mogollon peoples lived in semi-subterranean pit-houses made from poles covered with brush and mud plaster and arranged in large villages. Within their settlements in the southern part of the Southwest and in northern Mexico, the pit-house gradually developed into an above-ground multi-roomed dwelling built with stone masonry. The original form of the semi-subterranean structure came to acquire a new significance as a ceremonial meeting place, or kiva, for male kin groups.

They were a rapidly expanding group who were dependent mainly on planted crops, although hunting was also important, and they influenced the Hohokam and Anasazi to such an extent that the southern regions of the Southwest were to become a blend of Mogollon-Hohokam cultures, while those of the north were Mogollon-Anasazi. The groups maintained separate identities in mixed villages, where they coexisted peacefully but retained many of their own traditions.

Among the many achievements of Mogollon culture, the one that immediately impresses historians is the considerable amount of pottery they produced. Most of this comes from the area around the Mimbres River in southwestern New Mexico, where the majority of the pots are shallow bowls intended as burial goods to be placed over the head of the deceased. All of them were brand new; none shows signs of having been previously used, and nearly all have been ritually 'killed' by having a hole broken through the centre. What is striking about them is the beautiful rendition of human and animal forms, initially in black and white but later in polychrome. Birds, bats, deer, and other figures are exquisitely painted in a superb use of two-dimensional space; decorative borders and backgrounds intertwine with these figures in an interplay of foreground and background that both delights and confuses the eye; but the concept of balance and harmony is never lost.

Mogollon culture faded about 1100AD, and there are indications that part of the group may have left the area, perhaps going to northern Mexico, while others became so closely merged with the Hohokam and Anasazi that a separate cultural identity was lost. Modern studies, however, increasingly suggest that the Zuni Indians are their direct descendants.

Hohokam culture, on the border of Mexico just north of Sonora, was even more dependent on agriculture than that of the Mogollon, and was supported by extensive irrigation systems that utilized the floodwaters of the Gila and Salt Rivers. This area is very hot at times, and has sparse rainfall; but this means that soluble salts in the soils are not leached out, leaving the ground extremely fertile. Water is brought to the area by permanent rivers, fed by mountain streams in the east. The Hohokam took full advantage of seasonal river floods by building an extensive system of irrigation canals, as much as 9m (30 ft) in width and up to 3m (10 ft) deep. These were in use as early as 500AD, reaching their fullest extent by 1400AD when those of the Salt River alone had a combined length of more than 240 km (150 miles).

Large, straggling villages with little formal plan were built around the canal complex. Certain sites had greater importance than others, suggesting a political organisation based on some kind of central authority or chiefdom. They did not develop the pit-house in the manner of the Mogollon, a trend also followed by the Anasazi, but continued to utilize wood, brush and clay structures built over shallow depressions in the ground.

The most surprising thing about their villages, however, is the presence of ball courts similar to those in Mexico, and the discovery of rubber balls of Mexican origin. Copper bells and mosaic

The Hohokam mortar shown
in this photograph was used
by an ancestor of the modern
Pima and Papago for
grinding paint pigments.

plaques and mirrors from Mexico have also been
found. This raises a number of intriguing possibilities. Trade contacts are obvious, and these must
have been regular and important to influence the
Hohokam sufficiently to take over Mexican traits;
it could be that part of the population was an immigrant one from the south; or even that the
Hohokams themselves were actually a northern
outpost of Mexican culture. The border between
Mexico and the United States is, of course, an imposed rather than a natural barrier; in environmental terms, northern Mexico and the Southwest
of the United States are a continuous area.

About 1200AD some Anasazi groups amalgamated with the Hohokam. Villages often contain
two distinct house types, and there is evidence
that whereas the Hohokam were cremating their
dead, the Anasazi were burying theirs. It is possible the Anasazi came into these villages to gain
the security of the Hohokam's canal irrigation,
since crops were always marginal in the Anasazi
areas; but even the Hohokam crop yields started
to fall. The canals were extended to bring larger
areas under cultivation, yet successively poorer
harvests meant that people began drifting away
from the larger village sites. There was a serious
population decline; an almost total crop failure
about 1450AD finally caused the Hohokam to
disband, and led to the creation of the modern
Pima and Papago.

Anasazi contacts with the other groups of the
area were complex, and their development followed a very different pattern. Although they did
not at first form permanent villages and had little
agriculture, living essentially as semi-nomadic
cave dwellers, by 500AD they had started to use
the pit-house and were gathering into small villages. The Anasazi of this period are referred to as
Basketmakers as they relied almost entirely on
basketwork, although they did make an inferior
type of thin-walled pottery. They had domesticated the turkey and started to grow some additional varieties of maize, yet in terms of technical
advance they lagged behind their Mogollon and
Hohokam neighbours.

Between 750AD and 900AD, however, Anasazi
culture underwent a sudden flowering. By the end
of the eighth century AD they were growing cotton
and making cotton cloth, had many types of
painted and corrugated fire-baked pots, were
using elaborate decoration on their baskets, and
had started to build multi-roomed apartments
above ground using stone and adobe. The pit-
house now served a ceremonial function as a
clan kiva, in the same way as it did among the
Mogollon.

This development was to continue over the next
350 years. Multi-roomed apartments became vast
multi-storied complexes built in a rectangular or
D-shape around an open courtyard and containing
as many as 1,000 rooms. The most impressive
growth was in Chaco Canyon, northwestern New
Mexico, where a road system connected as many
as 125 different towns. Pueblo Bonito was the

biggest of these – and the largest apartment building in North America until the 19th century, when a bigger one was built in New York City.

Pueblo Bonito is a D-shaped complex, rising five storeys high, which housed perhaps 1,500 people. It was at the centre of an aboriginal trade route and probably had religious and ceremonial significance, since one of its main features is a number of very large kivas, called Great Kivas. These are far too massive to have served as clan houses even for a pueblo as big as this. If, however, Pueblo Bonito served as a religious focus for outlying settlements, then kivas on this scale would have been necessary to accommodate related clan members from several different communities.

Other pueblos, particularly in the area of Mesa Verde, relocated to the canyons. Villages on the flat canyon tops were rebuilt in natural recesses on the cliff faces, where they were protected by huge rock overhangs. Access to them was extremely difficult, often by ladder, and they would have provided excellent defence against even the most determined aggressor. Fields were maintained on the flat plains above the village, requiring a hazardous climb for them to be tended; water was obtained from rivers in the canyon bottoms or from springs, and could often only be reached by an arduous descent and even more difficult ascent. Why the people chose to move to these areas is not known, although the difficulty of access suggests there may have been severe pressures from hostile groups who had started to live in the area.

By 1300AD the populations of even the pueblos were dwindling. This is usually attributed to aggression from nomadic tribes and to a series of severe droughts between 1276 and 1299; but a different theory which has been gaining ground recently is that the peace-loving Anasazi had simply grown too large: that truly democratic processes were impossible to maintain in the big settlements, and that they chose instead to live in closer communities. Finally, for whatever reason, the cliff dwellings were totally abandoned. The Anasazi had moved into smaller villages in the Rio Grande Valley, where they established the modern Pueblos.

A new group of peoples entered the area some time before 1500AD. These small bands of nomadic hunters spoke a common language, Athapascan, but did not form any cohesive tribal units. They had begun a long migration from the far north, where many of their relatives still live, in about 850AD, slowly working their way south along the foothills of the Rocky Mountains and through the Great Plains. They lived in brush or skin shelters and used pack dogs to carry their belongings. Even though they were aggressive they did not form a serious threat to the stability of the pueblo groups, their constant raiding of pueblo fields must nevertheless have been a nuisance. They were the ancestral Apache and Navajo.

European contact began in 1539 when Mendoza, the Viceroy of New Spain, sent Fray Marcos de Niza, a Franciscan friar, on a voyage of exploration to the north. Mendoza had heard of fabulous riches in the Seven Cities of Cibola and was determined to obtain his share of the bounty.

Estevanico, or Esteban, a Negro slave who had been one of four survivors of a Spanish expedition to Florida, and who had escaped across the southern part of the Southwest, was to guide the Friar to these untold treasures.

The party reached Cibola, the Zuni settlements of New Mexico, in June, and Estevanico was ordered ahead to make contact with the inhabitants, thus making the first representative of a European nation to reach the Southwest a Negro. The Zuni were stunned by his strange appearance, for the skins of the A'shiwi, their name for themselves, were copper-red, as were those of all the other people they knew. When Estevanico managed to convey to them that a white man would arrive in two days' time, they concluded, after a long deliberation, that he must be a demon and put him to death.

As soon as word of Estevanico's fate reached de Niza, he fled back to Mexico. Here, in spite of the fact that he had not actually seen the Zuni towns, he gave a glowing account of the substantial settlements of Cibola, which Mendoza used as justification for a military expedition. Thus, in spring 1540, Francisco Vasquez Coronado, Governor of the Province of New Galicia, marched against Zuni where, after a brief but fierce battle, their principal town of Hawikuh was captured by the Spanish on 7 July.

This 900-year-old pottery olla, or water jug, is of a type used by both the Mogollon and Anasazi. It is painted with black and white geometric designs that are very similar to those still used by potters at Acoma and Zuni Pueblos.

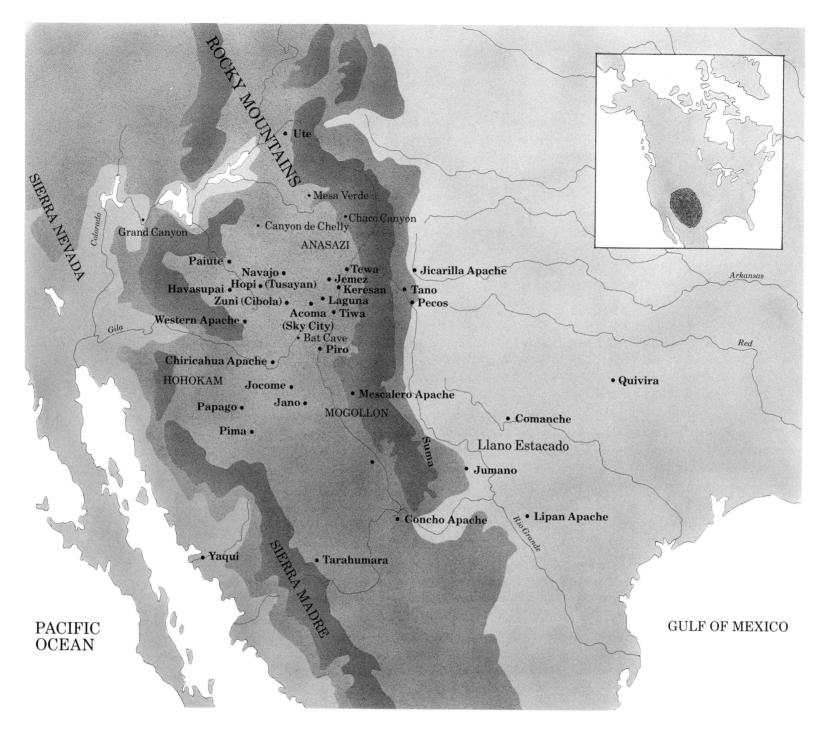

ROCKY MOUNTAINS

SIERRA NEVADA

• Ute

• Mesa Verde

Colorado

• Chaco Canyon
• Canyon de Chelly

Grand Canyon

ANASAZI

Paiute •

Navajo • • Tewa
Hopi • (Tusayan) • Jemez
Havasupai • • Keresan
Zuni (Cibola) • Laguna
• Acoma • Tiwa
Western Apache • (Sky City)
• Bat Cave
• Piro

• Jicarilla Apache

• Tano
• Pecos

Gila

Chiricahua Apache •

HOHOKAM

Jocome •

Papago •

Jano •

Pima •

MOGOLLON

• Mescalero Apache

Suma

Llano Estacado

• Jumano

Arkansas

Red

• Quivira

• Comanche

• Concho Apache

Rio Grande

• Lipan Apache

• Yaqui

SIERRA MADRE

• Tarahumara

PACIFIC
OCEAN

GULF OF MEXICO

Far right: Unmarried Hopi girls wore their hair in a distinctive butterfly style. After marriage, the hair was allowed to hang loose. The girl in this drawing is also wearing the typical Southwest Pueblo cape, and has thick leggings that offered adequate protection against the bite of the numerous venomous snakes found in this area.

No gold was found, and the disgraced de Niza was sent back to Mexico; but the people of Cibola spoke of much wealthier provinces than their own: those of Tusayan. Coronado decided this was worth investigating and sent out a small force under the command of Pedro de Tovar. De Tovar spent several days among the Tusayan, more properly known as the Hopi from their own name Hopitu, 'People of Peace', where he again found no gold but was told of a great river in the west. Garcia Lopez de Cárdenas was sent to explore, leading to the European discovery of the Grand Canyon.

A similar exploratory party was sent east, under the command of Hernando de Alvarado. At the pueblo of Tiguex, on the Rio Grande, he was told of 80 other villages like theirs in the region. Further east, he came to Pecos, the most easterly of the

pueblo group, where he was told there was a far wealthier province, called Quivira, further still to the east in the heart of the buffalo country.

Coronado assembled his forces in winter quarters at Tiguex, whose inhabitants had fled. Small exploratory parties were sent out throughout the winter, discovering a well-populated region with many small villages scattered at distances a few miles apart along the Rio Grande Valley. An expedition to Quivira in 1541 discovered nothing. No gold or other riches had been found, and in the spring of 1542 the disillusioned Spaniards returned to Mexico, leaving three missionaries behind to begin the work of conversion. One was to continue the search for Quivira, while the others were to establish missions at Tiguex and Pecos. All three were probably killed within a year of Coronado leaving the area.

The Spanish expedition had achieved nothing, except to burst in upon the tranquillity of Pueblo life. Perhaps no other peoples of the North American continent were as peace-loving and contented as were the Pueblos. Excess was unknown to them, and in all they did they proceeded in a gentle and quiet manner. Violence was permitted only against something that threatened to disturb the equilibrium of their lives or disrupt their ceremonial cycles, and even then this was undertaken reluctantly. It was the reason that Estevanico was killed, and almost certainly the reason that the missionaries left by Coronado met their deaths. We can imagine them protesting

strongly against the masked Pueblo dances, and the Indians deciding with genuine regret that this disruptive force must be permanently removed.

So non-violent were they that even in hunting they preceded the hunt by elaborate ceremonies during which the animals were asked for permission, and promises were made that they would only kill the minimum number needed for food and clothing. In these rituals the animals were spoken to as equals, and when game was brought into the village it was wrapped in a ceremonial robe and greeted by the people; anything less would have been disrespectful. After a deer had been consumed, its skull was painted with white clay, prayer feathers were tied to its antlers, and it was placed on the rooftop until such time as it could be blessed with sacred cornmeal and ceremonially disposed of in the Rio Grande. In farming, too, the crops were spoken of as friends and given personal names. Their staple crop, maize, was said to be the heart of the ancestral Corn Mother, and by eating it, the Corn Mother's own flesh became one with that of the people.

It was because of their gentleness that the ancestral Mogollon, Hohokam and Anasazi groups had been able to live so peaceably together, to the unprecedented extent of sharing each others' villages. This legacy had been handed on to the Pueblo peoples, who believed in living in harmony with the past, the present, and the future. In many ways it was an unchanging world: the cycles of nature creating a rhythm, like a steady heartbeat, which continued unbroken. They walked softly, unhurriedly, without the haughty demeanour adopted by some other tribes. Their pride was carried within themselves and not to be expressed loudly and proclaimed to others.

The Hopi Indians, whose village of Oraibi is the oldest continuously occupied settlement in the United States (a claim disputed by the people of Acoma Pueblo, who say that Acoma is older), believed that the world was created with knowledge, wisdom and love. People were given songs so that when they performed their ceremonies the rhythms they used would be in unison with the rhythm of the Earth; thus creating a harmonious vibration which embodied the essence of life. Though expressed in various ways, the Hopi view holds true in its essentials for the Zuni, and for Acoma, Laguna, Taos, Isleta, and all the other Pueblos of the Rio Grande Valley. Differences between these groups are a matter of detail rather than substance. The Keresan-speaking Pueblos, for instance who claim the world was thought into existence by Thought-Woman, and that the purity of harmonious thinking is the essence of life.

The permanence inherent in the Pueblo worldview meant that their culture was a conservative one, resistant to outside influence, and strictly ordered. The ancient songs contained the rhythms for the future and no one could interfere with these without disastrous consequences. Similar rhythms in their lifestyle, such as a steady pace rather than a frantic dash, could be equated with the songs; in this way, Pueblo ritual came to be incorporated in every aspect of life. The way one spoke, in an easy manner instead of a shout, was not only a means of communication, but also an expression of the deep inner belief felt by the speaker and shared with every member of the community.

Aggression, in a society like this, would strike a blow at one's own convictions and ideals far more effectively than it struck at the opponent. The opponent might be killed, but the aggressor had to live knowing that he had violated the most sacrosanct principle of Pueblo belief.

Pueblo society was organized into clans, with individual affiliation usually inherited through the female line. This meant an extended family had several kiva representatives since father and son would belong to different clans, as would any men who had married into the family. In many ways this helped to increase the society's cohesiveness. The majority of families had an involvement

60

in the activities of a number of ritual groups, whose responsibilities included duties of both secular and ceremonial significance.

The clans themselves were grouped into two distinct divisions, called moieties, which were responsible for the ritual cycle at different times of the Pueblo ceremonial calendar. Among the Tewa-speaking groups, for instance, there was a winter moiety, the Squash People, and a summer moiety, the Turquoise People, each of which was responsible for Pueblo organization during six months of the year. These divisions echoed the order of the spiritual world, and made each Pueblo a microcosm of the entire universe. Among the Hopi and Zuni the spirits, or Kachinas (from a Hopi word that means 'the spirits of the invisible forces of life') were believed to live in the Pueblos for half of the year and then to return to their homes in what modern commentators called the San Francisco peaks, but which the Pueblos thought of as the Grand Canyon, for the second half.

The secular divisions were not, however, a direct copy of the spiritual world: the people, after all, were human; whereas the Kachinas were the messengers of the sacred beings. Thus the Kachina half-year began after the Winter solstice, when they were said to arrive in the people's villages and where they were impersonated by dancers who could only have pure thoughts and who were said to lose their own personal identities as they became imbued with the spirit's presence. It ended in July – with a ceremony the Hopi call the Home Dance – when they returned to the mountains. Even after leaving the Pueblos the Kachinas maintained a presence there, in the form of small dolls carved from cottonwood root and painted in the Kachinas' own likenesses.

Arrival of the spirits in the Hopi Pueblos was announced by the sudden appearance of the Qöqölö Kachinas, who marked each kiva with a cornmeal design. By doing so they opened the kivas so that the other Kachinas could emerge. From now until they returned to their own homes the Kachinas were thought to have a continual presence in and around the villages. Prayer sticks of small painted boards, decorated with feathers, and offerings of sacred cornmeal would be left daily at places of religious significance, which the dancers who impersonated the Kachinas would visit. The entire Pueblo became inspired by close association with these visitors from the spiritual world.

In theory the Kachinas brought rain to ripen the crops; but every Hopi knew that in addition to this they came to bless the village and ensure its continued success, that they had other gifts to bestow – such as bringing the people together and uniting them as a single family – and that they would initiate joyful songs and ceremonies that made each member of the community feel glad to be alive.

There were at least 350 different Kachinas, and probably many more than this since new ones could be introduced at any time. A small proportion of them, the Chief Kachinas, appeared at specified times of the year, and their masks and costumes were considered to be sacred objects.

The Chief Kachinas were very powerful and highly respected. They danced singly, whereas the other Kachinas danced in groups. As an expression of their status, their masks were less elaborate than the others, in the Pueblo tradition of expressing greatness through moderation. The other Kachinas appeared in the Night Dances, dances held in the kivas during the hours of darkness, or came to the Pueblo at the people's request. Popular figures might be represented every year, simply because the people liked them, whereas others might make only very rare appearances. The atmosphere in the kiva on an occasion when the people waited for the Night Dances to begin would be an expectant one. A rattle sounded, and a voice called out in an unexpectedly high falsetto tone. There was a thump on the roof as the Kachina stamped his foot demanding admittance. The kiva clan chief called out to invite him to enter, and Poli Kachina, the Butterfly Spirit, descended the ladder.

The kiva was immediately imbued with the presence of the spirit. He wore a turquoise mask and had long hair hanging over his left shoulder. His body was painted in red, yellow and blue. Bells tied to his legs marked each movement, and were echoed by the sound of the rattle he carried in his right hand. On his back was a painted tablet hung with eagle feathers and bright red-dyed horsehair. Immediately behind Poli Kachina came Poli Kachina Mana, the Butterfly Spirit Girl, who wore an elaborate headdress painted with geometric designs and hung with feathers and gleaming turquoise pendants. In her hands she carried sprigs of evergreen, symbols of growth.

No sooner had they entered the kiva than a second pair of Poli Kachina dancers appeared. When four pairs had assembled, a masked chorus began a song, accompanied by a drummer, and the line of Kachinas swayed into a rhythmic pattern, a combination of sound, motion, and dazzling colour. At the end of their dance, the Poli Kachinas left to visit other kivas; but shortly after their departure there would again be a loud stamp on the roof as another group of Kachinas demanded entry.

Not all Kachina dances took place in the kivas, and there were frequent performances in the open plaza of the Pueblo. Sometimes as many as 60 dancers took part, performing synchronized movements that flowed along the line and created a rhythm which was marked by the sound of turtle shell rattles tied below the right knee of each dancer. In other dances, bells, voices, drums and the chanted songs of a chorus retold the stories of the spirits and their reasons for visiting the people. The rhythm of the dance was important, for it was an echo of the sacred world.

At the end of the dance the Clown Kachinas took over, giving a burlesque show in which they parodied the actions of any visitors from other groups, in a reversal of normal etiquette, and in fact, turned the whole world upside down. They were grotesque. All their movements were exaggerated, they washed in mud, people presented them with food which they grabbed with their hands and stuffed down their throats, they insulted the spectators, and were always extremely obscene. Their

actions seemed even more exaggerated in the context of Pueblo good manners.

Later in the day the Kachina dancers would reappear to give presents to the children, and it was then that the cottonwood root dolls were handed out, together with presents of food and other small gifts. Some specialized Kachinas, the Racing Kachinas, might challenge the children. If the child could beat them across the plaza they received a prize; but should they lose, then the Kachina might blacken their faces with soot or cut off their hair.

In all of these dances, even those of the Clowns, there was an unstated but ever-present feeling that the dances were directed by an immutable force going back to the beginning of time, which had the well-being of the people as its overriding purpose. This is demonstrated in the order of the Hopi dance cycle. It began with Wuwuchim, when the first fire was lit and life germinated; the second phase was Soyal, during which the Sun gave warmth to the germinating life; and it finished with Powamu, the purification in which plant life appeared and when the Kachinas initiated man into the sacred mysteries. These represented a

deep religious conviction, as is shown by the estimate that an average Hopi man spent about half his life directly involved in ritual activities intended to promote peace, harmony and goodwill. Many of these, of course, were also practical activities, such as tending the corn fields.

Although many Pueblos did not have Kachina dances as such, they had other masked and costumed performances in which the characteristics of the Kachinas were represented. At Santo Domingo, for example, the Squash and Turquoise kivas provided the Koshares and Kurenas, the invisible spirits of the deceased in much the same way as the Hopi dead lived with the invisible Kachinas in their mountain home. The Koshares and Kurenas opposed each other; one group was painted with horizontal markings and the other was painted vertically, and they functioned much like the Kachina clowns by making ribald comments and pantomimic gestures that mimicked the spectators, the chorus, or even other dancers.

Again like the Kachina dance series, those of the other Pueblos all had the stated intention of bringing rain to help the crops grow to maturity. Even some of the animal rituals that are more clearly connected with hunting often had this intention as a secondary purpose, since the deer, antelope, elk, mountain sheep and buffalo were all plant eaters, and the dance asked for plant growth so the animals could thrive. The request for rain was more specific in the Eagle Dance where the performer wore a painted tablet on his back which was trimmed with feathers and dyed horsehair and referred to as a 'moisture tablet'; thus acknowledging the Eagle's ability to control clouds.

Such, then, was the Pueblo culture the Spanish had blundered into in their search for material wealth. There was virtually no contact for 40 years after Coronado's visit, but during this period, Spanish interest in the area was growing. In 1596 Juan de Onate financed a private expedition to the Southwest and founded a church at the Pueblo of Caypa, which he renamed San Juan. He then proceeded to give the Franciscan friars authority over the other Pueblos, renaming many of them in the process. The Pueblos offered no serious resistance to Onate; the Spanish forces were strong, and they were a people of peace. They accepted the strangers' presence with resignation. Only Acoma, called Sky City from its majestic location on the top of a high mesa, tried to stop the Spanish incursion, and Acoma was stormed and its inhabitants

Mogollon peoples made pottery, such as this bowl from Mimbres, that served exclusively as grave goods to accompany the deceased. The hole in the centre was deliberately made as a ritual 'killing', whereby the soul inherent in the bowl was released.

Far right: Navajo weavers used on improvised loom that could be quickly erected on a wooden frame, or which might employ an overhanging branch of a tree. Unlike the Pueblos, where weaving was a male occupation, all Navajo weavers were women. The typical Navajo home, or hogan, can be seen in the background of this drawing.

When the Kachinas left the Hopi and Zuni villages to return to their own homes, they gave small dolls carved from cottonwood to the children to remind the people of their presence. The Kachina represented here is probably *Hote*, whose name derives from his characteristic call.

put on trial. Men over 25 received the punishment of the loss of one foot and 20 years slavery; women received only the 20 years slavery; children were handed over to the priests. As a warning to the other Pueblos, two Hopis who had been visiting Acoma were sent home with their right hands cut off.

In 1609 Onate founded Santa Fe as the Governor's principal residence. It was to be occupied over the next 71 years by a succession of different Governors who bought the office in the hope of finding the fabled riches of Cibola. Their searches were in vain, and many bankrupted themselves in this futile task. Meanwhile the priests were busy, converting thousands of Pueblo Indians, who became nominal Catholics but nevertheless continued to conduct the age-old rituals and ceremonies in secret. Spanish indignation at this deliberate disregard of the prohibition on 'idolatrous practice' was such that the priests of the kivas were regularly flogged, sometimes leading to deaths.

By 1680 the cruel punishments meted out to their religious leaders had exhausted the patience of the Pueblos. There was a general uprising, called the Pueblo Revolt. Five hundred of the 2,500 Spaniards in the area were killed, the rest driven out. The churches, Spanish houses and possessions, even their livestock, were all destroyed in a massive attempt to remove any influences they might have had. Characteristically, these

farmers of the Southwest kept the seeds and plants the Spanish had sown.

Twelve years later the Spanish returned in force, and after a war lasting four years they reasserted their authority. The Indians rebuilt many of the Pueblos in different locations and gave them new names, since the old villages had been defiled by fighting and could no longer be used as symbols of the ancient traditions of peace. Yet, remarkably, the old ways continued: they were too strong to die. The ceremonies continued in the kivas, while the cottonwood dolls kept alive the Kachinas' presence in the villages. Today, although the Pueblos are fewer than in their heyday, the ceremonies and ritual observances are still carried out, essentially unchanged from those of the sixteenth century.

To the southwest of the Pueblos the old traditions of the Hohokam peoples were being maintained by the Pima and Papago. Their scattered summer villages of domed brush-covered houses were still located along the Gila and Salt Rivers, whose flash floods irrigated small fields of maize, beans and cotton. In winter they moved to higher ground close to mountain springs where they could more easily hunt for deer.

These two groups lived in a very close association and considered themselves friends who shared ancient cultural links. The modern name Papago even comes from the Pima word for these people, Papahvio-otam, meaning 'Bean Growers'. It reflects the importance of this crop in Papago life; the Papago themselves used the name Tohono-o-otam, or 'People of the Deserts'. The origin of the term Pima has a rather more curious derivation. When missionaries first arrived among the Pima they asked them for their tribal name; but the missionaries spoke in a strange tongue and the Pimas replied by saying "Pinya-match", 'I don't understand'. Their own name is Ahkeemult-o-otam: 'People of the Rivers'.

Like the Pueblo groups, the Pima and Papago were unaggressive farmers and hunters who abhorred violence. Warfare and killing were considered unnatural acts, and it was believed that someone who had taken the life of another would become insane. Conflict was forced upon them by the intrusion of the Apaches into their lands, when they proved themselves able fighters in the defence of their villages; but to avoid insanity the warriors took only four hairs from the head of a slain enemy as a symbolic scalp which contained the soul of the defeated, and then underwent a 16-day curing rite in which emetics and sweat-baths were used to remove any contaminants that the body might have absorbed as a result of the killings.

The gentle manner of these tribes extended to friend and foe alike, and anyone seeking refuge – even though it might be an Apache – was welcomed into their villages. When the Spanish built missions and ranchos, here they found them willing converts to Catholicism and ready workers as farmhands and ranchers, and at a later date they were consistently friendly towards the Americans who came into their country. Both the Pima and Papago readily adopted ideas and beliefs from the

This photograph of Acoma
Pueblo, or Sky City, was
taken by Ben Wittick in
1885, Acoma claims,
together with the Hopi
village of Oraibi, to be the
oldest continuously occupied
settlement in North
America.

View in Pueblo Acoma N.M.

many friends they had in the region; but they did so without losing sight of their own traditions. Among all the products of Pima and Papago culture the one that has achieved most mention is their basketwork, and this has remained virtually unchanged since the very early days. Old and modern baskets use the same formal structures and arrangements of elements. They are stunningly beautiful. Spiral patterns and fretwork motifs are executed in perfect symmetry to create designs that play on the contrast of light and dark, reflecting the brilliant sunshine and deep shadow of the lands they occupy. Many of the baskets are shallow trays, used for collecting the beans of the mesquite cactus that were an important part of their diet, but larger storage baskets were also made. The visual impact of their basketwork is inspired by the desert environment and has the powerful attraction of the canyons and mesas woven into it.

Most of the tribes of the Southwest who, like the Pima and Papago, converted to Catholicism early, retained traditions which were either practised separately from Christian ritual or became merged with the ceremonies of the church. They saw no conflict between their older beliefs and the new ones that were being introduced. None of them, however, took this as far as the Yaquis, who had been subject to Jesuit missionaries in Mexico during the early 1600s, and who brought these influences with them when they moved into Arizona as refugees from a war being waged against them in the south.

The Yaquis' principal ceremony was held at Easter, when the Matachines – a men's dance group – defended the church against the attacks of the Fariseos. During this battle the Matachines wore headdresses covered with flowers and ribbons and carried wands decorated with feathers; their opponents wore grotesque masks and carried wooden swords and daggers. As the Fariseos charged the church they were met by a barrage of flowers, representing divine blessings, were defeated, and their swords and masks then burnt on a huge fire. The older Yaqui hunting rituals were reorganized to take place in the context of a fiesta, led by old men called Pascolas. In these, however, there is a clearer indication of traditional form, since the Pascolas are essentially clowns who entertain the spectators with jokes and horseplay. In spite of the strong Christian influence on them, the Yaquis have remained very independent. Their services are not run by ordained priests but by Yaqui men, who are the equivalent of shamans, and are conducted in a strange mix of Yaqui, Spanish and Latin. Even the Yaqui church is an exclusive domain and has no official affiliation with the Catholic church.

Spanish attempts to extend the mission system beyond the areas occupied by the Pueblos, Pimas and Papagoes had been thwarted in the 1650s by a loose confederation of the nomadic Apache tribes, who were well established in the area by then. Their country, Apacheria, was to remain unconquered for the next two hundred years. These people could not have been more different from their neighbours: aggressive and warlike, haughtily proud, and with a reputation for both ruthlessness and recklessness.

They were quickly to earn themselves a name as fierce guerrilla fighters. The Spanish feared them, as did the later Mexicans and Americans. Some

Below: Pueblo weavers used a narrow belt loom to produce these intricate woven wool and cotton sashes that were worn as part of their ceremonial costume.

Right: Pima and Papago basketwork are virtually identical in their motifs and weaves. There is a tendency, however, for Pima baskets to be predominantly light and to employ linear patterns, whereas Papago baskets are darker and the patterns more massed. The larger basket shown here is Pima, the smaller one is Papago.

Apache groups became mounted warriors, on horses they took from the Spanish; the word for 'Mexican' was an Apache epithet, and all Mexicans were considered by the Apaches to be loathsome and cowardly. Stories are legion of Mexican armies, being told the direction in which a gang of Apache marauders had gone, setting off immediately – in the opposite direction! The Apaches also fought with some of the other tribes in the region, particularly the Pima and Papago whose lands they had invaded; and they even managed to rouse some of the Pueblos to anger. The name Apache comes from the Zuni word Apachu, meaning 'Enemy'.

Perhaps the sincerest recognition of the Apache temperament was the grudging respect in which the early White Americans in the area held them. To be deemed tough by such as these was the highest accolade, for this was the true Wild West and many of its occupants came to the gunfighters' and

rustlers' hideouts of the canyons to escape the noose and the posse. In just one single year, 1877, the State Governor posted descriptions of over 5,000 bandits and outlaws who had sought refuge in the Rio Grande district. Apacheria, as far as the law-abiding citizen was concerned, was the end of the world.

Yet how had these straggling nomads managed to acquire such a reputation? They were small groups with little tribal authority or leadership. Each individual was free to come and go as he pleased, and although a particularly respected warrior might organize a war party or a raid against the Spanish herds and others would follow him, he had no authority other than respect. Even this limited leadership applied specifically to that single occasion. There were about three dozen of these groups, with names such as Jicarilla, Mescalero and Chiricahua, who, although friendly to each other, certainly did not think of themselves as a single entity. They were hunters of buffalo and other game on the grasslands and in the mountains, and raided their neighbours when opportunity arose; yet just as often they traded with them, exchanging meat with the Pueblos in return for corn. The Jicarilla were frequent guests at the ceremonies of Picuris and Taos Pueblos.

We might assume that tales of their ferocity are exaggerations by the writers of Western fiction; but we would be misled, for their reputation was often well-earned. It was also understandable as a consequence of the pressures placed on the Apaches and the atrocities committed against them. Their mistreatment began with their first contacts with the Spanish, when the Apaches were openly defiant. Instead of fleeing in terror at the sight of the Spaniards on their strange mounts, the 'Querechos' – for the name Apache had not then been coined – used their powerful sinew-backed bows to unleash arrows against these unknown beasts, which their shamans then dissected and studied, declaring that it was a marvellous animal with superior powers over their own dogs. Rather than instilling awe of the Big Dogs of the Spanish, this prompted a number of the Apache groups to acquire them for their own use by raiding the Spanish herds.

The Spanish, meeting only hostility, declared these tribes could never be converted to Catholicism and must always remain heathen. They declared a war of extermination, and wholesale slaughter of the Apaches began, culminating in a grand celebration in Santa Fe when the Palace of the Governors was garlanded with the severed ears of Apache Indians. Mexico and the American states were later to follow the same pattern, since both adopted policies of Apache extermination. To facilitate the extermination policy, some of the states offered high bounty payments for Apache scalps.

It was extremes like these that caused an Apache backlash during the 1800s. Hostile action against the tribes had been taken by everyone in the area; Indian, Mexican, Spanish and American, the only exceptions being the Pueblo groups, who defended their lands when necessary but never waged aggressive warfare. Sometimes the hostilities were reprisals, as among the Pima and Papago Indians who suffered similarly at Apache hands; but it would be true to say that the Apache character seemed to bring them into conflict more regularly than any other tribe in the area.

In the 19th century, however, the kidnapping of Apache children started, escalating as the century progressed and reaching its highest level during the 1860s and 1870s. Boys were enslaved, girls were forced into prostitution. These factors, particularly the prostitution of Apache girls – for chastity in their young women was rigorously demanded – set the tribes on the path of terrorizing their foes and brutally mistreating anyone who fell into their hands. It was at this point that Apache torture and mutilation of enemies began – and that the wars of extermination took on a new vigour.

At first the Apaches were almost universally friendly to the Americans, regarding them as allies in their battles with the Mexicans, with whom the Americans were also at war. These friendships broke down after the Treaty of Guadalupe Hidalgo in 1848, which put the Southwest in American rather than Mexican hands. The Apaches continued to raid into Mexico, and their refusal to recognize American dominance, coupled with the fact that the Americans came under pressure from the Mexican government to deal with the Indian menace, meant they were now a nuisance to be removed from the area.

In the fights that followed, the Apaches produced some outstanding leaders – Mangas Colorados, Cochise, and Victorio among them. The extermination policy continued until 1871, with the American army, vigilante groups, the Texas and Colorado Volunteers, town mobs, trappers and miners, and Pima and Papago Indian allies all arrayed against a handful of hostile Apache groups. When the war of extermination ended, however, not a single Apache band had been subdued. Fighting was to continue sporadically until 1886, under the leadership of Geronimo, until the Apaches were finally placed on reservations after surrendering voluntarily.

That they were courageous fighters goes without saying; their reputation for barbarism was earned simply for responding in kind to the treatment they received. Many of the qualities they credited to the White man – whom they called killers, gluttons, thieves, adulterers and liars – were exactly those which had been introduced into the world by the Trickster Coyote, and one of Coyote's characteristics was that he reversed the normal order of things. Apache life had been seriously disrupted by continual fighting, and in many senses their 'normal' world order no longer seemed to apply. There is no indication that they ever gloried in warfare, and even their earlier pattern of raiding was thought of as having an economic basis.

If they had been driven by some kind of 'war lust' we would expect to find elaborate ceremonials related to war and mythical characters of exceptional aggressiveness, but these are almost absent in Apache myth and ritual. There is a mythical figure called Killer of Enemies, who has a twin brother named Child of Water; but similar

twin characters are also found among the Pueblos and represent a struggle for survival and not a desire to wage war. The Twins are the opposing poles in the struggle, since all of nature has these dual aspects.

In ceremony, too, it is not a war ritual that takes precedence, but a girl's puberty rite, when she becomes of age, formally able to marry and have sexual relations which will ensure the continuance of the people. The Mountain Spirits, known as Gan, are analogous to the Kachinas; and the importance of this puberty ritual is shown by the appearance of the Gan Dancers, who live on

the mountain tops and in caves which mark the boundary of the Apache world. By dancing for the girl they effectively make her the centre of this world. They are similar to the Kachinas in some respects; they even bring clowns with them, who mimic their dance and make the people laugh.

Long ago, in the mists of mythical time, the Gan lived among the people; but Coyote, in his usual guise as a troublemaker, introduced death, and the Gan fled to their caves and mountains to escape the fate that humans would thereafter have to suffer. They remembered the pleasant times they had spent with the Apaches, however, and vowed to return to bring blessings to the encampments and to drive away any sickness or illness. Their appearance at the puberty rite is significant; the entire ritual is symbolic of the life journey the girl will take and the Gans' presence ensures this will be long, happy and healthy.

While she is influenced beneficially by the Gan, the girl is able to exert special curative powers

under the direction of the shaman who conducts the ceremony. She is unable to refuse anyone who comes to her for aid, since the Gan promised their assistance to all the people, but the shaman helps her by singing long chants that bring his own spiritual powers into attendance, reinforcing those already being expressed through the Mountain Spirits.

All the healing rites are conducted with a great deal of solemnity and seriousness. The activities of the clowns, however, deny this sombre aspect of the Gan spirits. Each movement of the Gan Dancers is echoed by them in an exaggerated form. When the Gan raise their painted wands decorated with sacred mystic symbols, the clowns wave worthless branches in the air; when the Gan Dancers stoop down to touch Earth Woman, from whom all life derives, the clowns roll in the mud and make obscene gestures.

One Apache band requires specific mention. They were initially just one of the many small groups who came to the Southwest in the 1500s, when they occupied the lands of an abandoned Pueblo called Nabajú. Their early history is the same as that of the other Apache tribes; but they took over some customs from neighbouring groups and from the Spanish and Mexicans. They started herding sheep, and planting peach orchards and corn fields in the canyons. Although they had a reputation for raiding, they adopted many of their captives and welcomed other Apache groups into an alliance that grew in numbers until the population was larger than that of all the other Apache tribes put together. These are the Navajo: a name which they, incidentally, are unable to pronounce since there is no 'v' sound in the Navajo language. In common with all the Apache tribes of the area, they refer to themselves simply as Dine, meaning the People.

Because of the size of the tribe, their raiding was seen as a serious threat to the stability of the region. In 1864 Kit Carson was sent to remove them to a reservation. Instead of engaging in open battle, he went to Canyon de Chelly and destroyed their crops. It took 300 men a full day to cut down the corn fields, 5,000 peach trees were felled, and the flocks were slaughtered. Starved into submission, the Navajo surrendered and were sent to Bosque Redondo near Fort Sumner, in eastern New Mexico, where they were to be trained as farmers. They were reluctant learners, and conditions at Bosque Redondo were squalid and inadequate, resulting in the deaths of 2,000 Indians. White authorities quickly realized it would be cheaper to supervise them as a self-supporting community on a small part of their original homeland than it was to keep them as prisoners of war. A tract of barren lands of mesquite and yucca in which the European settlers and farmers had no interest was selected for the reservation. Many of the White people who supported the return of the Navajo secretly hoped they would disappear. Each family was issued three sheep and sent back; they were expected to walk through nearly 300 miles of desert lands in which water and pasture were scarce before they could reach the reservation.

Remarkably, the Navajo survived. They were a

Above: This selection of Navajo blankets and rugs illustrates the use of basic geometric patterns to produce very different overall designs in which no two were ever alike. The contemporary Apache concha belt hanging over the blankets uses plain german silver discs (or conchas).

Right: Unlike the Pueblos, the nomadic Apache never produced significant quantities of pottery, relying instead on more easily transported basketwork. The basket shown here has a diameter of 33 cm (13 inches) and was used for storage.

Far right: The Southwest contains many dramatic landscapes; but perhaps no other had as much significance as Spider Rock in Canyon de Chelly. It was from there that Spider Woman let down the thread of life to create a human presence in the area.

progressive people who quickly picked up new skills, especially those of silverworking, which both they and the Pueblos took over from itinerant Mexican traders, and weaving, which they learned from the Pueblos. Their population increased rapidly as immigrant groups joined the tribe. From being a small band in the 1500s they numbered some 10,000 when Kit Carson rounded them up in the 1860s; but expansion in the post-Bosque Redondo days gave them a population of 60,000 in the 1940s and over 120,000 in the 1960s. Today they are by far the largest North American tribe.

It is a success story as remarkable as that of the Pueblos; but whereas the Pueblos survived by refusing change, the Navajo did so by wholeheartedly embracing it. Both groups, however, insist on entering a contemporary world on terms which they dictate rather than on terms which are imposed upon them. In spite of their progressiveness, the Navajo still cling to many of their ancient traditions, particularly the need of the nomad to be constantly on the move.

Their sheep farms and corn fields would appear to contradict the ethos of nomadism, as they have to be tended, and therefore require settled communities. The Navajo solved this in a unique manner, by not forming villages. Each community

Far right: The Gans were the Apache equivalent of the Hopi and Zuni Kachinas. In the depths of mythological time, the Gans lived with the people; but foolish acts of the people introduced death, and the Gans fled the villages so they might remain immortal. They remembered the dances, feasts and celebrations they had formerly attended, and regarded the Apaches with fond affection, so at certain times of the year, particularly during the girls' puberty ritual, they would return to the villages to confer blessings on their inhabitants. At this time dancers wearing elaborate headdresses and carrying wooden wands impersonated the Gan spirits.

Among the Apache, the most important moment in a woman's life was when she reached puberty. At this point she stopped being a child and came of marriageable age, and accepted her responsibility as the life-bearer who would ensure the continuance of the people. During an elaborate puberty ceremony, she wore this cap decorated with symbolic emblems representing the life-giving and healing rays of the Gan spirits.

consisted of a number of widely scattered log houses, called hogans, each of which was home to a single family. For any kind of social interaction it was necessary to travel, often for long distances over small pathways and trails. The cohesiveness of Navajo society, since everyone seemed to have friends or relatives everywhere, bears testimony to the frequency with which these trails were used.

In keeping with the nomadic ideal, much of Navajo belief was concerned with movement. Their land was defined by the travels of the First People, who named Turquoise Mountain as its eastern limit, Abalone Mountain in the west, Jet Mountain in the north, and White Shell Mountain in the south. Their songs and chants asked that they might 'walk in beauty', and the ideal of old age was to wander forever on a harmonious path in the company of grasshoppers, with dew at their feet. It is an enchanting image, suited to this enchanted country; for Navajoland is starkly beautiful, and seems to hold mystic symbolism within itself.

It is impossible to stand on the rim of Canyon de Chelly, looking across at the twin pinnacles of the monumental Spider Rock, without sensing something of the magic that inspired Spider Woman to lower the thread of life from its summit. Nor can one look down at the thin silver ribbon of the river hundreds of feet below without feeling the immense power that has been used to carve the canyon. It is a paradoxical feeling, since from here the river appears as an insignificant trickle. One need know nothing of Navajo belief to feel these things: they are in the earth, the sky and the rocks.

Within these surroundings the Navajos believed they unconsciously absorbed elements from the world about them. Wind breathed its own life into their bodies, Sun gave them energy and imbued them with his healing powers, Water gave them her strength. They, in turn, redirected these gifts into the things they made. A Navajo blanket contains the forms and colours of the deserts and the canyons, and its patterns derive from the symbiotic relationship between the people and nature. When worn, the blanket becomes a living entity: its colours glowing as Sun reanimates them, its patterns changing to conform to the body of the

wearer. Although worn by men, they were woven by women, who imbued them with their own qualities as the life-bearers of the tribe. So powerful were they that each blanket had a small mistake deliberately woven into the pattern to break its perfection: a reminder of human frailty. Such objects were never intended to be hung on museum walls or placed in dusty collections.

In all these things there is an order, or correctness, which gives them their power, and which underlies everything a Navajo does. Their religion is neither a doleful reverence for nor a thanks-offering to the gods and spirits; it is a joyful celebration of life and of all the blessings the world contains, and its only prerequisite is that the rituals should be carried out in a precise order. White visitors to a Navajo 'chant', more used to the semi-automatic repetition of hymns and psalms and the silent offering of prayer, are often surprised at the enthusiasm and exuberance of these events and the way in which 'non-religious' activities, such as horse racing and buffoonery, are integrated with them.

To the Navajo there is no contradiction. What can say more about freedom and the joy of living than a horse and rider? Blended as one, racing across the flat bottomlands of the canyons, the horse's hooves reflecting the fleetness of Wind, its bridle capturing the Sun, both man and animal take energy from and give energy back to the forces inherent in the world about them. The Navajo emphasize the privileges they have been given, and will always speak first of the gifts they have received and of joy to be obtained rather than of duties imposed on them.

They are, of course, acutely aware of the nature of these duties. Navajo life is based on taking no more than is needed, and always giving something back; on acting truthfully and honestly, and sharing good fortune with others; on being industrious, dependable, skillful and good-humoured; and, most importantly, in everything to follow the 'Right Way', the path of beauty and happiness which is strewn with sacred cornmeal and which leads ultimately back to the centre of everything.

In Navajo belief no god takes precedence, no force exerts greater influence than another, no element receives undue preference. Each and every constituent of the world has its own gift to offer and its own specific skills. Changing Woman, who created the people from scales flaked from her own skin, and whose sons, the Twin War Gods, rid this world of the monsters and other evil forces so that humans could live happily, is no more – nor less – important than Badger, who burrowed from beneath the earth to create an opening through which the people could step from a previous underground world into the country where they now live. We might expect this place of emergence to take on special significance; yet it is only an ordinary badger hole, in some unidentified place that may lie in the mountains of north-western New Mexico.

The Navajo concept of the universe is one in which all parts are interrelated through a harmonious balance. This is precarious and can easily be

Above: Yeis, like the Kachinas and Gans, were invisible spirits who conferred benefits. The Navajo recorded the Yeis presence in weaving, such as on this rug from 1880.

Far right: The Yaqui are a refugee tribe from Mexico who, although the majority now live in the Southwest, have no status as Indians in the United States. Many of their rituals and celebrations have been strongly influenced by the Spanish and incorporate European elements; but they also perform dances that are purely aboriginal, such as this buffalo dance.

upset: to touch a lightning-struck tree might bring on unbearable consequences. Illness is the result of disturbing the harmony. Healing rites are the remedy. To bring the world back into order, a shaman initiates a chant during which a sandpainting composed of symbolic designs that have spiritual force is constructed. By seating the patient in the centre, and placing elements of the sandpainting on his or her body, the patient's illness is redirected back to its source.

Sandpaintings are not unique to the Navajo, who in fact borrowed them from the Pueblos, but it is among the Navajo that they come to have particular importance as the principal means of restoring harmony. They are made with various coloured earths, charcoal and cornmeal, which are sprinkled on the ground to create symmetrical patterns up to 6m (20 ft) in diameter, depicting aspects of Navajo mythology. A 'Singer', or shaman,

conducts the ceremony and directs the making of the sandpainting, in which a dozen or more people might be involved. These ceremonies, which are also called sings, ways, or chants, take place after the sun has set, and the sandpainting is always destroyed before the sun rises; because it is believed to absorb and nullify the patient's sickness. Exposure to Sun's life-giving rays would, therefore, reactivate the illness.

There are 50 or more curing chants organized into six main groups, some of them requiring a complicated series of sandpaintings that are made over a period of nine nights. Prominent among them are the Blessingway, used to promote general good health and well-being; the Shooting Chant, for curing illnesses attributed to snakes or lightning; the Night Chant, which is a cure for insanity and paralysis – although we should bear in mind that in the Navajo way of looking at things,

No commentary on the Southwest would be complete without a picture of Geronimo, perhaps the most famous of Apache chiefs. This photograph was taken by C. S. Fly shortly before Geronimo's voluntary surrender to General Crook in 1871.

something which is 'out of order' may be thought of as an insane action – and the Windway, which is for disease caused by evil winds.

Colours used in the sandpaintings are directional and defined by the travels of the First People. White is used for the east, representing daylight or dawn; the west is yellow, symbolizing cloud and evening light; blue stands for the south and for the sky; while the north is black, for darkness. The centre, which is the health-restoring part of the sandpainting, is red since this is the life-colour, and representative of sunlight.

The most spectacular of the chants, and the one which takes priority over all others, is the Night Chant. It is also known as the Yeibichai, since on the eighth night of the Chant, the Yeis – or masked dancers – make an appearance. Yeis, like the Kachinas and Gans, represent mythical beings who return to the people to confer benefits. In the Yeibichai their specific function is to initiate children into the secrets of the supernatural world; but once their blessings have been conferred, the Yei dancers remove their masks, revealing that they are really human. Hastseyalti, the male Talking God, places his mask on the head of each boy initiate; while his female counterpart, Hasttsebaad, does the same for the girls. In this way they are able to view the world through the eyes of the Yeibichais, and gain an insight into the relationship between man and the spirits.

For the Navajo, as for the other Apache groups, this relationship is always a beneficial one; even though it may at times brings hardship and difficulty. By travelling along a hazardous path, one gains knowledge and spiritual growth; and if these difficulties can be borne with humour and mitigated through joyful song, they can be overcome, and their 'true' power for good may be realized. It is a fitting belief for this harsh land, where the yucca protects itself with sharp leaves and the cactus survives without water, but in which there is a monumental grandeur and power that words alone can never describe. Navajo strength and resilience are attested to by the fact that one can visit Navajo and Apache gatherings today, that continue to carry benefits from an ancient past forward along the sacred pollen trail.

Changes have, of course, taken place; but these have usually been absorbed without seriously disrupting the flow of traditional thought. Most important, perhaps, is that the Indians of the area have managed to hold on to their own world-views. They have not lost sight of the links that bind them permanently to the natural forces by which they are surrounded, and of which they are part.

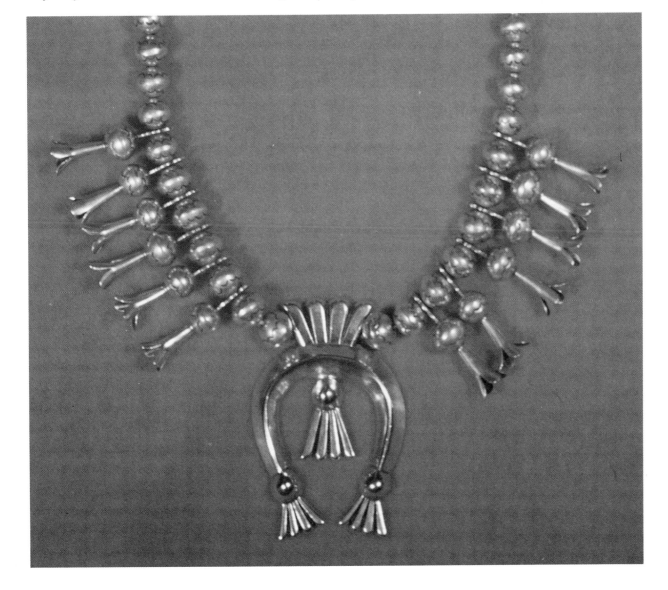

The squash blossom necklace is a symbol of Navajo identity, and is worn by both men and women. Silverworking was introduced by the Spanish, but the design elements of the necklace are ancient; even though the Naja, the horseshoe-shaped pendent, is often erroneously stated as deriving from Spanish bridle ornaments.

CALIFORNIA AND THE GREAT DESERT

Far right: The Hupa were one of many Californian tribes to suffer a severe decline from White incursions into their areas. Prior to this, they were a numerous tribe who lived peaceably in a land of plenty, and were able to spend time simply relaxing and enjoying the benefits their country had to offer. The woman shown here is dressed in a traditional costume of shell embroidered skirt and basketwork hat, and carries her infant in a cane cradleboard.

Below: Although most North American tribes made dolls as childrens' playthings, the bundled and painted grasses used here are typical of the Mohave.

This region comprises three distinct culture groups: those of California, the Great Basin, and the Plateau. The Californian tribes occupied an area that corresponds almost exactly with the modern state of this name. Great Basin culture centred on the arid, desert-like regions of Nevada and Utah. To the north of this, in the more mountainous areas drained by the river systems of the Columbia and Fraser, lay the Plateau.

Californian lifestyles were based on a hunting-gathering economy that ran continuously from the earliest prehistoric period until it began to be disrupted after the Spanish arrival in the 1600s. There were few changes over this long time-scale, mainly because the lives of these peoples were extremely rich and varied due to the abundance of natural resources and the widely different micro-environments found here. Parts of California contain huge redwood forests, whereas elsewhere there are oak parklands or chaparral growth, but the entire region enjoys Mediterrranean temperatures and a lack of climatic extremes. Stability was ensured since there was no need for groups to expand into other tribal territories and resources were more than sufficient to maintain large populations in localized areas.

The area attracted migrant groups from widely different backgrounds, as it still does today. About 500 small tribal groups, speaking as many as 100 separate languages, lived here, occupying very specific territories and relying on local products. Mussels, abalone and some hunting of sea mammals were important to the coastal tribes. Those of the interior were more dependent on seeds and berries, and, in certain localities, on the acorn, which was often a staple crop. They all supplemented their gathering with limited hunting, particularly of small game and wildfowl; but none of them practiced agriculture: the resources already at their disposal were so rich as to make this unnecessary.

There had been sporadic contacts with Europeans along the coasts for some 60 years prior to 1602, when three ships commanded by Sebastian Vizcaino sailed from Mexico and landed near Monterey. Vizcaino was clearly impressed by the Indians he met, claiming the men to be tall, handsome and strong, able to carry for a mile a burden which a Spaniard could barely lift. Their women he described as beautiful, among the fairest on

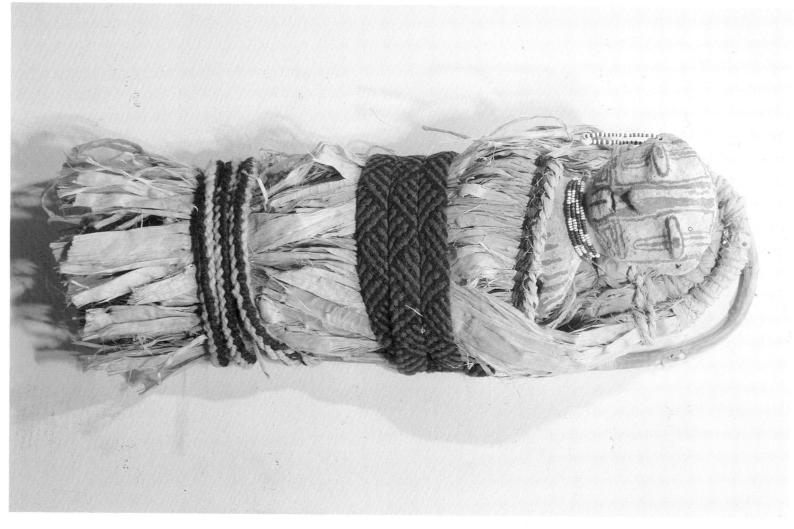

this earth. But he was most impressed by their friendliness, and was reluctant to leave when, so he says, many of the Indians wept as a demonstration of their sadness at his departure.

A mild disposition and a generous character were typical of all these peoples; a reflection of a country where extremes were unknown and in which there was an abundance simply to be picked up. There was no need for competition; although certain village leaders became wealthy through trading the goods of their locality to nearby groups, using shell money as a means of keeping count, there is no indication that any of them ever tried to exert authority over their neighbours.

They lived side by side, visiting, trading and exchanging goods, yet each retained its own distinctive customs and habits. Even when hunting they remained within their own well-defined tribal territories and did not intrude on those utilized by other groups.

More than half the total indigenous population of California resided in the central area, and this can be said to be characteristic of the region, since it was isolated from influences coming from elsewhere. Among the southern tribes there are cultural expressions which appear to have a connection with those of the Southwest, where trade links had been established; whereas the northern

ing, exchanging gossip, telling stories, laughing and joking. Small children ran in and out, constantly seeking favours. The men ate and slept here as well as smoking tobacco ritually, and performing ceremonies before undertaking other tasks, in order to bless them and ensure their successful outcome.

Women had no meeting house as such, but gathered together to work collectively when large undertakings required their attention. Often a group would sit together as they worked on making the baskets in which these tribes excelled. Few of these are made today, but from those in museum collections, and the comments of visitors to the tribes in the early twentieth century while the craft was still alive, we can be permitted a glimpse of the skill that went into their manufacture. Our first impression has to be of the uniformity that expresses itself. Baskets dating from an early period are indistinguishable from those made relatively recently; there is a continuity that is in itself remarkable, and we can often only attribute a date when the basketmaker is known and has permitted her name to be disclosed.

Such consistency reflects the extreme stability in the lives of these tribes. The absence of change and the continuation of the ancient patterns demonstrates a way of thinking in which power derives from constancy. These were not people who felt dissatisfied with their lives and sought something new. They knew exactly what they wanted, rooted in the traditions that had been

Californian abalone was far more vivid than the pallid Northwest Coast variety, and a lively trade existed at the Dalles on the Columbia River between the northern Californians and the southern British Columbia tribes. The pendant illustrated here is made from shell collected off the California coast.

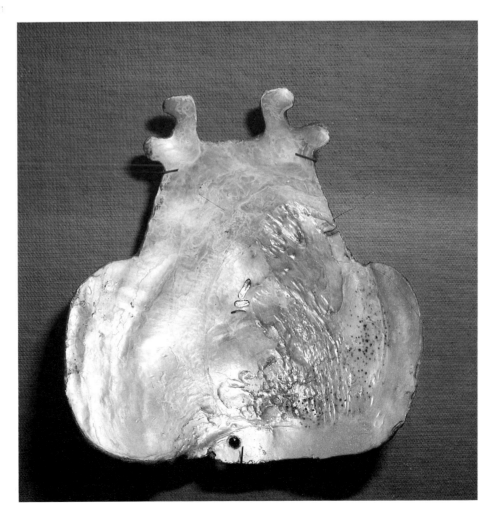

people were closely associated with other groups living in Washington and southern British Columbia, who introduced stronger ideas of wealth and status, and a somewhat more aggressive outlook.

The central Californian tribes included people such as the Pomo, Miwok, Maidu, Wintu, Wintun, Mono and Mariposa. Their villages were always small. A few dozen earth- or mat-covered lodges at the most were situated in what appears to be a random pattern, but which almost certainly had some formal structure that eludes modern scholars, around a larger structure which served as the men's meeting house. Much of a man's day was spent here, when he was not out hunting or fish-

Right: Map showing the approximate locations of the Californian, Great Desert, and Plateau tribes when first encountered by Europeans.

Far right: Throughout most of California fish were abundant in such numbers that lines and dip nets were more than sufficient to provide for a family's needs, although weirs and traps were also employed in some areas. The Karok fisherman shown here has paddled a dug-out canoe into the middle of a river, and is using a woven net of a type that would have been familiar to many tribes of the region.

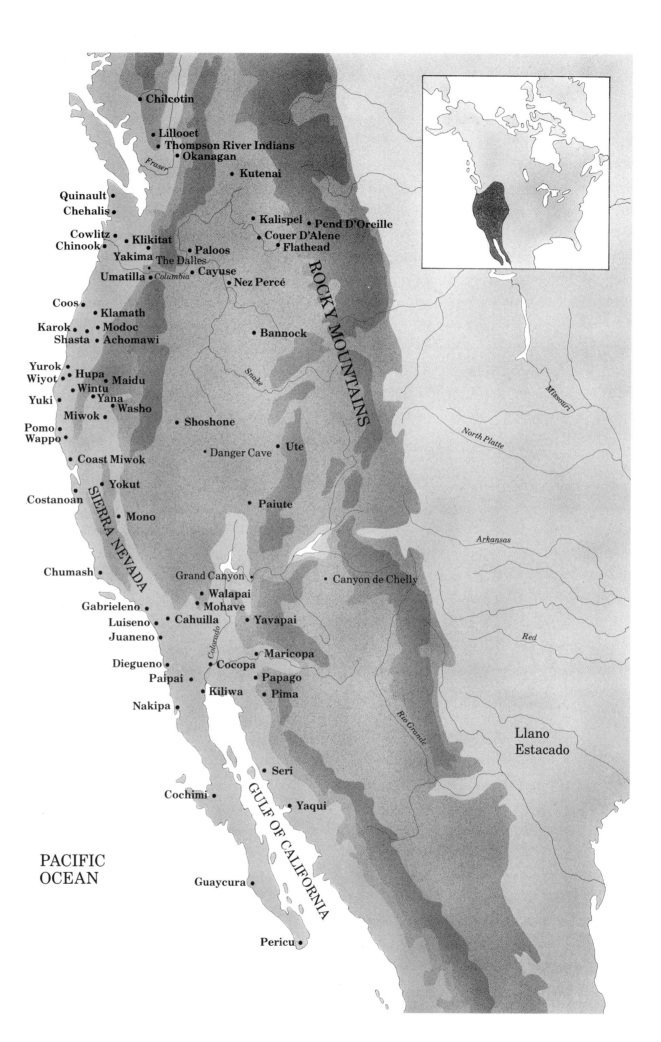

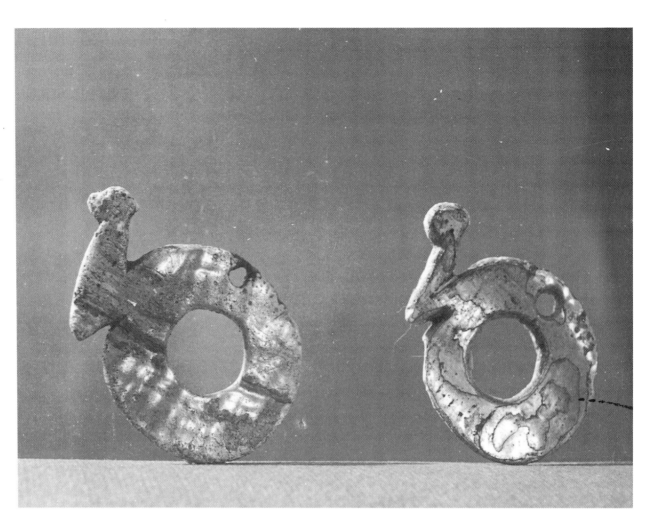

Right: The Sinagua occupied lands midway between the Southwest and California, and had a culture that incorporated elements from both regions. The ear ornaments in this photograph are made from abalone shell obtained in trade with the coastal tribes.

Below: Participants in the Kuksu cult of the Pomo Indians wore distinctive regalia which included the ear decorations depicted here.

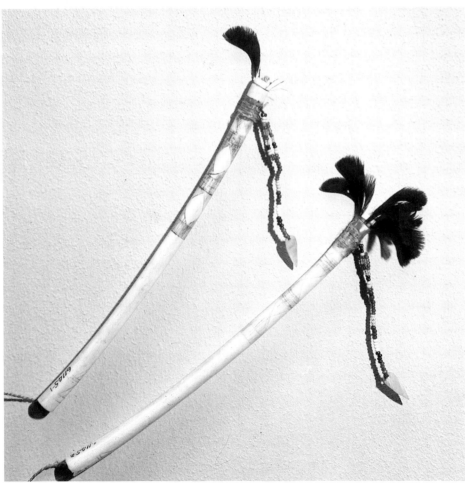

passed down over many generations.

Some of the baskets they made were so tiny that it was impossible to count the threads, and these were intended purely as demonstrations of skill. Others were so big that they stood as high as a man and were used to store the large quantities of acorns and seeds they gathered. It might take a year or more to make one of these massive storage baskets, and throughout this time the stitch and weave would be maintained in perfect balance. All the basketmakers thought of their products as being animate things, containing life from the grasses and rushes with which they were made. Perhaps the most beautiful were the gift baskets of the Pomo. Intended as presents, these were covered with the brilliant feathers of hummingbirds and woodpeckers, and adorned with shells and abalone. Long fringes hung with shells gave them a jewel-like quality, and they were often given a strap so they might be suspended. When hung up, they slowly turned in the Californian sun which flashed and reflected back from the highly polished shell surfaces.

Very often the women's social gatherings took place inside the family houses where, away from the men, they played stick and dice games. Most Indians of North America were keen gamblers and the Californian tribes were no exception. Extensive bets would be placed on the throw of split acorn dice inlaid with delicate shell inserts, or on the lucky guess of how many sticks might remain when a bundle of forty or fifty had been shuffled by the 'dealer' and then counted out in groups of four.

Plate 27

California Indians were renowned for the exquisite beauty of their basketwork, which is amply illustrated in this collection of baskets from various tribes of the area.

The stakes were usually household goods such as baskets; but at larger gatherings they might be made in the form of 'Kaia', shell strings of dentalium or clam, which the women wore around their necks and had sewn to the woven rush aprons that each of them wore. The shell strings acted as currency and indicated a woman's status, since the wife of a wealthy man might wear considerable numbers of these necklaces, often displaying them as an indication of the bride price that had been paid to validate her marriage. They were important, too, in maintaining the family's position in the tribe. By redistributing their wealth in the form of gifts and presents, the family could count on the support of others.

Shell strings would also be used if any disagreement had arisen in the village and someone's property had been damaged, or if tempers had flared and someone had been injured. In these cases the village leader was called to arbitrate, and to decide the indemnity in shells and other goods that was required to settle the matter amicably. Occasionally a family feud might get out of hand and another village would become involved, but this was the nearest the Californian tribes ever came to war.

Any act of violence was considered in a negative light. The central Californians had no weapons for warfare, and in a fight would resort to whatever happened to be lying nearby. The hunting bows, digging sticks, a convenient branch or a rock picked up from the ground – these were the weapons of these non-aggressive peoples. They had no war rituals or defensive items such as shields. If an opponent were to be killed, the scalp might be taken; yet this was done so that it could be brought back to the village where it would be mourned and given a proper burial; the incident would be resolved more rapidly by treating the dead with respect.

Inter-village disputes were very rare, and were usually caused by personal animosities and arguments rather than through any more serious cause. To ensure that these disputes might quickly be ended, the village leaders always made certain they did not become directly involved. In this way they could meet together as disinterested parties who would show no favour to either side in the argument, and who would therefore be able to decide a fair indemnity to be paid by each side in the dispute. Even so, the victors always paid considerably more than the losers, and the wealthy

93

suffered much higher penalties than the poor.

Usually, however, life ran very smoothly and the disapproval of the group if someone acted out of order was generally sufficient to prevent matters going any further. Banishment from the tribe could be used to ensure social control, although they only ever resorted to this solution with great reluctance, since such a course of action almost certainly constituted a death sentence. The tribal boundaries were so strictly defined that anyone who had been banished would have to move into another tribal area, to live among people whose language he did not understand and who would be unlikely to offer shelter to a known trouble-maker.

It was better to rehabilitate the offender. The village leader would counsel him and point out the error of his ways, and a prominent shaman would attempt to discover if he had been afflicted by some malignant spirit so that a cure might be effected. Only if these attempts failed would the whole village be called together to discuss the matter. After long deliberation, in which all the facts were exposed for public scrutiny, a vote was taken and, if this proved unanimous, banishment might then take place.

The role of the shaman in these affairs reflects the importance of shamanic activity among the Californian tribes, where the shaman, usually a woman, was responsible for the physical health of the community. The specific power a shaman possessed depended on the content of her power dream; yet, to a far higher extent than in any other area of North America, where they might be involved in ritual activities as priests or as diviners and seers, Californian shamans were exclusively concerned with healing and medicine. Some were specialized in curing certain diseases, others were skilled diagnosticians who were able to determine the cause of illness but required the help of another shaman who had the power to cure it.

Power dreams were given greater significance among the tribes of southern California, where they were often induced by the use of a narcotic derived from the Jimson Weed or Datura. So important was this that a cult developed around it, to which all male members of the society belonged. This Toloache cult was principally concerned with the initiation of young men through visions received as the consequence of taking an infusion made from the roots of the Datura. Dream-visions received under the influence of this drug were believed to control the initiate's mystic thought throughout adulthood.

Much of southern Californian life reflects that described for the central region, with the same

Alice Spot, a Hupa woman, is shown in front of a traditional plank house. She wears a shell-decorated costume that was typical of wealthy families from central and northern California.

abhorrence of violence and a similar organization into small independent tribal units with abundant resources. Some tribes such as the Seri – who lived just across the modern U.S./Mexico border in Baja California but who are a definite part of the southern Californian tradition – rejected outside influences and continued to live well into the historic period in the same ways as their forefathers had always done. The Seri made their clothing from pelican and swan skins, and refused to accept the introduction of cloth and of metal tools and implements. As far as they were concerned the ancient ways had always been adequate and efficient and there was no reason why they should disrupt these for the sake of unnecessary change. They continued to hunt sea turtles from their reed boats, using only stone and shell points and blades on their harpoons and knives.

Other southern Californian tribes were incorporated in the Spanish mission system and their own tribal designations have not been passed on. We know them by names such as Diegueno, the Indians of San Diego; Gabrieleno, who lived in the mission of San Gabriel near Los Angeles; or Juaneno, from the mission of San Juan de Capistrano. But it is clear that these peoples, prior to their contact with the Spanish, had trade links with the Southwest Indians, who exerted their influence on material goods. The manufacture of a limited amount of unslipped buff pottery decorated with simple red designs, frequently representing the rattlesnake, is a Southwest influence, as is their use of sandpaintings. Unlike those of the Southwest, the southern Californian sandpaintings depicted star movements and were part of an elaborate lunar-solar calendar that only the shamans were able to understand. Unfortunately, little is known of this area, since many tribal identities were lost when the mission system was introduced.

In northern California, influences came from the tribes of Washington and British Columbia. These reveal themselves in a greater insistence on wealth displays and a more aggressive attitude. They shared the same aversion to warfare as other Californian tribes, and made no distinction between war and murder, but feuding played a much larger part in their lives. This was most frequent among those tribes living in the northern parts, especially along the Klamath River where aggressive influences were strongest – to the extent that Klamath men developed a stone-headed mallet exclusively for fighting purposes, and had a form of armour made from elk hide to protect the chest. If fighting did break out, it was common for both men and women to become involved. The end of hostilities was always marked, however, by the traditional Californian practice of a dance, in which the antagonists came together to decide what payments would be made for damages, to offset the losses that each side felt it had suffered.

Contrary to the systems of the south, wealth was of overriding importance to the Klamath, Modoc, Hupa, Yurok and other tribes of the north. Displays of a family's assets contributed greatly to the status they enjoyed. Although these never reached the British Columbia extremes of the

deliberate destruction of wealth goods, to pay over and beyond the bride price demanded for a girl of impeccable manners and morals was normal for wealthy families. They lived in the best built homes in the best situations, and had treasure chests full of shell string money and of valuable white deerskin dance costumes and red woodpecker feather headdresses.

Only the wealthiest families could afford to sponsor the great celebrations at which these costumes were displayed, since the feasts and dances might last 20 days or more. Their daughters became the debutantes of the tribe; able to command high dowries and with the discretion to refuse any suitors who were unable to match their family expectations. Marriages between these high-ranking families created an aristocracy and a system of social class far removed from that of the other tribes of the area.

The unfinished basket tray shown here is Achomawi, and is one of the few artefacts from this tribe to have survived in modern collections.

Even so, they were still very much part of the general Californian cultural ethos. Essentially non-aggressive, all these peoples enjoyed eating, singing, dancing, and journeying to a neighbouring village to visit old friends and make new ones. Their lives were usually relaxed and comfortable; although winters might bring some shortages there was never any fear of famine or their being faced by starvation. There was always time to stop and dream, or simply to reflect on how good life was; little thought was given to the fact that it might be any different.

Far right: The Hupa and Wintu Indians relied quite heavily on proceeds from the hunt, and in recognition of this fact they held annual ceremonies at which the deer was honoured. To propitiate the animal spirits, they chose carefully selected skins of animals that were believed to have been specially marked as sacred. Among these, the white, or albino, deer was prominent. Such skins were stored in boxes together with other ritual paraphernalia and were only exposed to public scrutiny during the White Deer Dance, at which valuable offerings were made to ensure the animals' continued goodwill and to demonstrate respect for the animal powers.

Right: The Tulare Indians, who lived on the Tule River, wove representational forms into their baskets, and decorated them with the top-knots from Californian quail.

That it could be different was soon to be proven in the most shattering and conclusive manner as far as the southern tribes of the region were concerned. Spanish frontiersmen, priests, soldiers and Indian allies came to San Diego in 1769. Another expedition reached Monterey in 1770. San Francisco was colonized in 1776. Between 1769 and 1823, a total of 21 Spanish missions were established along the California coast. They were given names that roll off the tongue and evoke romantic ideals: San Juan Capistrano, San Buenaventura, La Purisima Concepción, San Francisco Solano, and San Luis Obispo. But the reality was very far from being romantic.

Indian tribes were rounded up and herded like cattle. If they resisted they were killed. If they succumbed they were enslaved. The missionized Indians frequently found themselves grouped together in adobe bunkhouses with other tribes whose language they could not understand and whose customs were alien to them. Resistance to the Spanish was met by punishments that included being shackled or placed in hobbles, put in the stocks, imprisoned, and flogged. Some Indians, refusing to give up their old beliefs, were burned at the stake. There are many tales of Indians being given an opportunity to convert prior to burning so that their souls might be saved and go to heaven. On enquiring whether the Spaniards went to heaven when they died, they were assured

that this was so; whereupon the Indians refused conversion, claiming it was better to suffer eternal damnation than to meet another Spaniard.

At the missions the Indians received instruction in the Spanish language, in Christian dogma, and in hymn singing. At other times they were put to work carding wool, tanning hides, preparing tallow, cultivating hemp and wheat, cultivating oranges, making soap and candles, and carving mission furniture. Resistance to Spanish domination was passive, executed mainly by the women, who employed traditional herbal skills to ensure that their pregnancies were aborted. The death rate among the missionized Indians was appallingly high, with many groups losing any sense of a tribal identity. Perhaps the most significant indication of the state of the Indians was the listlessness and apathy that was common among them. From being proud, independent people who always enjoyed laughter and song, they were reduced to people who walked with their shoulders hunched in abject resignation and who could never look anyone in the eye: totally humiliated and resigned to whatever fate the Spanish might mete out to them.

Between 1811 and 1825 many of the Spanish New World conquests won independence, and in 1834 the mission system was abandoned. The pathetic remnants of the tribes were left to their own devices, and even though 50 per cent of the

mission lands were theoretically given back to the Indians, most of these were immediately secured by the California ranchos. The Indians continued to work on these in much the same conditions as they had faced at the missions.

In 1846 America conquered California, and in 1848 the California gold rush began. California declared itself a state in 1850, with a non-Indian population of 260,000, compared with one of only 15,000 two years previously. The gold rush was to prove the end for the Californian Indians.

Mob rule dictated that if gold was found on

Californian tribes readily adopted new materials into their traditional artefacts, as in this Mohave collar which uses trade beads to create patterns that would formerly have been achieved by weaving different coloured grasses.

lands occupied by an Indian group, the massacre of that group was justified. Prostitution and venereal disease decimated the Indian communities. Gang rape of Indian women was so frequent and so blatant that even some of the Californian newspapers ran editorials questioning whether civilized people could condone this practice. The kidnapping of Indian children was regularly practiced. When the gold rush subsided, Californian farmers found it expedient simply to kill the Indians in their area rather than go through the lengthy process of getting state and congressional approval for their removal. From a population that may have exceeded 150,000 in the mid-1800s, the Indians of central and southern California had been reduced to less than 12,000 by the turn of the century.

Opposition was stronger among some of the

northern groups. The Modoc and Klamath tribes resisted attempts to move them from their homelands, and were settled on a reservation in the Klamath territories in 1830. Although these two tribes were related both by customs and speech, they never got on well together. The Modoc particularly resented the fact that the reservation was on Klamath lands, where they were treated as intruders, so they left the reservation to return to their own Lost River country.

Having shown their obstinacy, the Modoc were the obvious people to blame whenever friction between Whites and Indians occurred. When a group of Shastan Indians robbed a wagon train in 1853, suspicion immediately fell on the Modoc, and their camps were attacked by White mobs. The Modoc retaliated, and in the fighting their chief was killed. Kintpuash, known to the Whites as Captain Jack, was elected to the position of chief. He realized the futility of fighting, and by diplomatic bargaining managed to bring the war to an end and gained an assurance that the Modoc would be safe in the Lost River and that the boundaries of their lands would be protected from incursions by settlers and ranchers.

This was not to be the case. Friction along the borders was constant and a number of Indians were killed and molested. Modoc stock was regularly stolen, and ranchers started to graze herds in the Lost Valley. Yet somehow Kintpuash held his young warriors back and no settlers were killed. By 1864 the Lost River was becoming so thickly settled that the government decided to move the Modoc back to the Klamath reservation. Kintpuash refused to go, and the U.S. elected a more amenable Indian, Schonchin, as chief in his place. To avoid factions arising within the tribe, Kintpuash reluctantly moved his people back to the Klamath territories.

They were greeted with derision by the Klamath, who refused to let them hunt or cut timber. Eventually, in 1870, Kintpuash led 70 warriors and their families back to the Lost River country. For two years they remained there, avoiding contact with the settlers and living peacably, but then the Californian authorities decided to enforce the order returning them to the reservation. General Canby, who was in charge of troops in the area, strongly advised against this, but he was overruled, and a military campaign began. The Modoc had no heart for senseless bloodshed and agreed to surrender, but fighting started and the Indians fled in terror to the security of the lava beds around Tule Lake.

Meanwhile, another Modoc band led by Hooker Jim had been attacked for no reason by a group of civilians, and in retaliation had killed a number of settlers. Hooker Jim joined Kintpuash in the lava bed stronghold, where they held off the soldiers for nearly seven months. Eventually, General Canby organized a peace commission to negotiate terms for surrender. Under a white flag of truce, Kintpuash uncharacteristically – but almost certainly persuaded by Schonchin and Hooker Jim, who accused him of cowardice – murdered Canby and other members of the commission.

Hooker Jim and his followers then defected to

the U.S., leaving Kintpuash to defend the lava beds with fewer than 30 warriors. Under heavy artillery bombardment they surrendered. Kintpuash was sent to the gallows, Hooker Jim was pardoned, and the Modocs – what was left of them – were sent to Indian Territory, later renamed as the state of Oklahoma.

No Indian group with a strong cultural identity exists in California today. They have all been swept away by the Spanish mission system and by the American greed for gold and land, or their reservation areas have been broken up and sold off. It is a sad indictment of the values held by the so-called civilized societies, and it is sadder still that these tribes who lived in a land of plenty and who must rank among the gentlest peoples of the world have been so ruthlessly exterminated.

The last truly independent Californian Indian was discovered in 1911; a lonely, starving man whose hair was cut short to show that he was in mourning. The rest of his family had died and he was the only remaining member of the Yahi Indians. He is known simply by the name Ishi, meaning 'man', since Yahi custom forbade a person to utter his own name and there was no one else to tell it for him. He died in 1916 of tuberculosis, and with him the free Californian Indians ceased to exist.

To the north and east of California lay the Great Basin country. Separated from California by the mountains of the Sierra Nevada, this is an arid and inhospitable land, with no rivers, sparse vegetation, and little animal life. It appears utterly desolate; an area that one would, if possible, avoid at all costs. Yet, surprisingly, the archeological record indicates a very long period of habitation which, at Danger Cave in western Utah, overlooking the Great Salt Lake, dates back to about 9,000BC.

The Danger Cave people were never very numerous, since the resources of the area are too few to support a large population; but they were clearly industrious and productive, and able to utilize their environment fully. Over 2,500 artefacts were recovered from this site, more than 1,000 grinding stones, and a similar number of wood, hide and fibre articles. There are abundant projectile points and bone tools. Bones of mountain

Danger Cave in Utah is important to archeologists as one of the few Great Desert sites where a chronological sequence of events can be established. Artefacts recovered from this site indicate that early Paleo-Indians were living in much the same way as the first historic tribes encountered in this area.

Right: These feather-decorated hairpins were worn by a dancer in the Pomo Kuksu cult, and served to link the dancer with the hummingbird; thereby establishing a connection with this bird's independence and freedom of movement.

Far right: The Ute were typical of the Great Desert tribes, subsisting almost entirely on small game and the gathering of roots and berries. The Ute hunter shown here has killed a rabbit which will provide nourishment for his family. After the introduction of the horse, the Ute became equestrian and their hunting pattern changed to include seasonal movements on to the plains in search of buffalo.

sheep, deer, antelope, bison, jackrabbit, bobcat, dog, desert fox, and wood rat give us an indication of the diet of these people. Plant species found number more than 65, and some of these were fashioned into nets and ropes, textiles and basketry. The foraging and hunting way of life continued down to the historic period, and modern tribes such as the Ute, Paiute, Gosiute and Bannock were living in much the same way as their ancient ancestors when first discovered by Europeans.

In European terms these tribes were abysmally poor. Their belongings were relatively meagre, consisting mostly of rabbit skin robes and the occasional basket used for collecting piñon nuts. They hunted with throwing sticks as frequently as they used the bow and arrows. Their homes were shallow depressions in the ground, made by pulling earth out with their hands and covered with a few dry branches and anything else they could find that might serve as a windbreak. Much of their food was dug from the ground, but it was never planted. Perhaps most distasteful to the first Europeans was their custom of eating such creatures as lizards and grasshoppers. Because of the low esteem in which they were held, the Great Basin tribes soon came to be known collectively by the contemptuous name 'Digger Indians'.

We need to look a little deeper than this. The environment in which they lived was an extremely harsh one which would seem to offer no possibility of survival. A European in this area would succumb within a few days, if not within hours; but the Indians managed to eke out a living here, precarious at times, yet strong enough to have survived for at least 11,000 years. They knew every aspect of their world intimately, and had no reason to suspect that life might have been easier or any different outside their region.

None of the tribal ceremonialism found among groups living in richer environments is to be observed here; there was simply too little food to support a large gathering. Rituals were therefore family affairs, presided over by the head of a household and involving only immediate kin. Because of this enforced separation, beliefs became internalized, expressed through individual acts of supplication and personal gifts and offerings. We might call it a superstitious response, for fear of reprisal always lay behind an individual's actions. A few grains scattered to the Four Directions before eating indicated the spirits were being thought of, and placated them. Some blood from a killed rabbit, ceremoniously spilled on the ground, soothed the rabbit's spirit so that it would return to its own kind with reports of how well it had been treated and of the respect that had been shown; thus ensuring that rabbits would continue to offer themselves in the future.

To the Indian these were necessary rather than superstitious acts. Starvation was a constant threat and no chances could be taken that an essential resource might suddenly be withdrawn. This is not to say that they were unaware of the riches their environment held. All their senses were acutely tuned to the land. Many a White traveller has been astonished, when traversing these desolate wastes with a local Indian guide, to

observe the guide suddenly drop to his knees, take out a knife, and dig up an edible tuber in the midst of an apparently featureless landscape. Even when the guide pointed out the signs of the food source's presence, a slight hummock in the ground, and indicated numbers of similar tubers in the vicinity, the traveller would have difficulty recognizing them. At another time the guide would pause and sniff the air, then following the scent of moisture would lead the traveller unerringly to a distant pool of water.

Instead of thinking of the Great Basin Indians as objects of contempt because they possessed so little in material terms, we should think of them instead as model examples of how people can adapt to apparently hostile conditions without the need for sophisticated technical aids, able to live simply from their own skills and resources. Such skills were the tools of survival. To the person who is aware of his or her surroundings and able to detect the slight differences that indicate the presence of a food source, who can rely on the senses of smell, sight, touch and taste as reliable guides, no environment is a wilderness. Nature provides for those who are prepared to work with her on her own terms, and in this respect the Indians of the Great Basin were highly skilled practitioners. They had little recourse to long-range weapons and organized hunts, yet were perfectly capable of pursuing and catching such an elusive animal as the mountain sheep – a creature which even modern hunters with sophisticated technology will readily admit is extremely difficult to hunt.

The procurement of food was the major concern of all the inhabitants of the Great Basin and when the horse was introduced to the area many of the tribes considered it just another food source; but some of those in the more hospitable eastern parts of the region, particularly the Ute, quickly became equestrian. They began to expand rapidly; both in terms of the territory they occupied and in the organization of bigger and more powerful family alliances. They also started to ally themselves with other Great Basin tribes, such as the Paiute, and with tribes in nearby areas, such as the Jicarilla Apache and the Shoshone.

Their lifestyle underwent a total change, due to influences of the tribes they came in contact with, and from the 1850s on, they lived much like any other southern Plains nomadic tribe. Brush covered wickiups were abandoned in favour of skin tipis. Rabbit-skin blankets were replaced by fringed shirts and leggings of deerskin, decorated with beaded bands and embroidered seams, and supplemented with heavy buffalo robes when the winters set in and evenings became cold. They continued to spend much of their time hunting in the mountains for elk and deer, but they also held an annual buffalo hunt, when they would leave the desert areas and move as a tribe into the grasslands of the Plains. North of the Great Basin were the Plateau lands. Drained by the Columbia and Fraser Rivers, this is a region of staggering beauty, of mountain valleys, hot springs and snow-capped peaks. It is a mystic land, a country that the hand of man appears never to have touched; that doesn't know the contamination of

Bannock Indians relied on the proceeds of local hunting and crops of corn grown in small garden plots. Their name has been preserved in the Indian corn-bread common at modern Pow-Wows, where a request for bannock will result in one being served with unleavened corn-meal pancakes. The illustrations here show a typical Bannock village at top, and Bannocks threshing corn below.

towns and cities. This was the home of the Cayuse,
the Flathead, the Coeur D'Alene, the Klikitat and
Kalispel, the Wishram, Wasco, Umatilla, and the
Nez Percé, and of a host of other lesser-known
tribes. They lived comfortably, enjoying the rich-
ness of their land and feeling that they belonged
here. Their villages, stretched along the valley
bottoms, consisted of semi-subterranean plank
dwellings or lodges, covered with mats made from
the bulrushes that grew profusely along the edges
of rivers teeming with fish.

Many of the rivers were salmon-bearing, and for
some tribes it was a staple food, eaten fresh during
the annual salmon runs or dried and stored for
winter usage. Even tribes away from these rivers
often included salmon as a major part of their diet,
trading furs from the mountains for supplies of
dried fish. Roots and berries were gathered in
quantity, and most tribes supplemented their
diets with some hunting. For a few groups, hunting was the major means of procuring food, and
these tribes lived a semi-nomadic existence.

In common with the tribes of California and the
Great Basin, these peoples were never overtly
aggressive. Their country's abundance meant
there was little incentive for violence. Quite frequently the tribes were in such close contact, as
among the Nez Percé and Cayuse, that inter-
marriages took place and there was, in any case, a
great deal of cultural sharing. People travelled far
and wide, visiting other tribes whose languages
they may not have understood but where they
were made welcome and invited to feasts and ceremonies. Using a sign language known to many
tribes of North America, they shared in each

other's stories and myths, and learned the crafts
and skills that each had to offer.

Because of this process of exchange, the culture
of the area is remarkable for its mixture of beliefs
and manufactures rather than for the expressions
of individual tribes, since they borrowed freely
from each other and from the tribes of surrounding regions with whom they came in contact. In
the northwest, they made wooden grave markers
that are analogous to the totem carvings of the
British Columbia and Alaska coast. Other tribes
produced birchbark baskets similar to those made
by groups in the Subarctic area to the northeast,
while porcupine quill embroidery shows influences from the Athapascans in interior British
Columbia.

Most of the Plateau occupants were excellent
woodcarvers, making magnificient dug-out
canoes, and were skilled in weaving rushes and
grasses into baskets, bags and other goods. The
finest baskets were made by the Klikitat, who had
developed methods that could be used for producing large, rigid storage baskets, and soft, flexible
bags and hats; but superior quality basketwork
was also made by the Yakima, Lillooet, Shuswap,
and Chilcotin, and by the Thompson and Fraser
River Indians. The Nez Percé made flat woven
wallets decorated with false embroidery: a technique in which geometric and floral patterns are
added to the object after its initial weaving is com-
pleted. Some of these tribal groups carved stone,
or used sheep horn and antler in producing small
bowls, serving ladles, and other household items.
Personal ornaments, particularly necklaces of
seeds and shells were abundant; one tribe, the

Kalispel, even earning their European name of Pend D'Oreille from their habitual custom of wearing large shell earrings.

The most significant aspect of the area was, however, its location at the hub of a great trade network serving California and the Northwest Coast, and extending into the Plains. This trade centred on the Dalles in the valley of the Columbia River – named by the American Captain Robert Gray after his ship Columbia had put into the mouth of the river in 1792 – where Chinook tradesmen exchanged goods from the coastal

regions, such as conch shells, abalone and salt, for those of the interior, usually furs and skins. Before Gray's arrival the Chinook were already trading goods of European manufacture, via the Klikitat tribes, with those of the interior Plateau and thence to the Plains. A trade language known as Chinook Jargon – a mixture of Native languages, English and French – was spoken from California to Alaska during the 1800s.

With such a long history of sharing and assimilation, of trade and barter, and an eagerness to acquire new skills, it is hardly surprising that the tribes of the Plateau adapted rapidly when horses were traded up from the Spanish herds of the Southwest by the Comanche, Kiowa and Shoshone. By the early 1700s, both the Nez Percé and the Cayuse were mounted tribes; but not content with merely trading horses, and lacking the aggression needed to increase their herds by raiding those of their neighbours, they became horse raisers and breeders. Their dry, mountainous and rocky country, with its broad flat pasturelands, was ideal for horses, and similar to the Andalusian homelands from which these Spanish horses originated. Moreover the Nez Percé and Cayuse

affinity with animals was such that they quickly realized it was possible to practice selective breeding. From this they isolated the dappled pony, distinguished by its pattern of black and white markings, that we know as the Appaloosa. The Nez Percé villages in the breathtakingly beautiful Wallowa Valley on the Snake River were soon distinguished by their pony herds; literally hundreds of horses grazed the rich grasses of the valley bottomlands.

At the beginning of the 1800s, some strangers arrived in Nez Percé country. This was the Lewis and Clarke expedition, which wanted to find a route through the mountains to the seas beyond. The mountain passes could only be traversed on foot and by canoe, so the Nez Percé offered to care for the expedition's horses while they were away – and, incidentally, returned more horses to the party when they returned, since some foals had been born during their absence.

Within 50 years of the Lewis and Clarke expedition, settlers had begun arriving in the Plateau country. Old Chief Joseph of the Nez Percé negotiated a treaty guaranteeing them their beloved Wallowa Valley 'for as long as the rivers shall run' and continued to live in peace with the newcomers, on occasion even rescuing them from other Indians who were less inclined to treat these incursions leniently, and who found the manners of the White man both arrogant and insincere.

A second treaty was negotiated in 1863, at which the Nez Percé were not present and when the Wallowa Valley was ceded and opened for settlement. Although pushed into smaller and smaller areas, the Nez Percé kept the peace. Old Chief Joseph died in 1871 and was succeeded by his son, Young Joseph, who continued to promote his father's ideals that the White man and the Indian could live side by side and could learn and benefit from one another. Even when a number of Nez Percé were killed by settlers, Joseph refused to let this shake his belief in peaceful co-existence, and excused the Whites on the grounds that the trouble had been caused by a lawless faction; but large numbers of settlers were moving into the Nez Percé lands and the tribe was under increasing pressure to move. Joseph made an impassioned plea on behalf of his tribe in a speech which is one of the most quoted in books about the American Indian. It deserves to be repeated here:

The earth was created by the assistance of the sun, and it should be left as it was. The country was made without lines of demarcation, and it is no man's business to divide it. I see the Whites all over the country gaining wealth, and see their desire to give us lands which are worthless. The earth and myself are of one mind. The measure of the land and the measure of our bodies are the same. Say to us if you can say it, that you were sent by the Creative Power to talk to us. Perhaps you think the Creator sent you here to dispose of us as you see fit. If I thought you were sent by the Creator I might be induced to think you had a right to dispose of me. Do not misunderstand me, but understand me fully with reference to my affection for the land. I never said the land was mine to do with it as I chose. The one who has the right to dispose of it is

The Cayuse woman in this photograph is wearing typical Plateau costume. Her dress is made from buckskin and decorated with early trade beads, as is the bag she carries in her right hand. In her left she holds an earlier form of bag made from twined corn husks.

Far right: Plateau tribes adapted to an equestrian way of life very rapidly after Spanish horses were introduced to the area. Within a few years they had gained a reputation as horse raisers and breeders, and were regularly trading horses to tribes of the Plains. A Cayuse horse breeder is shown here, together with the spotted Appaloosa pony for which the tribe was well known.

Right: This Cayuse war club is unusual in that it carries a scalplock of white hair which is almost certainly European.

the one who has created it. I claim a right to live on my land, and accord you the privilege to live on yours.

His plea fell on deaf ears, and finally, in 1877, Joseph agreed to move the tribe out of the Wallowa Valley to avoid conflicts with the White people coming to the area. As they were preparing to move, settlers stole several hundred of their horses and a group of young warriors, disregarding Joseph's advice, struck back. Eighteen White scalps were brought into the villages; a defiant gesture by the warriors to show that they had been pushed far enough. The American response was to send in troops to curb the uprising.

Joseph had no desire to fight the people he knew as his 'White brothers', and realized the only possibility for the Nez Percé was flight. If they could reach the border and cross into Canada, the Motherland, he felt they would be safe and that the refugee bands of Sioux Indians who had been driven north the previous year, and who were now living there under the leadership of Sitting Bull, would offer them shelter.

With only 100 warriors and accompanied by their women and children, the aged and the infirm, the Nez Percé took to the mountain paths and struck north. For 1,300 miles, in bitter weather conditions and driving snow, they outwitted and outflanked four separate columns of U.S. troops that had been sent to intercept them. Joseph had ordered that no scalps were to be taken, no property was to be destroyed, and that White people who were not directly involved in the conflict were not to be harmed; it is a testimony to his authority and leadership that the only White casualties incurred during the Nez Percé War were of combatants.

Just 30 miles from the border, at the foot of the Bear Paw Mountains, the Nez Percé were halted by troops under the command of Nelson A. Miles. Joseph rode forward on a bay pony, the last horse they possessed – all the others had been scattered when they took flight, and the few they rode had by now been eaten in their desperate struggle to survive. He was accompanied by several other warriors who walked beside him, offering advice. Some distance from the troops his companions stopped and Joseph rode forward alone. Dismounting, he handed his gun to General Miles and walked into the camp of the Americans.

He obtained assurances that the Nez Percé would be returned to reservations in their own country that had been set aside for them. The government, however, broke its promise, and the tribe was sent instead to Indian Territory where they remained until 1885. Many died from exposure to diseases in this unfamiliar land, and by the time the tribe was returned to its own reservation at Lapwai only 287 captive Nez Percé were still alive, many of them too young to remember the valiant struggle of their predecessors. Joseph died on 21 September, 1904, on the Colville reservation in Washington, where he had been confined as too dangerous an influence to be allowed to live with his own people. The official report of the agency physician was that Joseph had died of a broken heart.

THE NORTHWEST COAST

Countless islands, innumerable fjords, rocky inlets covered with giant cedars, and always a constant feeling of moisture in the air – this is the Northwest Coast. It is a narrow strip of rain forest, not more than 160 km (100 miles) wide in places, sandwiched between the Pacific Ocean and the Coast and Rocky Mountains, and stretching from Washington in the south, through British Columbia, and thence into Alaska as far as Yakutat Bay.

Influenced by the presence of warm sea currents just off-shore, and protected by the mountains from harsher inland climates, the area remains mild throughout the year with plentiful rainfall. This combination of mild weather and high precipitation creates a very rich and constant environment, with an abundance of natural resources. There is no easy access to the interior except in the south, and the only other connections with the interior on the whole of the coastal strip are more difficult ones along the Skeena and Stikine River valleys. Due to its extreme isolation, the Northwest Coast is both culturally and environmentally unique.

In spite of the wealth it offers, there is little

archeological evidence for a long prehistoric occupation. A distinctive Northwest Coast culture starts to manifest itself only about 2,000 years ago, with a number of stone carvings in the form of bowls, pestles and animal figurines. One of the reasons for this paucity of early remains may be that many archeological sites are now well below the waters of the Bering Sea, since the thousands of islands in the region are the peaks of Ice Age mountains that were flooded when the glaciers melted.

The cultural institutions of the historic period, with an emphasis on wealth and status, were already firmly in place by 500AD. European influences, particularly the fur trade and the introduction of iron tools, caused an exaggeration of previous patterns, culminating in the large-scale production of surplus goods purely for status reasons, and a conspicuous display of wealth by which hereditary rights were validated. Unlike other Native peoples of North America, those of the Northwest Coast reached the peak of their attainment after European contact.

Russian explorers with the Bering expedition, in 1741, began limited trading in the far northern parts of the region, although this was carried out via the Aleut, relatives of the Eskimo, and without direct contact with Northwest Coast peoples. In 1774 Juan Perez sailed from Mexico and spent several days trading with the Nootka tribes on Vancouver Island. The year after, two Spanish ships, the Hecate and Bodega, sailed to Alaska in an attempt to claim the country as a Spanish possession.

These visitors came and went, recording some customs of the local populations and noting that several Indians they met were already using iron they picked up from the flotsam of European ships wrecked in the China trade which sea currents had brought to their beaches. But it was not until 1778, when the English ships Resolution and Discovery, commanded by James Cook, put in for overhaul near the villages of the Nootka Indians, that the Europe-China-Northwest Coast trade began. This was to bring scores of ships from many nationalities to this area over the next 25 years.

Cook engaged in a lively trade with the Nootka. He seems to have genuinely admired these Indians whom he described as industrious and totally honest except where metal was concerned, which they coveted. This forced him to keep a guard on his ships, since any metal item that was loose or could be prised free – nails, barrel hoops, even buttons – would have disappeared into the Nootkan villages. Metal was so eagerly sought because it was seen as a prestige item; but the tribes of the area also found it made more efficient cutting edges than the traditional blades of stone and shell. The goods they required in their demonstrations for achieving status, many of them carved from wood, could be produced much faster and in greater abundance using metal-bladed tools.

Nootka Indians of Vancouver Island's seaward shores were the first people of the Northwest Coast to be met by Captain Cook. This 1778 engraving is from a sketch made by John Webber, the artist accompanying the Cook expedition.

This Tlingit house screen was made about 1840 and depicts the brown bear clan crest of the house of Chief Shakes on Wrangell Island. The opening in the screen represents the vagina of the Bear Mother, and at ceremonial gatherings the clan leaders would emerge from here to be reborn by the clan ancestress.

Right: Map showing the approximate locations of the Northwest Coast tribes when first encountered by Europeans.

Far right: During ceremonies, Kwatiutl dancers often approached the village from the sea in massive and elaborately decorated, sea-going trade canoes. A costumed figure danced on the prow of the boat, while its crew sang songs and beat their paddles in rhythmic accompaniment to the dancer. The figure shown here represents the Thunderbird, as distinguished by the curved horns on the mask he is wearing.

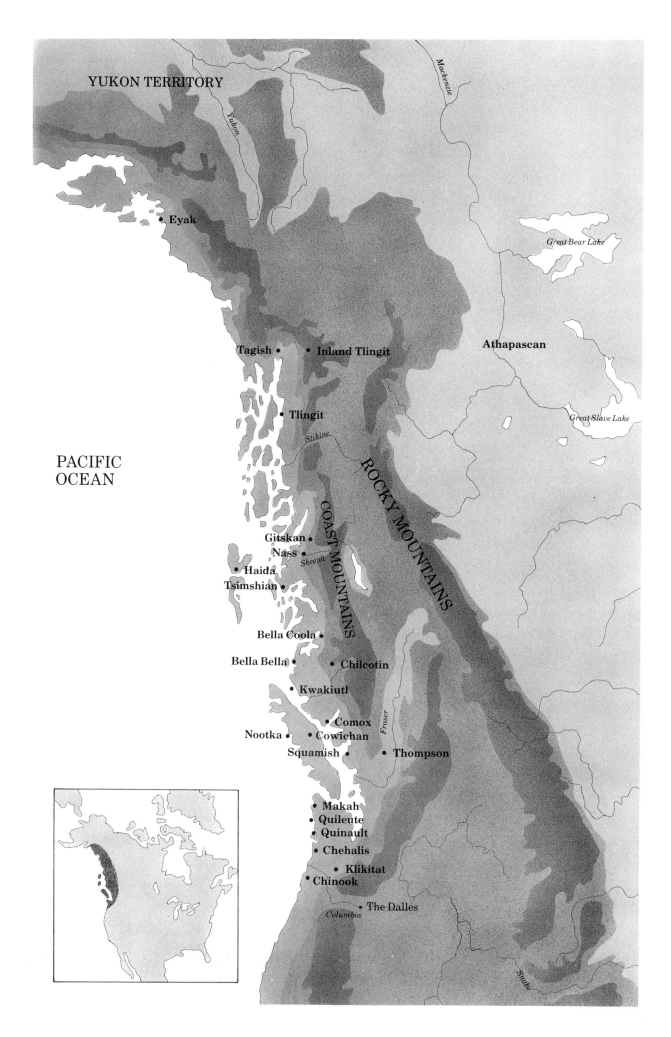

YUKON TERRITORY

Great Bear Lake

• Eyak

Athapascan

Tagish • • Inland Tlingit

Great Slave Lake

• Tlingit

Stikine

PACIFIC
OCEAN

COAST MOUNTAINS

ROCKY MOUNTAINS

Gitskan •
Nass • Skeena
• Haida
Tsimshian •

Bella Coola •

Bella Bella • • Chilcotin

• Kwakiutl

Fraser

• Comox
Nootka • • Cowichan
Squamish • • Thompson

• Makah
• Quileute
• Quinault
• Chehalis
• Klikitat
• Chinook
• The Dalles
Columbia

Snake

In exchange for the handfuls of metal items, beads, and pieces of copper they received from Cook, the Indians brought him sea otter furs that he was able to sell in China for $150 apiece. The proceeds from these sales could be used to make cheap purchases of tea and silk, which could then be resold in Europe at inflated prices. The money to be made from this trade was a commercial adventurer's dream, and after 1785 the coast was saturated with European products. Of the many trade items, the big iron chisels that made wood-carving easier were the most eagerly sought after by the Indians.

The first European traders were King George men (the English), but Boston Men (Americans sailing round the coast from New England) soon arrived and were to dominate the trade after the 1800s. French and Spanish ships also traded regularly, as did the Russians. By the turn of the century, overland routes across the Rockies had been found by Alexander Mackenzie, acting on behalf of the Northwest Fur Company, and trading posts, working through middlemen, were being established. After the Northwest Fur Company merged with the 'Governor and Company of Adventurers of England Trading into Hudson's Baye' (the Hudson's Bay Company) in 1821, a post was established at the mouth of the Columbia River specifically for the coastal trade, and the Hudson's Bay blanket became the standard 'currency' in the region. From then on everything was given a value determined by the number of blankets it was worth.

The Indians were past masters at trading. They quickly realized the motives for the European interest in their furs, and inflated their prices accordingly, readily adapting these new outlets to the aboriginal pattern. Soon the Nootka and Haida Indians were buying furs from tribes not yet contacted by Whites, and reselling these at a profit. In the 1830s, the Kwakiutl Indians set themselves up in opposition to the British-owned Hudson's Bay Company, by travelling along the coast buying furs at a higher rate than the British were offering, and reselling these to the 'Yankees'. On the Skeena and Stikine Rivers, trade was controlled by the Tlingit and Tsimshian, who refused to allow Europeans entry to the area since this would have broken their monopoly. Trading stimulated the Native economies, and brought the wealth required to underpin the increasingly competitive aspects of Northwest Coast life.

None of this involved competition for land or resources, since these were more than adequate to support the Native populations in a high degree of comfort, but were all directed towards the twin themes of rank and prestige. Even before European trade affected the tribes, the area had been highly populated with status-seeking groups who had hierarchies supported by the trading and distribution of rare goods.

Californian abalone shell, more brilliant than the pallid local variety, was traded into the area and used to decorate clan masks and other objects of value. Interior Athapascan tribes supplied porcupine quills and deer skins via the Tsimshian and Tlingit tribes. Dried salmon was exported to the interior Plateau in exchange for robes and furs. Fish oil, a rare commodity simply because its extraction was a labour-intensive process that required much time, was traded widely along the entire length of the coast. The northern groups even loaded 18m (60 ft) long dug-out canoes with trade goods and traversed 1,900 km (1,200 miles) of often dangerous seas to bring these to the Dalles trade centre on the Columbia River.

The Tlingit participants in the Northwest Coast culture on the Alaskan coast, divided into many smaller sub-tribes and occupying a number of different villages. Offshore, on the Queen Charlotte Islands, were the powerful Haida peoples, and adjacent to them on the British Columbia coast were the numerous Tsimshian tribes and the Bella Coola. South of the Bella Coola lived various groups speaking dialects of Kwakiutl, who were related to people living on Vancouver Island. The larger part of Vancouver Island, together with parts of the southern mainland, were occupied by the Nootka, who lived on the seaward coast, and by several small tribes who spoke variants of a common language known as Coast Salish.

All these peoples shared a very similar culture, and differences between them are only a matter of degree. Clan households claiming descent from an ancestral animal spirit were general in the north, whereas southern households tended to be organized along family lines with a direct blood relationship. All, however, depended on ostentatious display as an outward manifestation of their status within the tribe, and all vied with each other in attempts to gain added prestige and importance.

The display of clan and family insignia impressed early European visitors when they first came to these villages and saw the huge plank houses, some as much as 60m (200 ft) long, with their magnificient painted fronts showing the clan and family totems. Since the villages were sited on steep beaches in protected coves where they might only be approached from the sea, they could not be seen until one rounded a promontory and came suddenly upon them. The effect must have been spectacular. Brilliant renditions of the animal supernaturals from which the families claimed descent had a stark and powerful contrast to the dense greens of the forest climbing abruptly away behind the village. Brightly painted trade and whaling canoes were pulled up on the beaches in front of the houses, where the paintings were emphasized by massive carved houseposts made from sections of cedar trunk.

Along the top of the beach were rows of intricately carved welcoming figures, often including the Bear Mother, who faced the sea with their open palms extended. In this way visitors could tell that they carried no weapons and that their intentions were friendly. After the introduction of metal tools, many of the carvings were elaborated into the totem poles for which this area is famed, and the villages became festooned with these great towering cedarwood monuments. The poles were carved with images depicting a series of mythological events through which the family's ancestry could be traced; they were not objects of worship or adoration, as the early missionaries believed, but had a function akin to that of the heraldic crest.

People who shared the same totem ancestor, even though they might be from different tribes and speaking different languages, felt they had an affinity that transcended other considerations. Thus a member of the Killer Whales from one tribe knew that he could find food, shelter and protection among the Killer Whales of another village, in spite of the fact that the two tribes might be bitter traditional enemies. The paintings and carvings told him immediately which houses he could rely on for support, and those where he was certain to find a hostile reception.

Similar totem figures were carved or painted on

Copper plaques, or shields, acted as symbols of wealth, and increased in value each time they were publicly displayed at potlatch ceremonies. The totemic figure shown on this Haida copper is probably a beaver.

Far right: All tribes of the Northwest Coast region had an essentially marine economy and were accomplished fishermen and hunters of sea mammals. Only the Nootka, however, regularly hunted whales. The whaler shown in this drawing is holding a long whaling harpoon. The point and foreshaft of the harpoon were detachable, and fastened to them is a stout cedar bark rope to which a number of sealskin floats are attached. When a whale was struck, the line and floats were thrown clear of the boat to prevent risk of capsizing. The dragging effect of the float line would tire the quarry, and each time it surfaced to breathe, more float lines were struck home until it eventually became so exhausted that it could be easily dispatched and towed back to the beach.

Right: Although the Northwest Coast Indians are renowned for their work in wood, numerous other materials were also employed and richly embellished with totemic emblems. The spruce root hat shown here was made by the Tlingit.

virtually everything the Northwest Coast Indians possessed: from horn ladles to wooden boxes and chests, from feast bowls, dance costumes and plank house screens, to their canoes. Even a humble everyday object such as the halibut hook would be elaborately carved. Mountain goat and dog hair were woven into intricate patterns on Chilkat blankets, named after one of the Tlingit sub-tribes, while Killer Whales were depicted on Nootka basketwork hats. When woollen blankets came into popular usage, replacing the earlier ones made from shredded cedar bark, pearl buttons were used to outline the figures, giving rise to the popular name for one of the coast artefacts: the button blanket.

The village sites with their great arrays of totems were occupied only during the winter, which was considered the sacred season. In spring the people moved to summer camps along the banks of salmon-bearing rivers, where posts had been left standing ready to receive planking brought with them from the winter villages. Although many other foods were regularly eaten, including all kinds of fish and shellfish, larger sea mammals – the Nootka were especially renowned as proficient whalers – roots, seeds, berries, and even some inland game animals such as deer and bear, the salmon was caught in such prodigious numbers that it was the staple food all year round and was eaten both fresh and dried.

So reliable was this food source that it was one of the main reasons that the arts of the area were so highly developed. The people could spend winter comfortably, with vast excesses of stored food; time could therefore be spent on ceremonial activities which required the manufacture of large numbers

of masks and other carvings, as well as on the production of a great variety of goods that could be distributed at the feasts.

In addition to salmon fishing, spring and summer was a time for catching halibut and eulachon. Also known as the candle fish, since it is said they were so oily that they could be burnt as candles, the eulachon was rendered down for its rich oil that was an accompaniment to every meal. Each village had a number of old canoes that were used for this purpose. The canoe was filled with eulachon and water, hot stones were dropped in to bring the water to a boil, and after several hours, once the water had cooled, the oil could be scooped off the surface and stored in special grease bowls and boxes. Quantities of berries, particularly cranberries and blueberries, were also collected and preserved, as were camas roots. Typical of these summer villages were the huge fires built along the river banks, in front of which were wooden racks for drying salmon.

This time of year was a busy one, involving all members of the community. Particular sections of

This wooden potlatch hat was collected in 1879, and illustrates the northern custom of adding rings to the hat to indicate the number of successful potlatches its wearer had participated in. The crest is probably a bear, although it could also represent the wolf.

the river and areas bearing abundant berries were clan property, and every member of the clan worked together to gather in sufficient stores to see them through the winter, generally collecting far more than would actually be required. Surplus food was a form of wealth and would be needed for the lavish feasts held as a way of proving that one's resources were limitless. When summer drew to a close, the planking from the houses was taken down and lashed between canoes, to form platforms on which the proceeds of the season's work could then be transported back to the winter villages.

Summer was a purely economic season, whereas all winter activities were related to ceremony and to the elaborate gatherings intended to enhance status and validate the right to own and display particular rights and privileges. Everything the Indian possessed fell into the category of 'property', and could be assigned some kind of ranked value which might be related to the right to perform certain duties connected with ownership. Thus a name was a property to be owned and validated, some names permitting the performance of higher ranking dances than others and consequently conferring greater prestige. Similarly, ownership of a productive berrying ground gave higher status than one that produced a lower yield.

The principal means of gaining status was through the demonstration of privileges and the giving of gifts at a potlatch, derived from the Chinook word patshatl meaning 'give-away'. Small potlatches would be held for the validation of lesser rights, and every individual went through a series of events at which invited guests received gifts in recognition of their attendance. Potlatches were held when a new-born infant was wiped down with moss and released from the spirit world into that of the people. The first ear-piercing of a young girl required gift giving, as did the acquisition of an adult name at puberty. Formal approval of marriages demanded the attendance of the families of both bride and groom, when presents would be exchanged. At any occasion when someone obtained elevation to a new, higher, or different status, this could only be achieved by inviting people of recognized standing within the group, whose authority validated the procedure.

In all these events the status of the individual and the rank to which he or she aspired, determined both the number of prestige guests who would be invited and the extent to which other members of the family or clan might become involved. The ear piercing of a girl of relatively low status only necessitated the attendance of immediate relatives, who would be offered a meal and a few trinkets that they would take with them. For a girl of high status, however, it was essential to invite quite prominent members of the community and the gift giving could become so lavish that it needed the combined effort of several members of the clan to provide the quantity of gifts required.

For the highest ranking positions when, for example, a son of a clan leader might take over the status of one of his parents, the attendance of entire clans from surrounding villages might be requested. Their presence gave weight to the position being inherited, and the quantity of gifts they received was a reflection of the importance attached to it, as well as a demonstration of the host group's prominence and generosity. New wealth being generated through European trade made it possible to hold larger potlatches, and because clans and families vied with each other for status and influence within the tribe, these soon came to have a very competitive character.

Before long the competition potlatch was being announced as a challenge to a rival clan leader. A refusal to attend, rather than being seen as a denial of the status that was being claimed, was derided as an indication of the rival clan's inability to meet the challenge since they could only elevate one of their own members to a higher position by giving a greater potlatch in the future. These challenges even extended to other tribes, when the status of both clan and tribe were demonstrated in a provocative display intended to insult their guests by implying that they were unable to match the greatness of their hosts.

Invitations to competition potlatches were announced as though they were declarations of war. In fact, as the potlatches grew in size and importance so incidents of actual warfare decreased. The Indians recognized this by saying that whereas in the old days they fought their wars with weapons, they now fought them with property. Preparations for these major demonstrations might begin several years in advance of the actual date of the event, when the sponsor called on all his clan relatives to make items that could be given to the guests, and to store extra food for the feasts. In a way he was calling in old debts, since he would have provided similar items or services at previous potlatches they had held. Among the Kwakiutl this reached an extreme, in which assistance on an earlier occasion had to be repaid at double the original amount as a form of 'interest'; a practice they may have picked up from contact with Hudson's Bay traders. It was necessary to amass vast amounts of food, which would be served in enormous quantities that the guests had

The Chilkat, a Tlingit sub-tribe, were famous for their woven blankets of mountain goat and dog hair, which they traded to other tribes of the area. The design on this Chilkat blanket is of the killer-whale.

Far right: Supernatural
spirit ancestors and animals
were represented in the
ceremonies of the secret
societies by dancers wearing
characteristic masks. The
privilege of performing one
of these dances and of
wearing the society emblems
was an honour that had to
be validated through a
potlatch at which the dance
was performed before an
invited audience. Many of
the masks, such as the
Hoxhok, or supernatural
bird, shown here, were
articulated and had opening
mouths and other movable
parts. The body covering of
the dancer is made from
shredded cedar bark.

Right: The Northwest Coast
carver did not have to rely
on a realistic portrayal of his
subject when making a
portrait mask, since the
crest paintings on the face
would identify the person
immediately. This example
was made by the Haida, who
used portrait masks far
more extensively than did
any other tribe of the region.

to consume entirely. If the challenged tribe failed to eat all that was placed before them, they would be ridiculed for having appetites that were so small they could not match the generosity their host could offer. They couldn't even prolong the feast so that the total amount they were required to eat was less, since this would provoke the host into exclaiming that nothing angered him more than people who ate slowly.

In extreme cases, a feast might be followed immediately by another one, or an eating contest would be initiated, when a large feast bowl would be filled with some particularly indigestible product such as fish oil. The challenge was in reality against the clan, although directed as a personal attack on the clan leader as its representative, and he might call on other members of his group to help consume the food or even delegate a party of men renowned for their strong stomachs to act on his behalf. While the food was being consumed, the rival leader would hurl insults back at his host, proclaiming his own greatness and the miserly manner in which they were being fed.

The guests would also be presented with valuable gifts, accompanied by speeches such as 'I throw this canoe, worth 1,200 blankets, into your face; you, who do not dare to stand erect; the chief whom even every weak man tries to vanquish', again which could not be refused without humiliation. Accepting them was an implicit acceptance of

the challenge to hold a rival potlatch at a future date, when the former guests themselves would give back gifts in excess of those they had received thereby showing that they were capable of surpassing the extremes demonstrated by their host.

At its height, fuelled by excessive wealth acquired in the fur trade, the potlatch frequently featured the destruction of property instead of its distribution. The logic behind this was that if status could be achieved by distributing goods, when a return was guaranteed, then even higher status might be attained if the goods were destroyed and not repaid. In this way the clan's utter contempt for their rivals could be clearly demonstrated. The only means whereby they might rise to the challenge was to destroy a yet greater amount of property.

The escalation involved in these affairs was so great that the manufacture of goods could not keep pace with their exchange or destruction, so systems were devised whereby the potlatches might continue without stepping beyond the bounds of possibility. Marked 'tally-sticks' with assigned blanket values often replaced the actual goods, but more important were copper plaques, or shields, which accumulated value each time they were used. They were made from native copper, and later from trade copper. A copper which was worth, say, 1,000 blankets when it was given to a rival at its first potlatch – which would be the blanket equivalent paid in goods to secure it, since they were actually quite rare – could have a value of perhaps 2,000 blankets the next time it was used.

Coppers might even be partially distributed by cutting them into five sections: the four quarters and the T-shaped bar to which the sections were attached. These could be potlatched to five different rival groups. If a clan was then able to challenge each of these to obtain the pieces and rivet them back together, the copper acquired value from all the potlatches at which it had featured. The total value could easily reach several thousands of blankets. The ultimate action, of course, would be to destroy the copper with no hope of return; which was done by 'drowning' it: throwing it from a cliff top into the sea.

Large potlatches were, of course, great social events associated with any aspect of life that was of particular importance or merit, and a clan leader who sponsored a number of them rose to eminence among his own people and was regarded highly by others. Various means were used whereby tokens of eminence served as constant reminders of the chief's greatness. Thus among the Tlingit, basketwork potlatch hats were worn which had a series of basket rings attached to the crown. Each time a potlatch was sponsored a new ring would be added. Many tribes made carvings showing a figure holding a copper plaque, which would be placed in front of a house where one had been used. Since the coppers were so rare and so valuable, the house itself was said to 'groan with the copper's weight' and became an emblem of the clan's importance.

In many respects all major potlatches also had historical significance, since the displays of masks

and dances that constituted the privileged wealth of the clan or family had a chronology that traced a family line back to their original acquisition. The Haida carried this a stage further in their use of portrait masks, which were worn in a strict sequence that presented an accurate order of events in the family history. All these masks were painted with crests depicting the clan totem of the individual they represented, and the same crests, together with the story of their origin, were carved on their totem poles.

Among the northern tribes the family privileges were inherited through the woman, but could only be displayed and acted out by her husband on her behalf. Some very high-ranking Tsimshian women had so many of these privileges that they could not all be performed by the same husband, and in

these cases she would marry a second, or even a third, man 'to enable her power to be danced out'.

Although the potlatch was strictly a secular event, it nevertheless became associated with sacred activities since many of the dances, dance masks, and songs had religious significance but were still considered as forms of property to be displayed. Membership of the secret societies, with whose activities the sacred Winter Ceremonials were concerned, also required the sponsorship of influential families and the distribution of gifts at a potlatch to validate the position.

Secret societies were most highly developed among the Kwakiutl, Tlingit and Tsimshian, and membership was sometimes organized in clans or groups of clans. It was considered a society prop-

erty, together with the paraphernalia associated with it – its songs, dances and names – that would be inherited as a privileged right. To be able to perform a dance or song, and to wear the costumes and facepaints associated with it, one had to be of the specified rank that the dance position required. Higher-ranking dances could only be performed by leading members of the community, and ranked positions within the societies often followed the same hierarchies within the clans and households themselves.

Possibly the most spectacular of the secret society dances was that of the Hamatsas. For this to take place, the clan house was cleansed and ritually prepared. A red cedar bark ring was hung at the gable end of the house facing the beach, to

This photograph shows the Haida village of Skedans after the introduction of iron tools caused a proliferation of monumental carving in which house posts developed into free-standing totem poles depicting family crests. Shortly after this, however, missionary endeavours resulted in the cutting down and burning of the poles, which were mistakenly believed to be worshipped as idols.

125

Far right: Salmon was the staple food for most of the Northwest Coast tribes, and much of the summer was spent at seasonal village sites on salmon-bearing rivers. Fish were speared and netted, or sometimes caught in traps set across the rivers, and were then cleaned and split open to be dried before huge fires set along the river bank. The woman in the drawing is splitting fish and fastening them to twigs to hold them open, before placing them on the drying rack seen in the background.

Right: Many flying-frogs came out of a lake in Tsimshian territory together with Frog-Woman, to bestow supernatural power on the frog clan and to confer high status. The carving shown here was worn as a headpiece by a leader of this clan.

indicate that it was a residence for the spirits, while the society's 'caller' toured the village, inviting people to the house and warning them to stop using their summer names. From then on until the end of the sacred season, only winter names that had been sanctioned by the spirits might be employed. When the people had assembled, the house was closed while they waited for the Hamatsas to appear.

At first it was silent, except for the roar of the huge central fires. The quiet was broken when whistles, the voices of the Hamatsas, were heard far away in the forests, rapidly coming closer as the dancers approached, until they were sounding all around the house. Then pandemonium broke loose. There was a deafening beating on the outsides of the walls and roof. Unearthly cries screeched from the forests. Roofing planks were violently pushed aside and a spirit figure suddenly flew across the room at head height. Strange voices began calling from deep inside the fires.

There was a terrible commotion at the door, which had been barred against the Hamatsas; but the bar was lifted as the people attempted to escape. Immediately the door burst open and the Bear Dancer, wearing great grizzly bear claws on his hands, rushed in among the people, forcing

them back to their places. A Cannibal Song started outside and the Kinqalalala, a young woman who danced naked and carried a corpse in her arms to entice the Hamatsas, backed into the room. The Hamatsas, or Cannibal Dancers, followed her. One of them, a new initiate emaciated from fasting and in an almost hysterical condition, became frenzied at her appearance and began biting pieces from the arms of the people nearest to him.

He did not yet have the strength to control the spirit by which he was possessed and had to be held down, shaking violently. A cedar bark rope was tied around his waist to prevent him fleeing from or attacking the people, and when he became calmer he was taken to a secret room at the rear of the house, separated from the main part by a partition screen painted with a clan totem. Later he would dance again, this time a little longer, before collapsing once more and being taken back to the room. Each time he appeared he was visibly stronger, until finally he could control the spirit.

The Hamatsa society embodied elements intended to frighten and shock. Nunltsistalal, the Fire-Thrower, would take live coals from the fires and throw them around the house, and had a reputation for eating dogs, which every Northwest

Coast Indian knew were deadly poisonous when consumed by humans. Nan, the Grizzly Bear who threatened and charged the spectators, had a furious temper and would severely punish anyone who challenged his authority, while the Rat Spirit Dancers would grab people at any pretext and rip off their clothes. Meanwhile, the Chewing Spirit Dancer prowled about the village, destroying valuable property, burning canoes, and throwing sticks at anyone who dared approach too closely. Later, at a civil ceremony, the Hamatsas would sponsor a potlatch at which restitution was made for the damages they had caused.

Their performance was pure drama and high theatre, accomplished by a number of 'magical' tricks. The spirit that flew across the house was a realistic puppet suspended on strings, and the rapid approach of the Hamatsas to the village was indicated by stationing people at intervals to blow their whistles in succession. Voices came from the centres of the fires through hollow lines of kelp, the sea onion, that had been buried beneath floor level during the secret ritual preparations and which led back to the partitioned room at the rear. Kinqalalala's 'corpse' was an effigy, and even the havoc wreaked by the Chewing Spirit Dancer had been arranged in advance with the owners of the property he destroyed, for which they would receive payment.

Other dance sequences of the secret societies were not as macabre and violent as those of the Hamatsas, but still emphasized the principle of possession by the spirit forces. The supernatural beings who inspired the dancers were animal ancestors, Star, Cloud, Bird, and spirits associated with the Sky and the Sea, rather than the Monster Spirits by which the Hamatsas were possessed.

In many of these dances the participants wore elaborately carved wooden masks; some of them so large that the dancer required assistants to help him support their weight. Killer-Whale dancers, distinguished by the dorsal fin on the mask, glided in gently undulating movements, echoing those of the whale through the water. Mosquitoes darted fervently around, in rapid, uncoordinated motion. Many of the masks were cleverly articulated, so that a sombre aspect could suddenly be transformed – simply by pulling on a few concealed strings – into that of a brilliantly painted Sun face, resplendent with shining rays that picked up the glow from the fires.

Some of the dance series, particularly those of the Dluwulaxa – 'Those-who-descend-from-the-heavens' – were of even higher rank than the Hamatsas and might require a number of potlatches in which the dancers were honoured, and the mask-makers were presented with especially valuable gifts which did not require a return. In all of these the emphasis was on displaying the masks, dance movements and songs; this was generally associated with their transfer from a retiring member to a new initiate, since the number of dance positions was limited. During these transfers, the myth that told of the acquisition of power from a supernatural animal ancestor was re-enacted.

The Coast Salish, although they also had dance displays and a modified form of the potlatch, were quite different from the northern tribes. Few of their dances were masked performances, with the exception of Swaie-Swaie – a form of Creator figure – who had a distinctive mask and a dance that was performed by a single individual from a leading family, who had to inherit the right to perform. Most dances, particularly among the southern tribes, were believed to originate in visions as the consequence of direct personal spirit contact.

The nature of the vision was interpreted by a shaman, who used drum rhythms to determine the type of spirit that had been contacted, to which the facepaint, dance and song that the recipient would use were related. Although these visions were highly individual, the spirit powers could be ordered into broad groups depending on whether they were granted by, for example, the Water,

Animal, or Mountain Spirits. During the Spirit Dances – or 'Dramatizations of Dreams' – the drum rhythms were used to call the spirit power back, sending the dancer into a trance-like condition. At first, the spirit and the dancer struggled with each other and the dance movements were frenzied; but the drumming brought them into a state of compatibility and harmony, in which the exhausted dancer gradually recovered from the trance.

Sometimes several different groups would perform together, each with its own distinctive movements and songs, creating a cacophony of voices that was said to echo the strange and unintelligible speech of the supernaturals themselves. The Salish longhouse, already imbued with the presence of the Otter Spirits carved on its supporting posts, was transformed into an arena where the powers of the animal spirits could be demon-

A double-headed eagle, or Thunderbird, has been appliquéd in red flannel on a black Hudson's Bay Company blanket to create this Kaigani Haida ceremonial robe. Dentalia shell outlines the figure; but pearl buttons have been used to provide the border, replacing what would formerly have been dentalia decoration and giving rise to the popular name of 'button blanket' for this type of artefact.

129

Far right: Nootkan women gained an enviable reputation for the fine quality of their basketwork, in which dyed cedar bark and grasses were used either to depict clan emblems or to portray marine hunting scenes. The woman shown here has used red trade cloth to wrap her braids, and wears a ring through the pierced septum of her nose. Her cloak is woven from yellow cedar bark.

Right: The figure shown on this Tlingit shaman's apron is not a crest or clan emblem, as is usual in most Northwest Coast work, but a depiction of the supernatural power by which the shaman was inspired.

strated and expressed, and where there might be as many as 200 supporting drummers.

Spirit Dancing and a form of potlatch were often combined; but, although the potlatch was still the essential means of validating status, these occasions did not have the competitive character found among the northern tribes. Gifts were made to honoured men, old debts were repaid, and all women attending the ceremony received presents. The total amount of property distributed could be considerable; yet it was always given in recognition of attendance and of the witnessing of a claim to status and was never accompanied by the boastful rivalry found elsewhere.

One characteristic feature of the Coast Salish potlatch was the 'scramble', in which tokens representing gifts were thrown out and all members of the audience, regardless of rank, age, or gender, scrambled to gather them. Sometimes property such as blankets would be scrambled for, and it

often happened that in the struggle to obtain a blanket it became ripped into several pieces. These, however, could be collected from several scrambles and then unravelled, when a new blanket would be woven that was said to bring good luck, and was in fact more valuable than one which had not been scrambled for.

On the outer coast of Vancouver Island opposite the Salish and Kwakiutl were the Nootka, whose economy and lifestyle were based on sea mammal hunting to a much greater degree than that of any other Northwest Coast tribe. They always remained fiercely independent; resisting influences from the other groups, reluctant to embrace change, and maintaining a conservative approach to all they did until well into the historic period. Their main ceremony, the Nutlam, or Wolf Dance, was a very ancient one, recording the days when wolves taught people to live together in harmonious communities and gave them the hierarchies

131

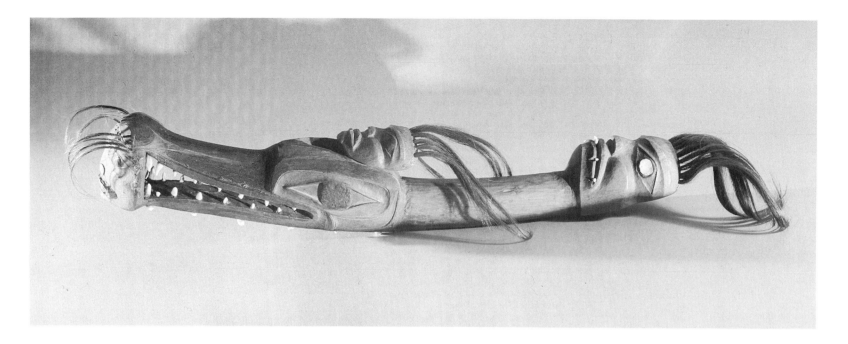

that were to be incorporated in human societies; everyone knows that wolves follow a strong leader and delegate responsibility according to individual achievement. Participants wore a distinctive mask and displayed non-human characteristics such as eating raw dog meat and sleeping by day. The dance featured the carrying away of the novice to the land of the wolves, where he or she was initiated into their customs, and their subsequent return to that of the people when they could pass on the knowledge and wisdom they had gained. Many of the elements in the Nutlam seem to be purer forms of the more exaggerated ceremonials found elsewhere, and this has led to speculation that it may be the ancestral form of dance display among all the Northwest Coast tribes.

Contrary to the world of human beings, that of the spirits, with the exception of animals such as wolves which lived in communal societies, was never organized into any form of hierarchical system. This served to emphasize the difference between the natural and the supernatural. A weaker spiritual force could easily usurp the authority of one considered more powerful; something unheard of in the human realm, where status and rank were the dominating features. Sun, for example, is often given the character of an almost supreme deity; yet Raven, the Trickster, could use a simple ploy to trap Sun in a wooden box and render him powerless. Even so, the impersonation of powerful spirits could only be undertaken by those of high rank. To become a Hamatsa, one had to be at least the son of a prominent clan member, and most leading Dluwulaxa dancers were the sons of clan chiefs.

All these positions required considerable quantities of masks and other goods, which traditionally limited them to the rich leading families; but wealth acquired through the fur trade meant that some individuals without high status were able to sponsor feasts and give-aways of extraordinary splendour. At the same time, introduced diseases were reducing the tribal populations, and numbers of privileged society positions remained vacant. Although these lower-status people had no formal claim to the unfilled places, they started to demand title to privileges which they would ordinarily have been denied. This created social problems within the tribes, as once-powerful families had their authority called into question. At the same time, the fur trade had a disruptive effect on previous economic and ceremonial patterns. From being self-sufficient fishermen many tribes had become dependent on fur trapping and sea otter hunting, and were increasingly reliant on goods obtained from the trading posts. Trade foods such as coffee, flour, sugar and butter constituted a significant proportion of the winter stores, often supplanting the traditional salmon, and men were often away from the villages during the sacred season, to hunt the thicker and more valuable winter furs.

By one of those strange acts of fate, the decline of the fur trade coincided almost exactly with the establishment of the colonies in 1849. The sea otter had been over-hunted and was becoming so scarce that it could no longer provide the income required to maintain rivalry at such a high level. Whereas the pre-1849 Indian had usually been considered as a necessary supplier of goods for the fur trade, the post-1849 Indian was seen as a barrier to European expansion. Indian morality offended the puritan ethic of the colonists, and their social institutions were simply incomprehensible.

The Indian was ripe for conversion; White populations found it increasingly difficult to accept this heathen expression on their own doorsteps. Russian missionaries had been active in the north since the early 1800s, but the middle of the century saw a sudden influx of priests and missions throughout the area. Jesuit missionaries were seeking converts in the 1830s. Other Roman Catholics were active in the 1840s. Anglicans and Methodists came in the 1860s. During the 1870s the Salvation Army arrived, and in the 1880s the Shaker Church established itself.

The effect on Native communities was to throw them into turmoil. Some new laws, such as the

Far left top: Captain Cook collected this Nootkan club in 1778. It features a wolf which holds a human head in its jaws, and was used as part of the ceremonial regalia of the Wolf Dance to depict the carrying-off of an initiate to the land of the wolves for instruction in their rituals.

Far left below: This typical Nootkan basket hat uses cedar bark and squaw grass to make a realistic depiction of a whaling scene.

Left: The Coast Salish had only one masked dance, at which the highly distinctive Swaie-Swaie was featured. The carved bird heads on the top of the mask, protruding eyes, and linear patterns representing feathers on the cheeks, are all characteristics of this type of mask.

Far right: The Tlingit chief in this illustration is dressed ready for a potlatch. He wears a Chilkat ceremonial blanket, and a wooden crest headdress, or frontlet, which has been inlaid with pieces of abalone shell. The crest figure on the frontlet is that of the beaver, indicating the clan of which this man was head.

Right: Raven rattles were employed by Tlingit shamans in effecting cures. The human figure on the back of this rattle represents the shaman, whose protruding tongue extends into the mouth of a frog to extract a powerful poison that frogs were believed to possess but which only shamans could use.

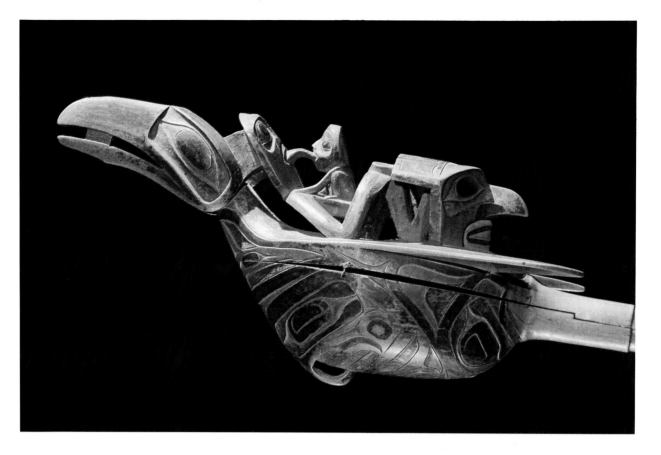

banning of the potlatch in the early 20th century, were simply ignored: the ban demanded the destruction – in reality the placement in White museums – of the ceremonial coppers, dance masks and costumes through which status could be obtained. The Indians circumvented this admirably. Lacking the actual copper shields they continued to use the names by which they were known. Even so, the potlatch decreased in importance, simply because the goods to support it at its previous high level were no longer available.

Meanwhile the missionaries were engaged in campaigns to convert the maximum number of Indians in the minimum amount of time, urged on by the fact that so many denominations were represented. In some areas, as among the Nootka, missionary efforts were doomed to failure because the power of the conservative shamans was too strong. Elsewhere the Indians found the contrast between what was practiced and what was preached beyond them. All the black-cloaked missionaries talked of peace and brotherly love, yet they argued bitterly among themselves as to how this doctrine should be interpreted. Most Northwest Coast Indians stood by as bemused observers, while the missionaries battled it out.

The shamans attempted to maintain their hold against the new preaching. They kept to the old values and the old hierarchies, denouncing those who claimed privilege to which they were not entitled and warning of terrible consequences for anyone who gave up their old beliefs to follow the Christian teachings. Baxbakualanuxsiwae, the Cannibal-at-the-north-end-of-the-world, assisted by Crooked-beak-of-heaven, would wreak vengeance and destroy the villages; while Hoxhok, the Monster-bird, would break open the skulls of errant humans and pick at their brains. Sisiutl, the Double-headed-serpent, would dislocate their bones, turn their heads backwards, and make their skins as hard as stones.

They claimed that the introduced diseases sweeping the coast were a punishment because the people had deviated from the true path laid down by their ancestors. Many Indians were persuaded by the shamans' rhetoric. These religious leaders were powerful people who possessed knowledge denied to others. They would not be buried at death, but would have their remains placed in special gravehouses where they would gradually sink into the ground to be reborn through the voices of younger shamans. They commanded the oceans, and no one would dare take a canoe through a cove protected by a shaman's spirit without first casting an offering into the waters to ensure a peaceful passage.

The missionaries recognized the shamans as the main opposition to their conversion of the tribes, and attempted to undermine their authority at every opportunity; even cutting down the totem poles in the mistaken belief that the shamans derived some kind of power from these carved 'idols'. But it was a medical rather than ethical revolution which was eventually to threaten shamanic influence. Smallpox struck the Nootka, and it quickly became apparent that those villages administered by the shamans suffered terrible casualties, whereas in those under the control of missionaries – who had the advantage of new vaccines – the numbers of deaths were relatively light. The smallpox epidemic spread rapidly, eventually killing about one-third of the population, and with its advance the shamans' power was seriously weakened.

Opposite: Tsonoqua, the Wild Woman of the Woods, was a cannibal woman who carried a large basket on her back into which she would place any children she was able to catch. She lived deep in the forests, and her voice could be heard in the wind sighing through the tree-tops.

Left: Haida carvers were known for the exquisite and refined quality of their work which, in contrast to the brilliant colours used in painting on Kwakiutl carving, tended to be restrained and understated. The carving on the left represents an owl; that on the right a mosquito.

An interesting example of this was the Tlingit village of Sitka, which had been the seat of the Russian government in the area since 1808. Very few Indians had been converted by the time of the first smallpox epidemic in 1835. The Tlingit, knowing the disease to be contagious, fervently wished for its spread to the Russian community; but soon realized that whereas the Indians suffered heavy losses, not a single Russian succumbed. Faith in the shamans was shaken; yet conversions to the Christian religion were slow – numbering only 20 by 1839.

When Russia sold Alaska to the United States in 1867, for approximately 19 cents per acre, it was claimed that hardly any of the shamans still commanded real respect and that the number of converts had increased to several hundreds. The conversions seem more dramatic in theory than in practice: each convert was promised a new shirt with a red cross on baptism, and it is known that many individuals possessed several of these shirts! It is quite likely that the shamans continued to have a strong influence but that this was not expressed openly for fear of reprisals. Some die-hard shamans were rather more direct in their opposition and refused to give in so easily. They attracted considerable numbers of followers in localized areas, exhorting the people to take to arms and drive out the intruders, before the White diseases, which rendered the supernaturals powerless by confusing them with conflicting arguments, should return to destroy the rest of the population.

Their predictions of doom were accurate. Following the smallpox outbreaks came epidemics of measles, influenza and tuberculosis. The twin evils of prostitution and venereal diseases again raised their ugly heads. Another debilitating introduction from the White man was alcohol, which the shamans saw as coming from the devil. Diluted and adulterated with a remarkable number of strange ingredients, alcohol was the direct cause of many Indian deaths.

Perhaps because of the precarious hold the shamans had on their followers, conflicts between Whites and Indians were surprisingly few. When they did occur, however, they were dramatic. There are instances of merchant ships being met and sunk by Nootkan war canoes, and of Tlingit villages sustaining heavy bombardment from offshore naval vessels. Throughout these incidents the White point of view was that the Indians were a vanishing race; a nuisance at times, but never a serious threat. From 1850 they were vanishing a little more slowly than had been expected; but with the establishment of schools and missions,

and under the guidance of the White government, it was expected that they would soon become Westernized and realize the futility of their old, pagan ways.

The Indians, however, saw things in a very different light, and had no intention of vanishing. For them, the White man was a devious creature who had one set of values for himself but another for anyone else. He was willing to take from the Indian when it was convenient, but slow to give anything back when it became necessary. To the Europeans all Indians were backward and uncivilized. The Indian, in a perhaps more realistic light, realized that some White men were good and others bad; but, even so, their judgement was clouded by a general distrust and dislike of the Whites, and a suspicion of the values they held. The Whites decided to conquer and take by force if need be; the Indians decided to wait and see.

White expansion was hampered by the same environment that had given the Indians such a rich culture. The countless inlets and fjords made even a short coastal journey a nightmare. Overland routes were barred by dense forests, tangled mosses, and the constant threat of stepping on what appeared to be solid ground only to find it was a mass of rotting vegetation rendered unstable by the dampness of the area. Communication between population centres could only be maintained by sea; and here the oceans came to the Indians' aid. Trapped between the peaks of Ice Age mountains, the coastal waters are treacherous. Smooth seas suddenly rush into narrow inlets, causing whirlpools, dangerous eddies, rapids, and high tides. Although the Indians in their dug-out canoes managed to traverse these with relative impunity, modern motorized fishing boats still have difficulty here, and a number of them are lost each year.

Today, most Indian groups still live in the lands occupied by their ancestors. Many things have changed, not least the abandonment of village sites as the populations decreased; some of the arts are lost and totem carving is now relatively rare. But tribal identities are strong and the sacred ceremonies still take place in a modified form. Most important, however, is that the 'vanishing' Indians have clearly demonstrated that they are here to stay.

Opposite: When someone became seriously ill, a shaman would often diagnose soul-loss and undertake a ritual journey to the land of the dead, where, if he arrived in time, he might snatch the soul back before it became irrecoverable. Bone soul-catchers, inlaid with abalone, were used as containers to carry the retrieved soul back. The one shown here was made by the Tlingit.

Left: Swaie-Swaie, a supernatural being, descended from the sky to spend his life at the bottom of a deep lake from where he conferred benefits on the people. The Coast Salish dancer illustrated here wears the characteristic Swaie-Swaie mask and a cloak of feathers to depict the spirit's power of flight. A clam shell rattle is held in the dancer's right hand, while in the left he carries a sprig of evergreen, symbolic of long life.

THE PLAINS AND PRAIRIES

I was born upon the prairie where the wind blew free and there was nothing to break the light of the sun. I was born where there were no enclosures and where everything drew a free breath.

This extract from a speech by Parra-Wa-Samen, or Ten Bears, of the Yamparika Comanche, sums up the the character of the Plains and Prairies in words so eloquent they could not possibly be surpassed. He expresses the true nature of these vast grasslands, where the eye can see forever and the Rocky Mountains in the distance might be 200 or 2,000 miles away. Distance is deceptive when there is no landmark to monitor one's responses, where the land seems to continue without end.

The Plains and Prairies are that immense space in central North America which extends from the Mississippi on its eastern boundary to the Rocky Mountain foothills on the west; from the edges of the Southwestern and Southeastern cultures in New Mexico, Arizona and the southern states north into the Prairie Provinces of Canada. Throughout this area the only distinctive feature is that it is grassland: long, prairie grasses in the east, that may reach the height of a man, and which flourish in the lowlands of the Mississippi River and its tributaries; shorter buffalo grasses in the west, that are capable of withstanding the long dry periods that are characteristic of this part of the region.

The whole area is marked by the absence of anything that might disturb the line of sight. Trees grow only along the banks and islands of occasional rivers; gullies and valleys are below the

sightline and can not be recognized until one stumbles accidentally upon them. Sudden outcrops of rock are conspicuous by their contrast to the surrounding areas, and are often accorded sacred significance simply because they seem so out of place.

Nomadic hunter-gatherers moved into the west of this area at the dawn of time. Their lives were dictated by the environment, which controlled the seasonal migrations of the animals on which they were dependent, and prevented the formation of large static populations. These highly mobile family bands occupied much of the short-grass Plains, and thought of themselves as autonomous groups, free to come and go as they pleased. They spoke a variety of different languages and shared no tribal identity, yet they all lived in much the same way, and had very similar cultures that were adapted to large game hunting.

Although the Plains grasslands can be thought of as the true home of the nomad, with its endless vistas and boundless spaces that made movement as much a part of the land as it was of the lives of the people, village tribes from the Hopewell traditions of the east started to enter the area in the early centuries AD. They established permanent villages, and planted fields of corn along the Mississippi-Missouri, in areas where flood-plains made agriculture possible. The influence of the grasslands, however, was not one to be ignored. Even these farmers, with centuries of settled history behind them, occupied their villages for only part of the year. From late spring until early

This Sioux effigy of a war pony bears red painted marks to indicate bullet holes, in commemoration of a favourite horse wounded in battle. It would have been carried in celebratory dances by a successful warrior.

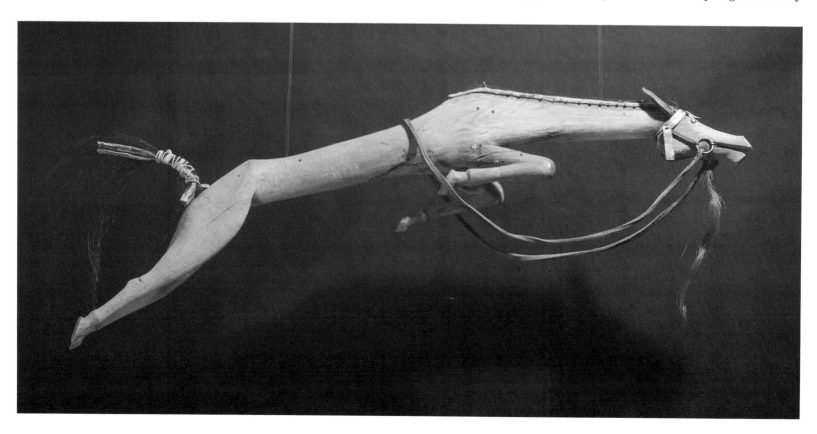

autumn they abandoned their permanent houses, and moved to the west in pursuit of the buffalo herds, living in a manner indistinguishable from that of their nomadic neighbours.

By about 900AD newcomers from the south had moved up the Mississippi, and introduced aggressive trends from the Mississippian culture. Prominent among them were the powerful and influential Caddoan peoples, who established a fully flourishing Mississippian outpost at Mound Spiro in Oklahoma. This, significantly, was the furthest north that direct Mississippian influence was to be felt, since it was at the limit where the species of corn developed in the Southeast could be grown. The Caddoans were, however, to continue to have a presence in the area through speakers of their language such as the Pawnee and Wichita.

Although these people were also farmers who adopted the semi-nomadic lifestyle of other Plains villagers, they were far more warlike than the earlier groups. Palisades and protective moats were established around the village sites, and,

when a series of droughts began in 1470 – which were to last 40 years – an internecine war developed for control of fertile areas. As the northern reaches of the rivers dried out and became untenable for farmers, the groups slowly coalesced into larger villages further south.

When the Spanish explorers Coronado and De Soto skirted the southern borders of the Plains in the 1540s, the compact villages of the historic semi-nomadic tribes were well established. The most northerly of these were the Arikara, Mandan and Hidatsa on the Missouri River in North Dakota. Below them on the Mississippi River and its tributaries were the Pawnee, Ponca, Omaha, Iowa, Missouri and Oto. To the south, in Kansas, Missouri and Arkansas were the Kansa and Osage.

The Plains and Prairies seem always to have attracted migrant groups and shifting populations. Even among the nomads, few were ancient residents, and most had moved into the grasslands from surrounding areas. Some tribes, such as the

The Comanche tipi and family group shown in this photograph are typical of the nomadic tribes who lived on the southern Plains.

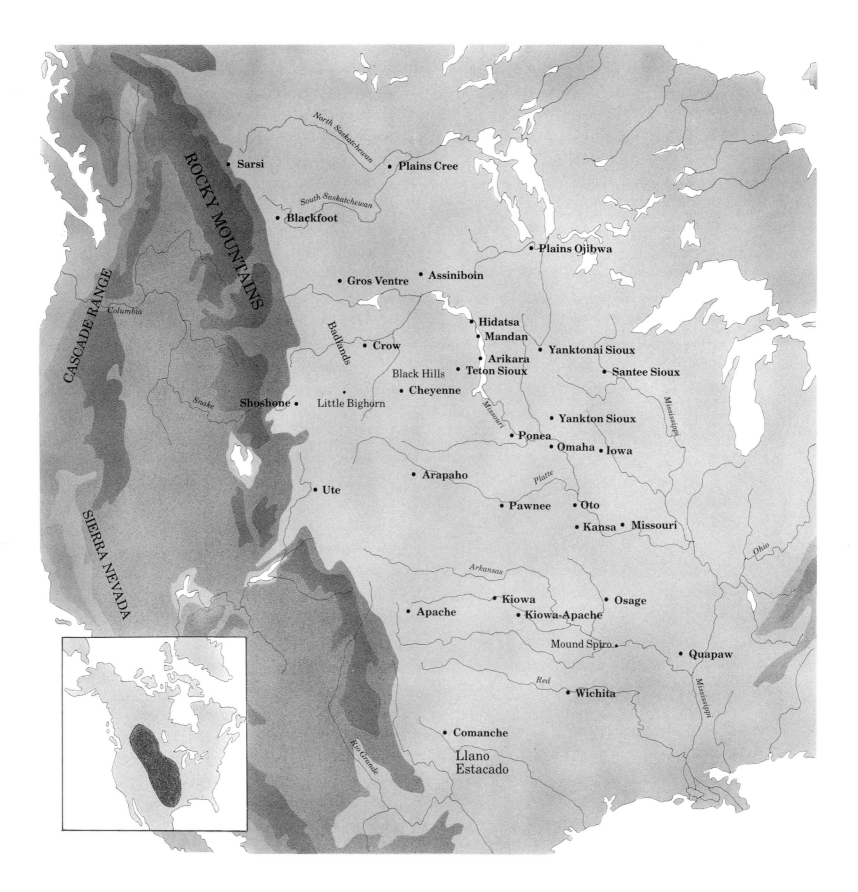

Map showing the approximate locations of the Plains and Prairies tribes when first encountered by Europeans.

Kiowa, speak ancient languages that cannot be traced back to any other, or linked with one of the major language families. This has given rise to speculation that they may be direct descendants of the first hunter-gatherers to have lived here. The movement of other tribes on to the Plains is clearer.

The Comanche, Ute and Shoshone came from the Great Basin country of the west. The Blackfoot moved from the Great Lakes into the north-western territories, while the Sioux tribes came from the Woodlands in the mid-1700s. Cree Indians came in from the north, separating from their Subarctic relatives in the Canadian forests and tundra. Arapaho tribes had lived in the northern foothills of the Rocky Mountains for as long as they could remember, but they moved on to the Plains with the introduction of the horse at the

142

The Pawnee were one of the most powerful and formidable of the semi-nomadic Prairie tribes, and were in conflict with many of the other groups of the region. The warrior shown here carries the short bow of these equestrian hunters and fighters, designed specifically for use from horseback, and wears a bear claw necklace that distinguishes him as a prominent man of proven bravery.

beginning of the 18th century; at the same time, the Crow separated from the village Hidatsa to become mounted nomads. The most recent arrivals were the Cheyenne. They were settled farmers in North Dakota until 1770, but Lewis and Clark met them in the Black Hills in 1804, and by then they were a fully equestrian tribe who practiced no agriculture of any description.

Even before White people started to enter the region in significant numbers, their indirect influence was being felt and dramatic changes were taking place. The horse frontier was moving up from the Southwest, while the gun frontier moved in from the Eastern Woodlands, and they met on the Plains. The small groups of wandering pedestrian nomads and their village equivalents were transformed into mounted warriors and powerful tribes, seemingly overnight.

The introduction of the horse had begun in 1598, when Onate's colonists moved thousands of head of livestock into New Mexico. Apache Indians frequently worked as stockmen on the Spanish ranchos, and every so often a few horses would go missing, turning up later in the Comanche and Ute villages. When the Spanish were driven from the area by the Pueblo Revolt in 1680, Santa Fe became the centre for a rapid dispersion of horses to the tribes of the north. By 1690 the Northern Shoshone in Wyoming were mounted. In the early 1700s they were riding out from their mountain strongholds on fleet-footed war ponies against their bitter enemies, the Blackfeet, who, fighting on foot, soon found themselves being pushed out of their rich hunting grounds. The Blackfeet sought help from the Crees and Assiniboines to the east, who came to their aid with another introduction from the White man: the gun. Within 30 years the Blackfeet were well supplied with horses, obtaining many from the Nez Percé of the Plateau lands who had by now gained a reputation as breeders of the Appaloosa, the famous black and white 'painted pony' of the Plains warriors. Both the horse and gun frontiers were rapidly enlarged to encompass all tribes of the grasslands, creating the short-lived (it was all over within 150 years) but spectacular culture of the Plains Indians.

Extensive European contact began with the semi-nomadic tribes of the east, who were closest to the frontier of White civilization. Treaties were being made between them in Nebraska by 1816, and in 1821 a delegation of Indian representatives travelled to Washington, at the invitation of a

Pawnee villages consisted of earth-covered lodges, which were large enough to house an entire extended family; but twice a year the complete tribe moved on to the grasslands for buffalo hunting, when they lived in hide-covered tipis similar to those of the nomadic groups.

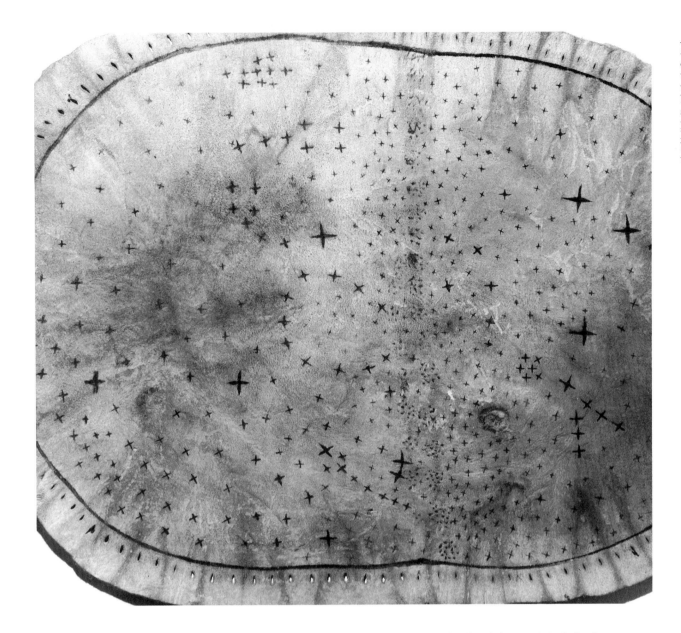

Although most of the Plains and Prairies tribes had elaborate myths concerning the stars, the cosmology of the Pawnee is said to have been the most complex. The star chart shown here was part of the Big Black Meteoric Star medicine bundle, and refers back to the origin of the tribe.

government that wished to secure passage along the Oregon Trail. At this time the American interest was in ensuring safe movement between the populated centres of east and west rather than in securing land, and the country seemed big enough to accommodate the needs of both Whites and Indians. These semi-nomadic tribes were proud and warlike. They were not meek and submissive people who could be trifled with, nor were they inclined to accept the notion of European superiority. Early American observers attached to survey and mapping expeditions often wrote in glowing terms of the reception they received at the Indian villages. John Treat Irving, travelling with a U.S. expeditionary force in Pawnee country in 1833, described their party approaching the Pawnee village and finding the hills surrounding them 'black with masses of mounted warriors' who sat motionless watching their approach.

A lone rider, the Pawnee chief, rode out to meet them on a pony that seems to have possessed almost magical qualities. It breathed fire, had a gait that was inspired by the wind, and a boundless energy that could not be contained; yet the chief controlled his mount with the greatest ease. His appearance and bearing left no doubt as to the pride of these 'lords of the prairies', for he sprang from his pony's back when he reached the soldiers and walked fearlessly up to them to shake the commandant's hand. Irving noted that he wore dark leggings trimmed with hair taken from the heads of his foes, and that a complete head of hair dangled from his horse's bridle.

At a wave of his hand the motionless warriors waiting on the hills raced down the slopes towards the U.S. forces, their wild cries and shouts were piercing, and Irving commented that 'there is something in the fierce, shrill scream of a band of Indian warriors, which rings through the brain, and sends the blood curdling back to the heart'. The warriors had paint 'profusely smeared over their bodies and arms, and many had even bestowed it upon the heads and limbs of their horses'. Feathers of the bald eagle hung from long plaited scalp locks, and dangled from the bridles and tails of the ponies. Many warriors had shaved their heads, which were adorned with red-dyed 'crests' or roaches made from deer hair; they wore necklaces of grizzly bear claws, and some had white wolf skins draped across their shoulders. As they neared the troops, the warriors split into two parties; urging their ponies on, they began a mad

Right: This exquisite Sioux woman's dress dates from about 1830, and is of an early style in which the cape-like upper part is made separately and then sewn to the longer skirt. The decoration is made from porcupine quills and red wool tassels, with an added fringe of copper cones.

Far right: Wichita women were often elaborately tattooed, as is the figure shown in this illustration. She is using a pestle and mortar to grind corn into meal that will be used in a variety of ways: as a form of bread, mixed with meat or fruit as a dumpling, or to thicken soups and stews. The manner of wearing her robe about the waist, leaving the bosom exposed, was a characteristic custom of the Wichita before European notions of 'modesty' introduced the full-length dress.

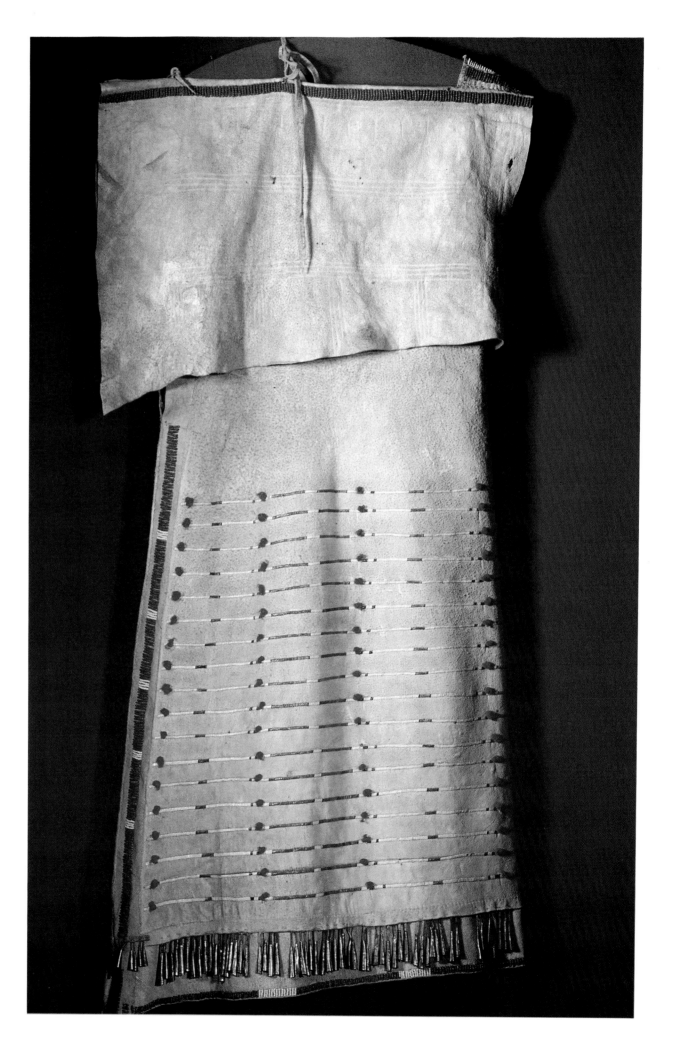

Buffalo were an important part of the diet of both the nomadic and semi-nomadic tribes, and were of major significance in dances and rituals. The Buffalo Bull dance shown here in a George Catlin drawing made in the 1830s, was part of the creation cycle of the Mandan O-Kee-Pa ceremonies.

encircling race around the soldiers. With another wave of his hand the chief brought this movement to an instant halt, and the warriors leapt from their mounts and seated themselves in a silent circle. Such displays were intended to impress their visitors and demonstrate the strength of the nation. That they had the desired effect on Irving's party is certain, since he tells us they proceeded to the Indian village 'nervously and in a tight group', in spite of the fact that the Indian greeting had been friendly rather than aggressive. As they approached closer to the village, their movement was impeded by the numbers of women and children who jostled round them, curious to see these strange White men. Others crowded the roofs of the mud and thatch lodges so they could obtain a better view over the heads of those in front.

Their reception in the village is typical of the Plains and Prairies tribes. They were taken first to the chief's lodge where the principal men were seated in places of honour at the rear of the

building, and a pipe was lit and passed around the group before anyone spoke, thereby binding them together in friendship and ensuring that only true words could be uttered. The chief addressed the group, telling them he was glad the White men had honoured them with their visit. When he had finished, the leader of the White party, Mr Ellsworth, made a similar speech emphasizing their friendly intentions and their desire to travel peacefully in Pawnee country.

At the conclusion of the speeches and smoking, Indian women brought in huge quantities of buffalo ribs and urged their guests to eat as much as they could. The White party, who had been living on somewhat meagre rations, set to with a gusto that astonished their Indian hosts. Towards the end of the meal, an Indian burst in upon the gathering to announce that the leading War Chief invited the White men to his lodge where another feast had been prepared. Later expeditionary groups, learning from the experiences of people such as Irving, realized that it was essential to eat only the minimum amount required for politeness at each lodge, since one could easily be invited to seven or eight similar feasts in the course of a single evening. Indian notions of hospitality centred on giving generously. The pipe and food offered in copious quantity guaranteed safety to anyone who had smoked and eaten in friendship while in the village, and an escort of warriors to lead them out of the country when it was time to depart; but other gifts were bestowed just as liberally. Irving notes that several warriors came up to their party before its entry to the village and pledged themselves to give away a considerable number of their horses. Some old men, who possessed no horses of their own, harangued these warriors for not being generous enough with their gifts, proudly boasting of how many horses they would have given if they had had any! Quite frequently, additional presents were placed with those that had been formally pledged. These were usually buffalo robes, other furs, and dressed deerskins, or particularly fine items of skin clothing.

All the semi-nomadic village tribes relied heavily on proceeds from the hunt, especially buffalo, and supplemented the meat with crops raised in small garden plots close to the village sites. Underground storage caches were dug in which surplus foods might be kept and utilized as a winter supply. Leadership was democratic, with representatives of the tribe gaining recognition through popular support. Even though some

tribes had a form of hereditary rank, being the son of a chief was no guarantee that one would become chief in turn; it was an advantage to have status, but popular support and proven capabilities were essential.

Among some of the groups, such as the Osage, village government was organized in ways similar to those of the Woodlands tribes, and the offices of War and Peace leaders were separated out. To become a War Chief one needed resolute courage, the ability to face fear without flinching, and the determination to overcome difficulty even against hopeless odds. Such people were highly respected, as they provided an example for the warriors and maintained the fighting strength of the tribe. The Peace Chief, although also noted for outstanding bravery, had to be able to negotiate and judge a situation accurately. It was his task to settle disputes amicably through arbitration and, if necessary, by restitution.

Together they formed a complementary pair who had the same objective in mind: to ensure the strength of the group and its ability to withstand hardship or opposition. But because they pursued this aim in such totally different ways, they were often in disagreement. Neither, however, had complete authority. They were given attention in councils of all the leading men, at which they would express their respective points of view; but decisions were taken by the council as a whole, and both the War and Peace Chiefs were under an obligation to facilitate the council's decision, even

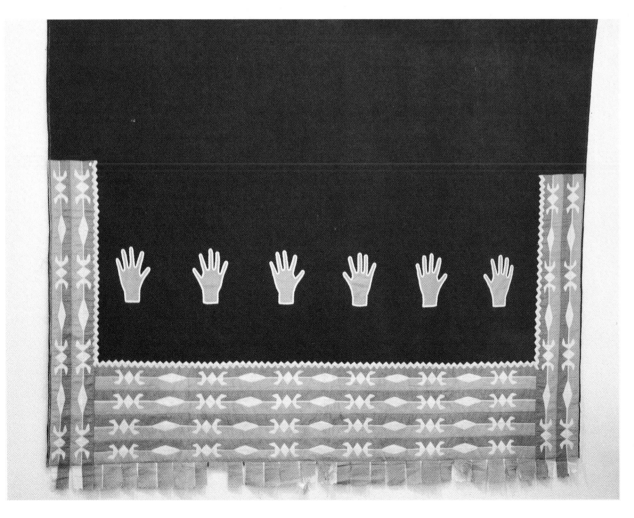

Although most tribes readily utilized trade items in the decoration of their artefacts, ribbonwork became – and remains – characteristic of the Osage. The hand patterns on this blanket are a traditional Osage design element.

149

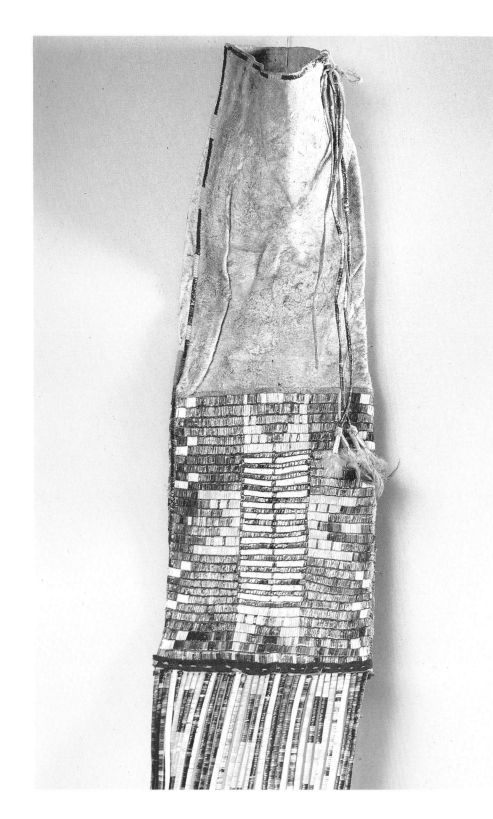

Even though smoking for pleasure was unknown to most North American Indians, every Plains man owned a pipe through which the rituals of friendship and greeting could be carried out. When not in use, the pipe, together with tobacco, a tamping-stick and a 'strike-a-light', were kept in elaborately decorated pipe bags such as this.

gained respect in a different manner were the medicine men, or shamans. Their power stemmed from the supernatural, and they not only had a rapport with the spiritual forces denied to others, but also possessed knowledge of the sacred rituals which ensured the survival of the group. In many ways they were a combination of philosopher and magician, tribal historian, priest and doctor, although in some cases their powers were more specific. One individual might control, say, healing powers, while another was able to prophesy events from signs that the spirits gave him.

In all cases their power stemmed from supernatural knowledge and control, and not from the possession of material goods or of any remarkable human skills. The spiritual tokens that ensured the continuance of the tribe were kept in animal skin wrappers, known as medicine bundles, which among the Skidi Pawnee were entrusted to the safekeeping of hereditary chiefs. These could not be used, nor could their powers be invoked, except through the consent of the shaman-priests, who alone possessed knowledge of the sacred rituals that would reactivate the tokens and render them effective.

Much of tribal lore was known only to shamanic fraternities, and was passed on through lengthy initiation rites during which the initiate was taught the secrets of the shamans' societies. It was often so complex that a shaman's training continued throughout his life, and no single individual could ever hope to understand it in its entirety. Among the Skidi Pawnee, only the Evening Star Priest may have known all the bundle ceremonies. His role was a passive one, since it was to oversee the other priests and to ensure that a correct ritual order was maintained; but his knowledge was the most powerful, because he alone could combine the powers of all the major bundles, thereby uniting the spiritual forces of both Earth and Sky. In recognition of this power, he had status even above that of the Skidi Head Chief. Skidi ritual life was based on the movements of the stars. One of their most important medicine bundles contained a sacred star chart, painted on deerskin, which was said to relate to Pawnee existence since the beginning of time. Their lodges were arranged according to star formations, and their placement in the village formed a pattern that echoed the constellations. In the Chiefs' Council, their chiefs 'sat above the people like stars sit over the earth'. So complicated was the Skidi Pawnee ceremonial system that they are said to have had the most intricate cosmology to be found on the entire North American continent.

Other village tribes employed different methods of tracing history and regulating their lives. The Osage saw a division between the powers of the Earth and the Sky, as the Earth controlled activities related to the material aspects of existence, and the fertility and continued success of the people, whereas the Sky controlled the souls of individuals and directed their spiritual needs. Both were essential and inter-related. Material progress had no purpose unless it could be applied to some higher level of meaning, but a purely spiritual existence relegated one entirely to the

when it conflicted with their own.

The Chiefs attempted to maintain support through example and generosity. Horses captured on a raid by the War Chief might be given away to other members of the raiding party, and he would keep none for himself; the Peace Chief lent or gave horses for the hunt or when moving camp. Both sponsored lavish feasts or gave robes and meat to the poor and needy. Among some tribes it is even said that the chiefs were noted for their poverty, since they had given away almost all they possessed.

Other leading members of the communities who

This Oto man, seated on a log bench in front of his home, is wearing full ceremonial dress. The buffalo robe around his waist has been carefully prepared and smoked to ensure it remains soft and supple, and is painted with dyes prepared from vegetable juices. The otter hat, although also used on occasion by some other semi-nomadic groups, is nevertheless highly characteristic of the Oto.

151

The cradleboard in this photograph of a Pawnee family was cut from the heart of a living tree, and bears a Morningstar design to ensure that this sacred power would watch over the health and well-being of the child entrusted to his care.

realm of the ghosts.

This dichotomy was resolved by organizing the year into two parts; one controlled by the Sky People, the other controlled by the Earth People. In some respects this was a carry-over of the Woodlands concept of separate War and Peace Chiefs, where different individuals had responsibility for maintaining the conflicting interests of the group; in this way both material and spiritual needs could be incorporated into Osage ceremonialism. This, in turn, had a direct bearing on the day-to-day life of the people, who looked to their chiefs and shamans for guidance and direction.

The rich culture of the semi-nomadic villagers was affected at an early date by their proximity to European influences. Their shamans were scorned for being more show than substance, their chiefs were criticized for not exerting control over factions within the groups, and their beliefs were belittled by the missionaries. By the time White people started to move into their areas the tribes were already decimated from trade contacts that had introduced smallpox and alcohol, and were able to offer only token resistance. Although they continued to wage war against other Indian groups, this was often accomplished by acting as

The Wichita were a small confederacy of village farmers and hunters, who built villages of domed grass thatch lodges such as that seen here. They are often said to be the occupants of the fabled province of Quivira visited by Spanish expeditions from the Southwest in 1541, although the records indicate the Spanish were told that Quivira lay even further to the east.

mercenary scouts and soldiers with the U.S. forces and was frequently a consequence of established tribal enmities: the semi-nomadic Pawnee had fought the nomadic Sioux for generations, and it was a relatively easy task to enlist a battalion of Pawnee scouts to lead American soldiers to the Sioux villages.

In the early days of White exploration relationships with the nomadic tribes were tense, yet for the most part there was little bloodshed. Throughout the first half of the 1800s, increasing numbers of White people travelled through the Plains and Prairies, adding to the population of mountain men and fur trappers who were already in the region. Emigrant wagon trains started to cross the grasslands to the settlements and gold strikes of the west. Agreements with the tribes were frequently ignored, and some of the emigrants began to think of settling down in these wide spaces that were 'wasted' by being reserved exclusively for Indian use.

Small detachments of U.S. troops were stationed here to keep the wagon trains moving and to prevent settlers from establishing themselves. The Plains were beyond the 'permanent Indian frontier' and the soldiers were to protect the Indians, not to fight them. It was an uneasy peace,

Because the buffalo was the life-sustaining animal of the Plains Indians, it was held to be sacred and played a significant role during ceremonies. This painted skull was used as an altar by the Arapaho during their annual life-renewal rituals.

153

Far right: The hoop and pole game was a test of skill and concentration, and was a popular pastime among many of the Plains tribes. The Sioux contestants pictured here are attempting to thrust their long lances through a hoop which has been rolled across their path. Coloured segments on the hoop served to indicate a score, and heavy bets would be placed on the outcome of the game.

since few of the tribes thought of themselves as subject to anyone else's demands; but it was a peace. Some Indians were killed in misunderstandings, which the tribes overlooked; yet when the U.S. army suffered its first casualties in 1854 the Plains Indian Wars broke out. The numbers of books and films made about this period, and the names that have become legends of the American West – Sitting Bull, Crazy Horse, Black Elk, General Crook, George Armstrong Custer, and William (Buffalo Bill) Cody among them – are testimony to the desperate struggles that were destined to take place.

Much of the conflict was ideological. The Indians thought of the land as sacred, a gift from the Great Spirit which they and all other aspects of creation merely travelled through. The Europeans, however, saw it as something they could own, and which might be put to economic use by fencing it off and raising crops and cattle. For all the Indians, nomads and villagers alike, regardless of their diverse origins, the environment embodied the very essence of freedom and independence. Thoughts and ideals of limitless possibility could be projected into its vast spaces. It was a land in which nothing stood still; where the constant wind, unimpeded by any natural obstacle, set every element into movement, and where the individual was answerable to no-one except himself and the forces of nature that shaped his life. But it was also, in another sense, a country that summed up the pioneer attitude. The land could become a monument to each man's achievement, where he carved a name for himself through the

labour of his own hands and the sweat of his brow. 'Look West, young man' was the rallying cry of the new America.

The Indians had no need to look West. They were already there, with democratic institutions that the early pioneers could admire but never emulate. No Plains Indian was ever subject to another, since their chiefs had no authority or jurisdiction. People followed a wise leader through choice, and the chiefs merely acted as the voices through which the wishes of the people were made known. They were great orators – their speeches at treaty gatherings, even in poor translations, attest to this and have a majesty and grandeur that amply demonstrates their wisdom, intellect, and perception – but they were never rulers.

It was a man's world, at least superficially, in which honour and respect were actively sought. Each warrior tried to attain a position in which the people would look up to him, where children would stand open-mouthed as he passed by: a great man among a nation of great men. Yet this denies the power of women. Women held absolute rights over anything to do with the household. All the family belongings were theirs; a man owned only his weapons and clothing. Even the meat secured on hunts became the 'property' of women as soon as it was brought into the village.

A woman could divorce an unreliable husband simply by setting his belongings outside the tipi, and in any domestic dispute she could turn to her own family for support and protection. A man would think carefully before raising a hand against his wife, since her brothers would come to

Men recorded their hunting and war exploits in pictographic paintings, which were frequently applied to tipi covers and often recorded the exploits of several family members. This model buffalo hide cover comes from the northern Plains.

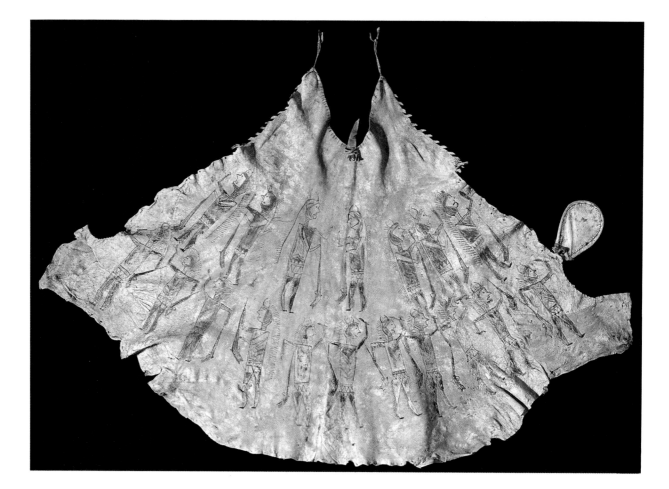

Quanah Parker was a war leader of the Kwahadi Comanche who advocated armed resistance in a desperate attempt to save the last of the buffalo from White hunters.

her aid. Much of women's influence was exercised within the domestic sphere, but few men would speak openly in council without first consulting their families as to what they thought was the right course of action. Elderly women were thought to possess particularly potent powers. Warriors sought their adulation and praise, and if cursed by them would immediately offer lavish gifts to placate their wrath and bring themselves back into good grace.

It was, too, a world in which compassion and humour played major roles. Early White observers saw only the display of war honours and the straight-faced demeanour of the Indian in a public context, where no emotion was displayed. They

concluded from this that the Indians of the Plains and Prairies lived only for glory in war; that they were cold-hearted savages who knew nothing of the 'civilized' emotions of happiness and love, sadness and loneliness; who were unable to engage in carefree laughter and who brought up their children to be ruthless and cruel.

If these early observers had stayed in the tipi camps and made friends, they would quickly have noticed the true character of the Indian, and realized that the bold face put on for public display was often a cover for deeper conflicting emotions and was adopted only as a matter of tradition. At home, families were close, and a great deal of affection and humour was demonstrated.

Children were expected to show their respect for older members of the community, but they were rarely punished. Most Indians were indulgent parents and even more indulgent grandparents.

A young boy could always rely on his grand father to stop whatever he was doing and join him in play-tracking a waterbird along the river bank, or engaging in an hilarious chase after a particularly elusive lizard or butterfly. When the boy was about five years old, his grandfather would make him his first bow and arrows, which were presented at a solemn and dignified ceremony which important members of the tribe were asked to attend, and the proceeds of his first hunt – even though it might only be a bird or rabbit – were formally prepared and eaten at a feast in the boy's honour.

Girls were similarly spoiled by their grandmothers, who praised their skills in porcupine quill embroidery and called elder women of the tribe who were renowned quillworkers to look at the girl's work and to offer advice and gentle criticism. The girl's first 'real' piece was proudly displayed. If, for instance, she had made a quilled shirt strip, then her father would make a point of having this sewn to his shirt and wearing it in the village so that others might admire his daughter's achievement.

In adolescence the young men and women were encouraged to take the initiative, and their wishes and desires were always given serious consideration. The boy who crept out of the tipi late at night against his parent's strict orders not to join a hunting or war party, provided he carried spare moccasins and cared for the horses, was admired for his determination and self-reliance rather than punished for his disobedience. In marriage, which among most of the tribes was arranged by the fam-

When the various bands of a Plains tribe gathered together, they pitched their tipis in a circle-camp which was imbued with ritual significance as the representation of the sacred circle that sustained life and ensured harmony.

ily heads and in which the prospective bride and groom had no theoretical say, there was usually a great deal of behind-the-scenes manoeuvring to ensure that the young couple's wishes were met.

Such people can hardly be called 'savage' in any sense of the word; yet war and warfare were always part of their lives, and war honours were something that every young man eagerly sought. To understand this, we need to consider the Indian concept of warfare, since it is very different from that held by Europeans. War was never a matter of conquering and defeating an enemy, or of expanding one's own territorial claims. It was a necessary condition of living in a harsh environment where individual skills meant the difference between survival and death.

The Plains and Prairies are subject to sudden and unexpected changes. A mild, sunny and calm spring day can change within a matter of hours to one in which driving snow storms sweep down from the Rocky Mountains and reduce visibility to a few inches; when anyone, even within a few miles of the camp, can become totally disoriented. A distant rumble can herald the oncoming rush of a herd of life-sustaining buffalo, numbering many thousands, but it can also mean the onset of a prairie fire set off by lightning, and from which the only escape is immediate flight.

For the Indian, war was a way to show oneself capable of withstanding such rigours, and demonstrated the ability to act immediately and decisively. It was never carried to excess and – at least until the last desperate struggles with the United States – was always bound by strict codes of honour. The duties of the warrior were laid down in the tales told around the winter camp fires, which make it clear that they were there to safeguard the people: to throw a protective shield around the camps which the opposing forces, whether those of the environment or of man, would be reluctant to penetrate.

To this end the Plains warrior set out to prove his superiority over the forces by which he was opposed, which could be measured in terms of dangers overcome rather than enemies killed. It is significant that the greatest honours went to those who had ridden against an armed warrior, and who had touched the enemy and then ridden away without causing injury to either party. This was clearly far more dangerous than waiting in ambush and shooting an opponent as he passed by, which did not expose the attacker to any particular danger.

In the scale of war honours, touching an armed foe ranked highest. Next was rescuing a comrade who had fallen in front of the enemy. Third was seizing an opponent's weapons or horses. The actual killing of an enemy or of taking his scalp was lower on the scale, and among some tribes was of little significance. Among the Blackfeet, for instance, the warrior boasted of the numbers of guns and horses he had taken, yet rarely mentioned scalps. Even with tribes such as the Sioux, among whom the scalp was a first-class trophy, its value was estimated in terms of the danger to which one had been exposed in the course of taking it. A scalp taken from inside the lodge of an enemy, which

Opposite: Hoof marks incised on the tubular bowl of this pipe indicate it was used by the leader of a Crow horse raiding party. During the journey to the enemy camps, he would often sit to one side and smoke the pipe in an attempt to establish communion with the spiritual powers to ensure a successful outcome to the raid.

Left: The buffalo chase was a thrilling and exciting pursuit. Mounted on highly trained horses, known as buffalo runners, the hunters rode close to the right of their quarry where they attempted to use lances or hunting bows to penetrate the soft body parts of the buffalo and pierce its kidneys. Their aim had to be swift and sure, for the spot they needed to hit was small and the buffalo was a fast-moving, unpredictable, and highly dangerous target. Should a rider be thrown, his buffalo runner was trained to stop and could be swiftly recovered by the long trailing line seen in the drawing.

Scalps were frequently treated with great respect and honour and given ritual meaning. The Crow hooped scalp shown here was used in their renewal ceremonies, and symbolizes the myth through which this ceremony came to the people. Talons from a bird of prey are attached to the beaded strip on the front, while on the reverse a cross of beads symbolizes the Morningstar. The contrast of red and black between the two faces indicates the scalp's importance as representing both life and death.

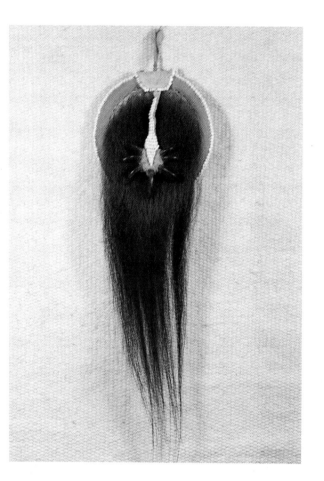

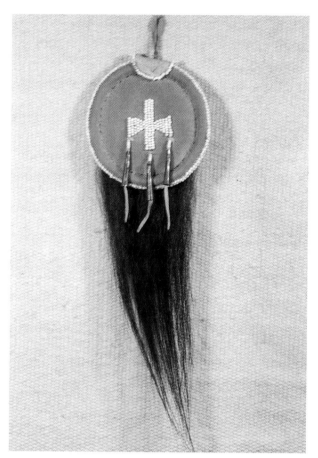

necessitated entering the village, had far greater value than one taken elsewhere.

Most young men would join a war party at some stage in their careers. For many, this never extended beyond raiding for horses, when a small group of six or seven people would set out under the leadership of someone who had proven himself successful on previous occasions. With horses one could attain status within the tribe. They were needed for the marriage payments; the more horses one could offer, the greater the respect that was shown towards the bride's family. An excess number of ponies made it possible to loan them to others for war or for the hunt, or to demonstrate generosity by giving them to the poor and elderly when camp was moved, thereby making their lives a little easier.

A few of the horses were trained specifically for war and hunting. These 'buffalo runners' were selected for their fleetness of foot, their ability to react immediately to a rider's commands, their stamina and endurance, and especially their courage. It was on such ponies that the Indians chased down their principal food source, the buffalo. Riding close to the right of the buffalo, where the spear or lance could be used most effectively, the pony would instinctively veer to the right away from the dangerous thrust of the buffalo's horns as the arrow or lance struck home. Since the Indians rode bareback and used no rein so that their hands would be free to handle their weapons, a man's life was dependent on the responses of his mount. A slow horse would be impaled on the buffalo's horns, or its rider spilled beneath the hooves.

Buffalo runners were highly valued. The village

tribes stabled them within the household's dwelling; the nomads picketed them outside the tipi, often with a line attached to the owner's toe so that he would be immediately awakened if anything untoward happened. Raiders seeking glory would gain much more from taking one of these highly trained ponies than by running off several of the ordinary pack horses herded outside the camps. Not only did they gain a pony whose qualities were assured, but they also demonstrated their ability to creep silently into the enemy camp – even into the enemy's house – and snatch this valuable prize without disturbing anyone.

War parties went out either for horses or for scalps. The Southern Cheyenne and Arapaho fought the Kiowa and Comanche bitterly, while the Northern Cheyenne were at war with the Crow, who were also under threat from the Blackfeet. Pawnee warriors coming into the grasslands from their villages to the east had no friends on the Plains; neither did the Shoshone, who raided from the west. Sioux Indians made enemies of all their neighbouring tribes and enjoyed only brief respites during occasional alliances.

In all these battles, the war parties were small, often consisting of only three or four warriors. Killings were opportunistic ones, intended to enhance status and honour, and once the party had gained a victory of this kind, it immediately returned to the village. There was rarely any follow-up to an attack, and quite frequently no deaths occurred. If, for instance, a member of the war party dreamed of misfortune, then the search for an enemy was immediately abandoned. The same would happen if any token of bad luck was

160

observed. Deaths from ventures of this nature were always very light, and there was never any kind of blood lust driving the warriors to excessive killing.

Occasionally large-scale war parties set out. These were usually organized to atone for the death of a tribal member. Among the Crow Indians, for example, a war party that went seeking vengeance could only be organized after the annual renewal rites. During the rites, the pledger of the dance, someone who had suffered a family loss during the previous year – although not necessarily through the actions of an enemy tribe – sought spiritual guidance whereby a scalp might be brought into the village and dedicated to the deceased. In a way it was a kind of spiritual replacement; the distress of the family bearing the loss could be ritually transferred to their foes. At the same time, the soul of the defeated enemy could be captured and brought into the service of their own deceased.

Usually these scalps were treated with extreme reverence. Brought into the camp by the victorious warriors, they were stretched on wooden hoops and painted before being paraded in the scalp or victory dance. This was not a celebration of the defeat of an enemy, as it has so often been depicted, but a rejoicing in the fact that mourning could now be set aside, and that normal life could be resumed. The Santee Sioux are said to have treated the scalp with dignified solemnity. It was

painted and decorated with honorific emblems, combed and set with feathers, and finally buried with ceremonies befitting a chief. Many of the dances associated with the scalp were joyful ones, expressions of the people's release from sadness at their own losses; but these were always intermingled with tears and sorrow for the necessary loss their enemy had sustained.

Perhaps such a view paints an over-romantic picture of the Plains Indians. There were people among them who lived only for the joy of killing, people who would never share their wealth in ponies, people who cared only for themselves and never gave a thought for others; yet all the evidence indicates that these people were in a minority, more likely to be driven from society than accepted by them. Among many tribes a person who was overtly aggressive, who joined in too many scalp raids, would never be elected as a chief or spokesman for the tribe. Bravery was an essential prerequisite for any position of honour, but this was tempered by the need to show restraint and clear and unbiased judgement.

The Plains Indians were people who had to live in a harsh environment, and who accepted harsh and immediate demonstrations of their ability to survive. A weakling had no chance here. Men proved themselves by their actions in battles against the environment and in battles with their enemies. They waged war on those they considered equals, rather than against weaker or

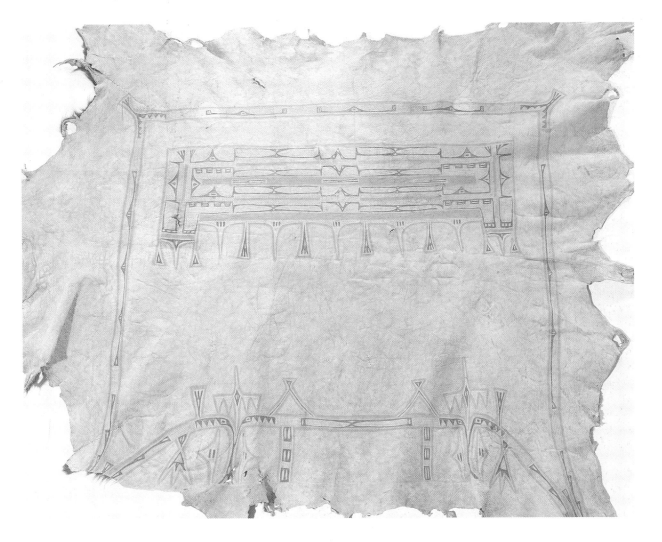

This buffalo robe was made by the Hidatsa in about 1850. It bears a 'box and border' design that designates it as a woman's garment, and which was said to be illustrative of the fertile and productive period of a woman's life.

The young Plains Indian child spent its early years in a cradleboard while its mother was working. This Sioux example is decorated with porcupine quills, and has a base of stiff rawhide to give it support. The soft deerskin pouch would be filled with dry moss before the child was placed inside and safely secured by tightening the leather thongs that closed the front opening.

carried out to maintain the world in balance. By the same token, only man had the power to throw everything into chaos.

The responsibility for keeping things in order fell on the shamans, or medicine men. Because of their extraordinary powers the shamans were both respected and feared. If they were able to interpret and utilize forces for the good of the people, then, surely, they were just as able to use these forces against someone with whom they disagreed. It was widely held that the shamans possessed power for evil as much as for good, and few people would dare question a shaman's judgement. Whenever a war party went out, a shaman was asked to guarantee its success and to give some token by which his power could be carried with the group. Hunting was sanctioned by the shaman, often to the extent that in major hunts he would perform ceremonies to draw the herds closer to the camp, and no council was complete without his spiritual guidance.

When a Blackfoot tribe moved camp, the shaman travelled in front holding the sacred pipe, decorated with eagle feathers and mallard heads. Its stem pointed forward to clear a safe passage and to remove any negative influences that might hamper progress. In most tribes the authority of the shaman was at least equal to that of the chief. The awe shown for the shamans' contacts with the other world, and the fear this instilled in the tribes, is indicative of the hold that the supernatural had over every Plains Indian. White observers called this superstition. The Indians called it common sense.

No Indian would travel into unknown country or brave the fury of lightning and sudden storms without some kind of protective talisman. This was obtained during a vision quest, when the seeker would go alone to some high bluff that was the home of the ancestors. Here, surrounded by the wind, the voices of animals, and the ancient relics of his forefathers, the Indian sought spiritual guidance. Through fasting he attempted to induce a dream in which he asked for a token that would both guide and protect him. Many people have written that the Indian humbled himself and begged for the spirits' assistance; but his calls for the 'Grandfathers' to pity him were never signs that he belittled himself. Grandfather was a term of respect, which the ancients deserved; but the Indian faced his gods and challenged them, and, if he were strong enough, demanded a gift from them, together with the facepaints and songs through which this gift could be reactivated. Such favours were not given easily, and were never passed on through pity; they were powerful forces that derived from the animal ancestors and which only the strong could manage.

The spirits usually made their presence felt through animal intermediaries. A man might dream that they spoke to him through the hawk or the badger, the wolf or the mouse. Whatever animal appeared became the medium through which the spirits might be contacted at a future date, and his first concern after obtaining a vision was to secure the skin of the animal in the dream to make a medicine bundle. A medicine bundle,

refugee groups, to whom they offered protection. The Sioux held the Pawnee in great respect, even though they were their traditional enemy, because they knew they could, and would, fight back.

Most importantly, all tribes stood by the belief that the land was created for the enjoyment of all the world's creatures. Man was no more nor less important than the white-tailed antelope, the buffalo, or the grizzly bear. When Wakan Tanka, to use the Sioux term, created the world, he divided it equally between all the products of his creation. No single element took precedence. Man existed at the same level as the animals – gifted, perhaps, with a superior intellect, but this superiority also brought its obligations. Only man could disturb the harmony of the world; only man had the responsibility to ensure the sacred ceremonies were

When nomadic Plains Indians moved camp they had to carry everything they owned with them. In former days, burdens were carried on the women's backs and in pack bags strapped to their dogs, men carried only their weapons so they would be immediately ready to defend the family if need arose. The introduction of the horse made life easier. The Blackfoot family in this drawing is using an A-shaped pole framework, or travois, which has been tied across the withers of a gentle pony, to transport their possessions. The travois poles themselves will later be used as tipi poles when a new camp is made.

163

Annie Berry, a Kiowa woman, is shown here wearing a fringed buckskin dress decorated with elk teeth. The teeth could only be obtained through trade contacts with the people of the north, and the number used on this dress indicate that Annie's family were well-to-do and possessed sufficient goods to acquire this rare commodity.

literally 'something wrapped up', contained tokens of various elements from the vision. If he had dreamed of lightning, it might contain blue beads; if the dream was of the earth, then dried grasses would be included. None of these had power in themselves; it was only in combination with the paints and songs of the vision that power could be invoked.

Most men, and some women, had personal power bundles of this kind; but there were also tribal bundles, far more powerful, that were handed down from generation to generation. The majority of these were invoked to promote the general well-being of the tribe. In many ways they were tribal talismans which, by being ritually opened during major ceremonial gatherings, helped to unite the various different bands that constituted the tribe.

This was important on the Plains, where most of the year was spent in small family groups scattered over a wide area. Winter was too harsh for the bands to remain together, since there were inadequate supplies of food, timber and water to support large groups, and the bands came together only in the spring and summer when the tribal rituals were carried out and when they engaged in communal buffalo hunts. The village tribes, with their stored corn, pumpkins and melons, could afford the luxury of large winter encampments; yet even they felt the need for some kind of unifying force such as could be obtained from the tribal bundles.

For much of the year, the tribal medicines remained in the care of highly respected individuals. Although it was an honour to be a bundle-keeper, it was also a difficult task. Taboos relating to the bundle had to be rigorously observed for it to remain effective, and many of these placed a heavy burden on the bundle-keeper, his family, and all who came in contact with them. The taboos reflected the importance of the bundle itself. In some senses it contained a 'history' of the tribe, and the bundle-keeper was therefore the keeper of the tribal lore. Most of the bundles could never touch the ground but had to be kept in a sacred place within the household, or were placed on special tripods outside the tipi and moved during the day so that they always faced the sun, the source of life and energy.

The power of the tribal bundles was invoked in summer, when the nomadic tribes started to gather together for their annual buffalo hunts and the village tribes began preparations to move out of the villages *en masse* in pursuit of the herds. At this time the powers inherent in the tribal bundles took on particular significance, since the well-being of the tribe and its identity as a unified group depended on successful hunts for the major rituals to be carried out effectively. If the hunts failed, it spelled not only economic disaster, but threatened the spiritual life of the tribe as well.

In the old days the hunts were almost always successful. Buffalo roamed the Plains in their millions, forming herds so vast that one might wait a week for one to pass by, during which time the ground up to the horizon was a solid seething mass of animals. There was such an abundance that

little difficulty was experienced in securing the quantities of food necessary for the feasts, or in collecting the buffalo tongues that would be consecrated as offerings in the most sacred rituals, and every part of the buffalo was utilized. The hides provided robes and bedding, as well as skins for making tipis. The meat was eaten, tendons were twisted for cordage and bow strings, the bones were made into a variety of implements and tools, the hooves boiled down for glue and the tail used as a fly whisk. Even the rib cage made a sledge for young children, and sometimes for adults too, on which they would race each other down grassy slopes.

So important was the buffalo in the life of the Indians of the Plains and Prairies that it would be no exaggeration to say that their traditional cultures were ultimately destroyed not by military actions but by the indiscriminate slaughter of buffalo for their fur and hides. It has been estimated that in the three years of 1872, 1873 and 1874, over four million buffalo were killed on the southern Plains alone. At a single 1874 killing site on the Republican River there were 6,500 carcasses from which the hides had been stripped; the meat was simply left to rot. By the 1880s, the herds had disappeared, and the Indians were starved into submission: 600 Montana Blackfeet Indians, for example, died from famine in 1883 because they were unable to find a single buffalo in their previously rich hunting areas.

When buffalo was plentiful, the summer camps might contain several thousand Indians. Allied tribes, such as the Kiowa and Comanche or the Arapaho and Cheyenne, often pitched their tipis together, attending one another's feasts and dances and joining in one another's ceremonies. In larger tribes, the circle camp – so named because the tipis were pitched in a circle, leaving a central space in which rituals might be carried out – could have a diameter of half a mile or more.

Among all the tribes, the major event of the circle camp was the annual renewal ceremony in which the world was 'made over', and rituals performed to ensure success and happiness for the forthcoming year. The Blackfeet held this ceremony when the chokecherries were ripe, at the end of July. For convenience, the renewal ceremonies are known by the generic term 'Sun Dance': a name applied by Europeans after observing the Sioux 'gazing at the sun' during their ritual. The dances did not, however, have any particular reference to sun worship; in many cases the sun featured only in a very minor way if at all.

Among the Cheyenne, a prominent feature was the sacred 'earths'. Spiral patterns by which the forces of nature could be drawn into the centre and concentrated within the circle camp were incised on a ceremonially cleared patch of earth. From there, the power inherent in these forces could be absorbed by the dancers, and from them could spread to the people. At the conclusion of the ceremonies, all these forces, now enriched with the wishes of the people themselves, could be dissipated and distributed throughout the world, via a reversed spiral which radiated force instead of drawing it in.

This exquisitely beautiful sewing awl is made from a short length of trade iron set in a bone handle. The iron has been filed to a point so that it would penetrate the tough and durable, but difficult to work, semi-rigid rawhide used in many Plains artefacts. Prior to the introduction of iron, awls were made from bone.

Far right: The Mandan were a numerous and influential semi-nomadic tribe who occupied strong villages on the upper Missouri. The man shown in this drawing wears a horned headdress that indicates his rank and status. Suspended from a roof support beam behind him are a buffalo skull and painted shield, both of which had sacred significance and were imbued with spiritual force. In the background to his left is a backrest made from willow rods lashed together with sinew, while the opening at the apex of the lodge acted as a smoke-hole to vent smoke from the fire and permitted light to enter.

The Omaha war shirt shown in this photograph bears beaded bear paw designs that derive from a personal vision of its owner. Such shirts could only be worn by leading warriors, and the right to wear them had to be granted by a prominent war leader.

For the Crow, the central object of veneration was a highly sacred doll-like effigy, which represented the mythical child who first brought the blessings of the spirits to the people. Among the Blackfoot, the Sacred Woman took precedence. It was she who married a star, from whom was obtained the sacred Natoas Bundle containing tokens of all the elements necessary to ensure the tribe's success and growth. Her son, Scarface, was given power as a warrior. By these means the essential aspects of both the Sky and Earth could be brought together and ritually unified for the benefit of the people.

Even among the Sioux, gazing at the sun was only a minor part of the total ceremony. Young warriors who had made a vow during the year, usually at moments of extreme stress or danger, pledged themselves to undergo trials of endurance by having incisions cut into the skin of their chests through which a stick would be passed. This was attached to a thong tied to the central pole of the Sun Dance lodge, and the dancer would move around the pole facing the sun while he attempted to tear himself free. If he succeeded, or fainted in his attempts to do so, he would be granted a vision. This was, nevertheless, a personal vision, although other members of the community might benefit indirectly. The essential aspect of the Sioux ceremony for the whole tribe was the painted buffalo skull altar and rawhide cut-outs of a man and buffalo attached to the central pole of the lodge, since it was through these that the people would ensure their continuation and an abundance of buffalo.

Apart from its ceremonial significance, the circle camp was the major social gathering of the year, marked by continual feasts and dances. Marriages were arranged and old friendships re-established, goods were bartered and exchanged, and games and gambling took place. There were horse races every day, on which heavy bets might be placed. Some shamans actually possessed 'Horse Medicine', which they could apply either to breathe fleetness into the pony they favoured or to throw ritual obstacles in the path of the challenger, to slow its progress. These were often

166

herbal treatments that the shaman might paint on to the pony's neck or breathe into its nostrils, and all race ponies were carefully guarded for four days before the contest to prevent these medicines from being applied. Should the pony which the shaman had favoured win, he would receive a part of the bets that had been placed.

Just as exciting, and just as heavily gambled on, was the hoop and pole game. In this game a wooden hoop, marked into segments with paint and rawhide thongs – and often elaborately decorated with featherwork and netted sinew to create a webbed 'dream catcher' – was rolled along a path between two opposing players. Each had a long pole which he attempted to thrust through the hoop. When the hoop toppled across one of the poles, a score was awarded according to the segment in contact with the pole. Several tries were made, and the winner was the one accumulating the highest score. This game often became a contest between rivals from visiting bands, which heightened the tension and made a thrilling spectator sport since the competition was certain to be fierce.

In late summer the circle camp started to break up. The separate bands each made their way to traditional camping grounds along the wooded banks of rivers that offered shelter from the severe Plains winters, while the village tribes returned to the security of their permanent lodges after the annual hunt. In these protected areas, with brush and timber piled against the tipi sides to maintain warmth, piles of firewood close to hand and mounds of cottonwood bark ready as an emergency winter feed for the ponies, the people settled down to listen to the old stories. Winter was the traditional time for telling these tales, as it was considered bad luck to tell them in the summer. It was through these that the people could be reminded of the reasons why the world had been created, and of Coyote the Trickster, who fooled himself more often than he fooled others.

The stories carried various meanings according to their audiences. For the children, they explained the way people should live and what they should and should not do, and taught them respect for their elders and for the animals. Young warriors learned more about their responsibilities as the protectors of the group. The middle-aged listened carefully to understand the sacred significance of the acts depicted in the stories, while the Elders, who told the stories, and knew them backwards, reminisced and tried to ensure that everyone followed the 'true path' that had been laid down for them by the ancients.

This true path had existed since the world began, but it was being blocked by carcasses left by buffalo hunters, and rutted from the wheels of emigrant wagon trains during the early 1800s. At the same time, the permanence of the 'permanent Indian frontier' – that part of the United States west of the Mississippi in which traders could only operate under licence, where none could permanently reside, and where White persons were not permitted to establish ranches – was being questioned in Washington. America needed land. The country of the village tribes had been overrun and most of the tribes subdued by the late 1830s, but the vast reaches of the western Plains were still controlled by a few bands of nomadic Indian hunters. Under increasing pressure from potential emigrants, the government legally established the principle of Manifest Destiny in 1848. This stated that Europeans and their descendants were ordained by destiny, as the superior race, to rule all of America, and removed any legal right of appeal from the Indians.

The stage was set for a trivial incident to trigger the Plains Indian Wars in 1854. In that year a lone Sioux hunter killed an emaciated cow that he found wandering on the prairie. The owner of the cow, an illiterate emigrant, turned down the compensation offered him by the Sioux, and a U.S. cavalry force marched on the Indian village to demand that the 'thief' be turned over for punishment. When the Sioux chief refused, explaining that the cow had been abandoned, the lieutenant in charge of the troops ordered him shot. The Indians retaliated by killing the lieutenant and the 32 soldiers accompanying him.

This started a series of fights, interspersed with treaties, that gradually drew in more and more of the western tribes. Fuelled by the popular press, which described every Indian success as a 'massacre' and every U.S. success as a 'victory', there were calls for the removal or annihilation of the Plains Indians. Even tribes on the periphery of the area, who submitted to U.S. authority and accepted reservations, often found life intolerable. They were starved into submissive obedience while the granaries and stores at the forts remained full. Promised provisions never arrived, and even annuity payments which would have enabled them to purchase food were siphoned off by 'Indian rings' in Washington or diverted from the tribes by unscrupulous merchants.

In 1862 the Santee Sioux, under the leadership of Little Crow, rebelled against their broken treaty agreements, and in a few days killed 700 settlers and 100 U.S. troops in their Minnesota homeland before fleeing west to join their Teton Sioux relatives beyond the Mississippi. Meanwhile the Kiowa and Cheyenne had put aside their long-standing enmity, and formed an alliance to save their hunting grounds and protect the hard-pressed buffalo in Colorado and Wyoming. When a peaceful Cheyenne village, consisting of women, children, and a few elderly men, was massacred in 1864 by Colorado Volunteers, led by the self-styled 'Colonel' Chivington, a former Methodist minister, the Sioux, Arapaho and Comanche joined the Kiowa and Cheyenne alliance.

White expansion, far from decreasing the power of the Plains Indians and undermining their war leaders, was forging new, more powerful, unions and alliances. What was seen in Washington as the 'Indian problem' suddenly became very real.

Under the leadership of Roman Nose, the Cheyenne Dog Soldiers – a fearless warrior society, dedicated to selling their lives rather than accepting defeat – besieged the forts in Cheyenne country. Emigrant wagon trains were halted, mail riders were unable to get through, trappers and hunters were killed wherever they were found,

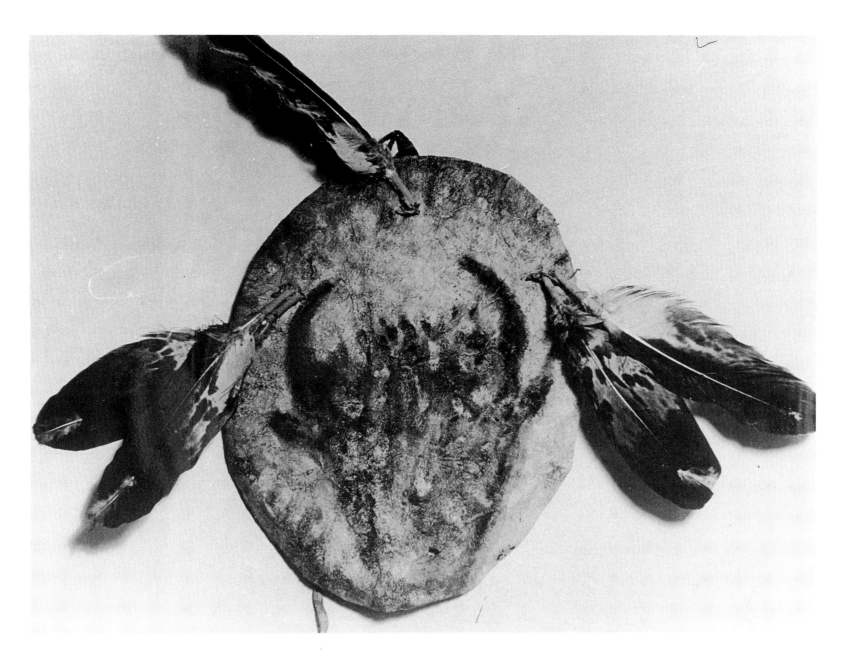

and even towns were attacked and burned. To their north, the Sioux, led by Red Cloud, and the Northern Cheyenne, under Dull Knife, laid siege to the forts of the Powder River country. This forced the abandonment of the forts and the closure of the Powder River emigrant trail in 1868, and obtained for the Indians a treaty that guaranteed their lands in perpetuity.

Treaties were also made with the Southern Cheyennes, Arapahoes, Kiowas and Comanches. By 1868 most of these were living on reservations. They were under military jurisdiction, but with guarantees that they were free to leave when they wished to hunt buffalo, and that they remained on the reserves only by agreement and not as prisoners. When the military authorities refused to allow the Kiowas to go to their buffalo hunting grounds between the Arkansas and Red Rivers, they pointed out that their treaty of 1867 permitted them to do so and left the reserve. Hard Backsides Custer – as the Indians knew him, since he never left his saddle when in pursuit of hostile tribes – arrested the Kiowa leaders, Satanta and Lone Wolf, while under a flag of truce and announced

they would be hanged if the Kiowas did not come to Fort Cobb and surrender.

For the next few years there was an unsettled peace, during which the Indians officially resided on reservations but frequently left to hunt buffalo or to conduct raids into Texas, which they considered to be more Mexican-Spanish than American, and outside the scope of the treaty agreements they had made. Red Cloud's and Dull Knife's peoples continued to occupy the Powder River country, unmolested by Whites. Unfortunately, gold was discovered in the areas under Sioux control in 1874, and hordes of miners began to re-invade their country. To make matters worse, the gold was in the Paha Sapa, the sacred Black Hills where the ancestors lay buried, and which was the home of the spirits. General George Crook marched troops into the Black Hills and advised the miners to leave, but he took no other action. The tribes were faced with no alternative if they wished to save the Black Hills from desecration: Red Cloud and Dull Knife reopened hostilities.

They were joined by a Sioux war leader named Crazy Horse, and by a shaman called Tatanka

Far left: The recurved bow was reserved exclusively for buffalo hunting and for display in parades. This Crow example is made from Osage orangewood – a straight-grained wood that is ideal for bow-making, but which the Crow could only obtain in trade. When in use, the twisted sinew bowstring would have been pulled to the right of the photograph.

Above: Shields of rawhide, reduced and thickened over fires, could stop an arrow and deflect bullets from early muzzle-loading rifles. To the Indians, however, they owed their efficacy more to the painted designs they bore than to the practical use they served. This shield is inspired by the buffalo, making its owner as difficult to kill as this tenacious animal.

Far right: The Crow were a small tribe, but they occupied and successfully defended the richest hunting areas of the northern Plains. The warrior in this drawing bears a society lance which pledges him to act bravely even in the most dangerous circumstances, and his horse is painted with horseshoe tracks to indicate his success in capturing horses from within the villages of his enemies. In the background is a burial scaffold. The Crow, like other tribes of the region, would abandon any locality in which their deceased were laid to rest; the warrior here is paying his last respects prior to the complete tribe relocating in a new area.

Yotanka, but whom the Whites knew as Sitting Bull. Battles and indecisive skirmishes flared up all over the Plains, until General Crook marched against the alliance, burning the villages of the Cheyenne allies; but even his strong force was routed by a combined war party of Sioux, Cheyenne and Arapaho in 1876. This humiliation was too much for Crook, who ordered more troops into the area and sent armies out to surround the Indian camps and claim a final victory.

One of his commanders was General George Armstrong Custer. Custer's Crow Indian scouts soon found the Indian camps, stretched along more than three miles of the river valley in the Little Bighorn and containing perhaps 12,000 people of whom some 3,000 to 4,000 were warriors. The scouts advised him to wait for Crook to bring up reinforcements; but Custer decided to ignore this advice. He thought his small column of troops was sufficiently strong to punish the Indians severely, and force Crazy Horse and Sitting Bull on to reservations.

He accordingly divided his forces, sending part under the command of Major Reno to attack one end of the camp while he struck at the other. As dawn broke, the troops charged. Reno's troops were stopped and routed, while the fight with Custer's division was over in less than an hour; his entire command, Custer among them, were killed.

White people called this a massacre. Congress clamoured for revenge and flooded the area with cavalry and infantry reinforcements. The Indians scattered. Sitting Bull led his people into Canada, where he hoped the British authorities would provide a reservation. Crazy Horse stayed in the mountains and river valleys, but the buffalo were gone and the camps were constantly harassed by troops.

At the same time, conditions in the regions to the south of the Sioux that were occupied by the Kiowa, Southern Cheyenne and Comanche tribes were rapidly deteriorating. The Comanche, who had always been guests at the ceremonies of other tribes in the area, organized their first Sun Dance in 1874; but as the tribes travelled to Elk Creek for this great renewal ceremony, they passed through endless stretches of prairie where White buffalo hunters had been at work. The grasslands were 'a desolation of bones, skulls, and rotting hooves', the air itself stank of putrified meat. At the Sun Dance, a young Comanche war chief, Quanah Parker, spoke out for a war against the White men: a war that would finally drive the buffalo hunters away; that would clear the Staked Plains, the Llano Estacado of western Texas and southeastern New Mexico of these crazed people who killed only for profit.

Quanah Parker's words had a sympathetic

Right: Virtually every item used by Plains Indians was decorated in some way. The moccasins shown here are probably Kiowa and employ trade beads to create geometric patterns that had significance only for the maker and for the person who wore them.

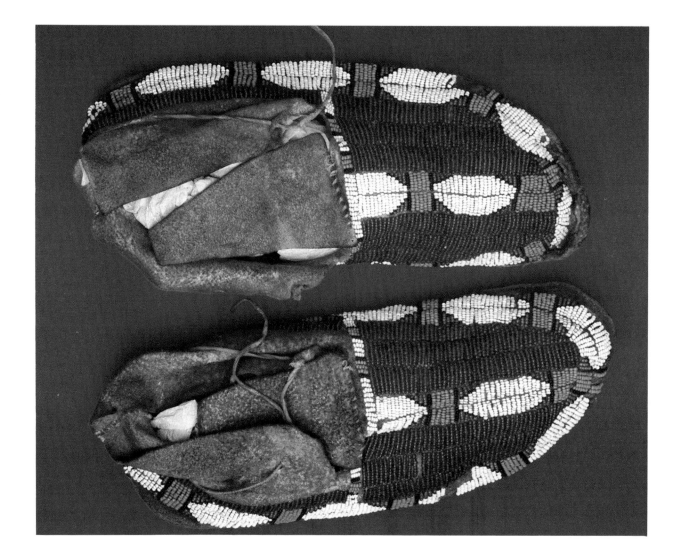

Sitting Bull, exiled in Canada.

Canadian authorities regarded Sitting Bull's band as a liability for which they had no responsibility. They refused to give them lands, would not offer provisions, and discouraged them from hunting; but Sitting Bull held out until 1881, when he led his people back to a captive life on the Standing Rock Reservation in South Dakota. For some years Sitting Bull remained the most prominent Indian on the reserves, much to the chagrin of the Americans, who attempted to undermine his authority by refusing to invite him to council meetings or letting him speak. Even so, no decision was made by the Sioux without prior discussion with Sitting Bull.

Then in 1889 a new craze swept the Plains reservations. A Paiute Indian, Wovokah, claiming to be the risen messiah, introduced the Ghost Dance. If the Indians would dance continuously until they fell into trances, then buffalo would return, their dead would be resurrected, and the White men would be swallowed by the earth. It was a non-violent movement; although it derived its inspiration from Christian beliefs, it was a last chance for many Indians to regain some pride and put meaning back into their lives, and the Ghost Dance spread rapidly.

Sitting Bull wanted no part of any religious revival that introduced Christian teaching; but in the democratic tradition of the Plains Indian he could only advise. He had no power to stop the dancing, and Standing Rock became the focus of Ghost Dance activity. White authorities regarded his refusal to stop the Ghost Dancers as an active encouragement, and decided to place him under 'precautionary arrest'. In the process of his being arrested he was shot through the head.

Without Sitting Bull, the Indians at Standing Rock felt vulnerable. A minor chief, Big Foot, left the reservation to go to Pine Ridge where he felt his people would be safer with Red Cloud. They were stopped by the U.S. Seventh Cavalry, Custer's old command, and Big Foot, dying from pneumonia, surrendered meekly. Under military guard the Indians encamped at Wounded Knee. Four Hotchkiss guns, capable of firing explosive shells at the rate of one per second, were set up on a hill overlooking the camp.

In the morning the Indians were disarmed, handing in a few rifles and some bows and arrows. One warrior, a deaf Indian named Black Coyote, began waving his Winchester above his head, shouting that he had paid a lot of money for it. A shot rang out, no one knows from which side, and the Hotchkiss guns opened fire. Half an hour later, 300 of the 350 Indians in Big Foot's band, himself included, were dead or dying.

The Glorious Seventh, as the Seventh Cavalry thought of themselves, had atoned for Custer's death by mowing down disarmed Indians in a bloodbath that has few historic parallels. By an irony of fate it was the same band of Minneconjou Sioux who inadvertently started the Plains Indian Wars by skinning an abandoned cow, who now ended them by being massacred at Wounded Knee. Indian armed resistance was finally over.

audience. The buffalo hunters were on territory reserved for the exclusive use of the tribes, and the need to save the buffalo was far more important than adherence to the petty restrictions and regulations of life on a reservation. They rebelled and struck back, resulting in thousands of 'bluecoats' being thrown into the area to suppress the Indian uprising. The tribes retreated to Palo Duro canyon, the last stronghold of their independent way of life, where the remnants of the buffalo herds had also sought shelter. They were found here by Mackenzie's 'pony soldiers', who slaughtered more than a thousand of the Indians' horses. The tribes scattered, without food, clothing or shelter, and the soldiers hunted them down. In the following year, 1875, Crazy Horse led his band on to a reservation, having received assurances they would be fed and protected. On arrival Crazy Horse was arrested and, in a brief struggle to avoid being manacled, was bayoneted. The only Sioux Indian leaders of any note were now Red Cloud, who was living in peace on the Pine Ridge reservation, and

THE ARCTIC AND SUBARCTIC

Although the Subarctic and Arctic can be thought of as two separate cultural areas, they are put together here because of their geographical proximity, and because they share the characteristic of being extremely severe environments with exceptionally harsh and bitter winters.

The Subarctic is that part of northern Canada, including some of Alaska, that lies mostly above the latitude of the Great Lakes. Much of it is pine forest, but to the north this gradually gives way to a transition zone – the 'land of little sticks' – in which the trees, though of the same species as forests further south, are affected by much colder winters and are dwarfed and stunted. Above this latitude there is tundra which is underlaid by permafrost: a layer of ground, sometimes only a few inches beneath the surface, which remains permanently frozen and does not thaw out with the arrival of milder summer temperatures.

In a few places the permafrost cover is thin or absent and stands of conifers have taken root to create what is known as park tundra. Further north still is the Barren Ground, which lies wholly above the tree line. It is characterized by tundra which supports only Arctic plants, that are inured to permafrost conditions, and that can complete their annual growth cycle quickly during the short summers. Beyond this are the extensive ice and snow sheets of the Arctic itself.

Both the Subarctic and Arctic have very protracted winters with little daylight, and short summers with long days when, in the far north, the sun may merely skirt the horizon and never actually set. Much of the year is spent in a kind of twilight. January temperatures in the north can easily be −40°C (−40°F), rising to a maximum of about 2°C (36°F) for a week or so in July. The south is warmer, but even the central forest lands may only have a short period during July and August when there is no frost.

Although apparently inhospitable, these regions were home to Algonkin– and Athapascan–speaking Indians, and to the Eskimo and their close relatives, the Aleut. The prehistories of these groups are diverse, and our earliest evidence is from the western Subarctic where a hunting, fishing and gathering economy was well established by about 7,000 years ago, and from which the historic Athapascan Indians of the Yukon and Northwest Territories, interior British Columbia and parts of Alberta are descended.

The early peoples had a very widely scattered population – estimates are for about two people in every 100 km^2 (39 sq miles) – living along rivers and lakes and utilizing the waterways of the area for passage. Localized resources forced a nomadic lifestyle, and created innumerable small 'tribes' that were essentially extended family groups. These are known by names such as Dogrib, Tanaina, Carrier, Slave, Beaver, Yellow-Knife, and Kutchin; but nearly all these are names that others apply to them and they refer to themselves by derivatives of Tine or Dine, the People.

Between 800AD and 1200AD some groups split off and wandered south, one group, the Sarsi, settling near the Blackfoot in Alberta, but others moving down to the Southwest to become the Apache and Navajo, who are generally referred to as the Southern Athapascans. Others moved on to the Northwest Coast to form the Tlingit – although this was so long ago that only a persistent linguist would ever be able to trace any connection – and one group travelled into California, ancestors of the Hupa Indians.

But the majority stayed in the north. None of these formed a tribal group, since the environment would not support larger communities, although occasionally they gathered together for a collective caribou hunt. Even in these circumstances the maximum number of people that the environment might have sustained, and then only for a short period, was about 200. Their modern descendants are still among the least known of the North American Indians: their country offers few incentives for White people, other than the occasional seasonal logging or mining camp consisting of three or four caravans and a cleared space as an airstrip, and one imagines that the rigours and hardships of the Subarctic have been sufficient to deter all but the most determined anthropologists.

Because they have been protected in this way

Far right: Athapascan hunters lived in a region where the climate could be harsh and uncompromising. Although their own skills were highly attuned to the environment, they often needed to rely on the superior sense of smell of their dogs to locate game successfully. The hunter shown in this drawing has killed a deer which his dogs have tracked down. Packs strapped to the dogs' backs contain the hunter's supplies, the most essential of which were spare moccasins in case those he wore should become wet.

Right: The grizzly bear possessed immense physical and supernatural power. To overcome the grizzly and acquire a symbol of his strength was, therefore, a potent indication of an individual's worth. The bear tooth medicine shown here is Athapascan from the Rocky Mountain foothills of the western Subarctic, and has remarkably fine porcupine quillwork decoration.

from European influences, many contemporary Northern Athapascans continue to live in much the same way as their forefathers and are dependent on a subsistence level of hunting and gathering, spending by far the larger part of their year as small family groups. Yet to dismiss them as relics of a past age would be to miss completely the significance they have for the student of American Indian culture. All American Indians came into the continent as Subarctic hunter-gatherers, but only the Northern Athapascans still retain their ancient heritage and live according to the original beliefs.

For the Athapascans, living in an uncertain world, every activity was fraught with difficulty and potential danger. Much of their habitat is enclosed, since trees grow thickly in the southern parts, and mists and frosts often transform areas so totally that it is impossible even for someone who has lived here for his or her entire life to recognize them and gain a bearing. Streams and small rivers twist and turn between banks overhung with vegetation, forming dark and narrow passageways. The forests have a quiet beauty, yet it is a quietness that barely manages to hold back forces of a savage and malignant tendency; forces that can bring starvation, or sudden temperature changes, forces which might, without warning, withdraw the resources on which survival was so delicately balanced.

It is a human response to imbue such landscapes with supernatural significance, and early White trappers in the area often awoke at night in terror when they felt the tangible presence of the Ice or Hunger Spirits hovering at the edges of their camps. The Athapascans dealt with these more successfully and with a deeper understanding of the nature of the land. When dangers are known and recognized, then rituals can be performed to keep them at a distance, since it is the unknown and the unexpected that cause injury, accident and disaster.

Nearly all their rituals were intended to avert danger, and to bring about a desired result by keeping the negative forces away rather than by asking the spirits to intervene directly on the people's behalf. Whenever an animal was killed, there were specific duties to be carried out by the hunter while butchering, for the disposal of the bones, and for returning any uneaten or inedible portions of the animal to the spirit world where it could be reborn.

These acts did not guarantee that the hunter would find game in future, in the sense that the animal would willingly give itself up because it had been treated with respect. Instead they ensured that the hunter could track and capture game without encountering difficulty. Such precautions were necessary in a land where game abounded, for the Subarctic has a surprisingly large animal population, but in which sudden freezing blizzards were a possibility even in summer, and where an accident that immobilized the hunter at any distance from the village spelled almost certain death.

In many ways, these ritual acts, clearly set out in the myths and tales, formed a code of rules which, if followed, kept the people free from harm. They operated at the individual, family and group levels. Every person – man, woman, and child – carried personal talismans. These might be granted in a dream or vision, but could also be blessed by a shaman, or given by an elder member of the tribe who had proved their efficacy in his or her own use of them. Many of the talismans carried by children were of this last kind, although

Left: The upper Skeena River was one of the few places where trade between the coastal and inland peoples of the north could take place. Tlingit Indians of the Northwest Coast learned quillworking techniques from the interior Athapascans in this region, whereas the Athapascans were able to acquire dentalium and abalone shells from the coast.

Left: The winged object shown in this photograph was probably used as a bannerstone on an *atlatl* shaft by a Bering Sea Eskimo in the early centuries AD.

they might also include hair from a highly respected medicine man or woman, which was woven into a bracelet, or emblems of the animal powers that took a particular interest in the child's welfare.

At the family level, many household heads knew ways of appeasing the spirits, especially those of Cold, Hunger and Death. They also knew how to soothe the spirits of the Land and calm those of the Waters. Often, for these means to be effective, the entire family had to abide by certain taboo restrictions, which might govern the order in which food could be served, the bank of the river on which their shelters could be erected, or even the time of day most propitious to a successful undertaking.

There were also group rituals which came into effect when a number of bands camped together. Many of these were concerned with hunting animals such as the bear and wolf, both of which were highly respected and considered as ancestral to the people themselves. If one of these animals was killed, it was accorded the same honours shown at the death of a leading member of the human community. The Slave Indians offered the same respect to the otter, the chief of the animals.

During these ceremonies valuable gifts were left at the site of the animal's grave. It would be revisited from time to time when offerings of food were made and the spirit of the deceased animal asked for help and guidance.

Other group gatherings took place at the solstices, when the 'long and short days meet'. Like the gatherings of other North American Indians, the ritual aspects were only part of the activities carried out at this time. There was a great deal of feasting, dancing and singing. Foot races took place. Wrestling matches were arranged and bets placed on the outcome. Marriages were conducted, establishing stronger alliances between particular families. Old debts were repaid. Such gatherings lasted only a short time, perhaps a week at the most, before the groups separated and returned to their family pattern of hunting and foraging.

As we might expect, in this world of mysterious spirits and constant threat, shamanism reached a very high level of development. Both men and women could be practicing shamans, or 'Dreamers', and they exercized a considerable influence over all other members of the community. This

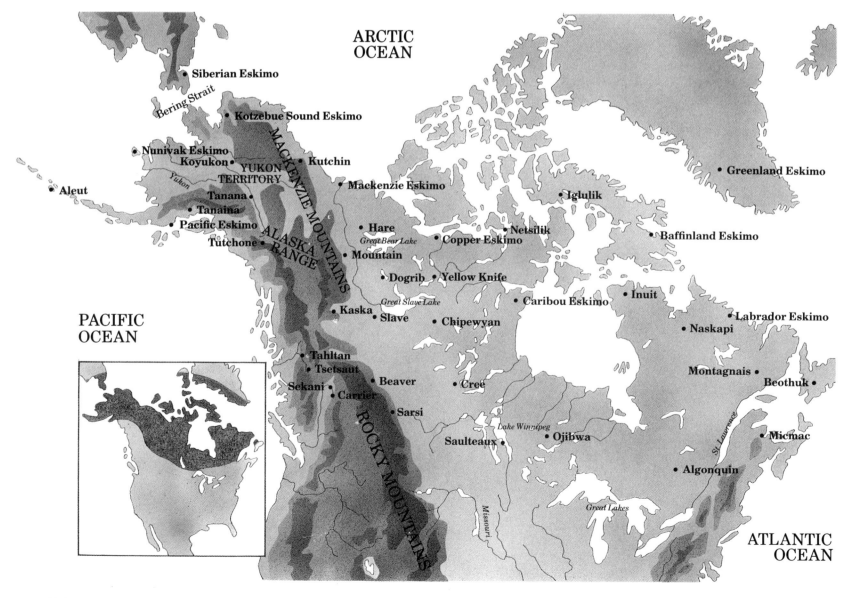

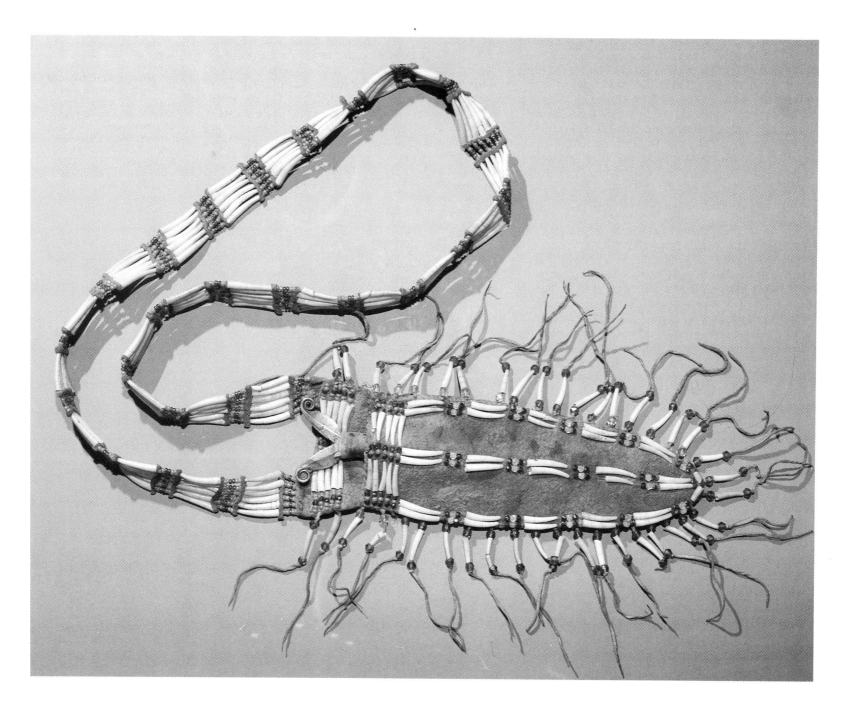

Cedar bark was commonly employed by the northern forest tribes to make containers. This 18th-century pouch is Athapascan, and was made in the western Subarctic. It is decorated with glass beads obtained from the Russians and dentalia shell from trade with the Northwest Coast, and also has dyed porcupine quill embroidery.

influence might even be felt at considerable distances. The Dreamers were thought to possess some kind of 'telepathic' ability by which they could direct events many miles away; or they might communicate telepathically with a local shaman who carried out rituals at their behest.

Shamanic powers might be inherited, when lengthy initiation procedures were called for; but more frequently they simply came while the potential shaman was sleeping, and were not actively sought. The Dreamers were believed to have an extraordinary sensitivity to and understanding of the spiritual world, and were granted power because they were open to it; even so, they never possessed any form of individual or direct spirit control but were simply the medium through which power could be expressed for the well-being of the community. These spirit forces were usually manifested through animal intermediaries, and the shamans were regularly thought to leave their human bodies, and to spend much of their time

roaming the country in the form of the animal by which they were inspired. During this time, the human aspect of the shaman was spiritually powerless, and he or she lived in the same manner as any other member of the community, unable to perform rituals or to effect cures.

At other times, shamans cured illness and disease, predicted the weather, decided where game might be found, conducted wars in both the physical and spiritual senses, helped ensure success for individual hunters, and advised the family and group leaders. They would regularly seek out someone of whom they had dreamed to warn them of impending misfortune or forthcoming good luck. Even in modern communities, the power of the dream is widely accepted, and family members may consider themselves to remain in some kind of dream contact when they are separated from each other and travelling in different parts of the country.

Through dreams, family ties could be maintained theoretically even when individual members resided in different bands, as happened after marriage when the man went to live with his wife's family and to provide for them. In this way no one lost sight of their roots and close friendships bonded a number of otherwise disparate bands together. In a sense, the dream transcended the environment. The forest lands are closed in and vision is always localized: one simply cannot see what lies beyond the next bend in the river or what lurks in the frequent mists. The dream, however, does not know these barriers and can carry as far as a thought: to eternity if need be. It can contact both the living and the dead, the near and the far, and is not subject to any form of enclosure.

The Athapascans travelled in their thoughts and dreams more widely than they did physically, as although they were nomadic, these movements always took place within well-defined limits and were dictated solely by the availability of resources. In spring they moved from winter camps, which in the western part of their range consisted of log cabins, and in the east, of birchbark lodges, to temporary dwellings near the muskrat lodges, hauling their belongings on sleds and toboggans or carrying them in canoes. This often ended a period of near starvation and was a time for joy and celebration. Birchbark was collected to make the numerous household articles that were needed, the older ones having been patched beyond further repair, and to furnish the materials for canoes and house coverings.

As the long thaw continued, and the river and lake waters started to reopen, the bands moved to their fishing sites, where weirs and traps left from the previous year required tending. At this time they could shoot or net numbers of migratory birds that were beginning to arrive from more southerly climes. Much of the summer would be spent here or on the shores of the larger lakes, where several families might camp together. Fishing continued to be a major activity but, since many of the men spent much of their time out hunting, the fish traps were usually left under the care of a few elders who specialized in their use.

The Athapascan hunters were highly proficient, and possessed an acute knowledge of the country and the animals. A track would tell them not only the species of animal and the direction in which it travelled, but also the animal's age, how much time had elapsed since the track was made, the speed at which it was moving, and even its gender. Hunters frequently studied the tracks, then set off in a different direction; knowing the animal's behaviour so well they could interpret its intentions, and predict where it would be found. All the hunters knew exactly how many animals of whatever species could be found within a mile or more of the camp, simply from reading the signs contained in their tracks.

While the men were away hunting, the women took advantage of the light available during these long summer days to prepare hides for both clothing and shelter. Deerskins were sewn into tailored shirts and leggings, a practice they may have learned from the Eskimo to the north, and

were decorated with coloured strips of dyed porcupine quills, in geometric patterns of red and yellow ochre. The heavier skins, such as those of moose and elk, could be used for fur parkas that would be needed in the winter, or, with the fur removed, might be sewn together as covers for their summer conical or dome-shaped lodges. Excess food brought into the camps was preserved and dried as a winter store.

At the end of summer, berries were collected and the families separated, returning once more to

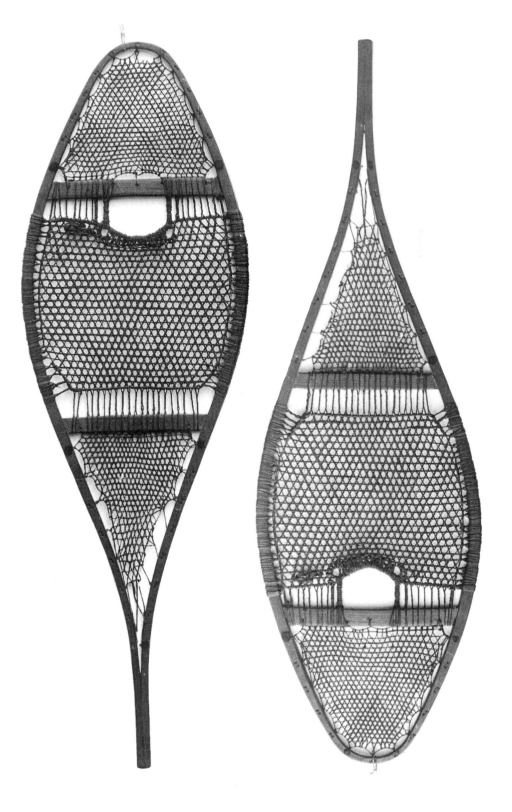

Travel in the Subarctic and Arctic was often only possible with the aid of snowshoes that distributed the wearer's weight over a larger area and prevented him sinking into soft snow. The snowshoes depicted here, designed for use in forested areas, could have been made by any of the Athapascan or Algonkin groups of the region.

Part of the Cree living on the southern border of the Subarctic region began to venture on to the Plains, where they hunted buffalo. Broken Arm, a chief of one of these Plains Cree bands, was painted by George Catlin in 1831.

distributed their weight and prevented the hunter from sinking. At times they could often walk up to the side of an animal that had become mired in a snow drift with no possibility of escape. Fishing also continued through holes cut in the ice, at least until the very severe mid-winter cold made the ice too thick for this method to be employed.

As the days grew shorter and darker, activities centred more on the household. If hunting had been good, it was a time for feasting and ceremony and for playing games, things that were given a secondary place during the food-gathering parts of the year, or which were considered to be proscribed by the spirits, who would be angered if frivolous events occurred during the productive summer period. Prominent among the games played by both adults and children were string-figures, and a kind of cup-and-ball game using a pierced bone attached by a thong to a pin. The object was to swing the bone round in the air and catch it on the pin. Such games were purely for fun, and everyone joined in.

European contacts with these groups began in the 1670s with the establishment of Hudson's Bay Company trading posts on the Great Lakes. It was, however, an indirect contact for most Athapascans, who traded some furs via middle-men in an extension of old aboriginal trade routes. Certain interior tribes of the far north had no direct contact with White people until the late 19th century, and even then it was sporadic. Many of these continue to live according to their old ways, and White people are still a rarity in their areas.

In spite of the fact that direct contact was not always apparent, indirect contacts were causing changes in the Indian societies. The most dramatically affected were those closest to the trading posts. They quickly became dependent on goods of European manufacture. Steel traps and knives replaced the traditional ones of wood and antler, while the gun replaced the bow and arrows. Gradually these influences spread to other groups, who acquired them from the middle-men in trade. European goods quite often made life easier and more efficient; but this has to be weighed against the fact that the use of a gun required regular supplies of ammunition which could only be obtained from the trading posts. The Indians were gradually thereby forced to rely on trade to support their own economies.

The overall effect of this was that indigenous lifestyles changed to accommodate the new trading patterns and to allow for visits to Hudson's Bay posts that might be many hundreds of miles distant. More seriously, when the fur trade declined many of the groups were unable to obtain the supplies they needed, and found themselves in over-hunted areas with few means of subsistence. This was alleviated to some extent among tribes of the Yukon by the Klondike gold rush. Few conflicts occurred with the strangers coming into the area: the harsh environment kept many of the more opportunistic Whites from becoming involved in the gold rush, and many of the local Indians were employed as woodcutters and suppliers of provisions to the mining camps. When the mines were played out, the Europeans left, since agriculture

their own fishing rivers near local hunting grounds. Here the men continued the pursuit of game, but also spent much of their time in repairing and making snowshoes and sleds. By the time these were ready, the caribou migrations had begun. In some areas, traps and compounds were erected across the migration routes so that large numbers of animals might be secured; elsewhere they were hunted with the bow and arrows.

Winter, although intensely cold, did not bring an end to the hunting season. In some ways it actually made hunting easier, since the tracks of the animals were clear and a large animal such as a moose or caribou would be hampered in its progress through deep snow. The hunters could easily catch up with the animals, travelling lightly over soft snow with the aid of snowshoes that

This Cree Indian hunter is venturing out on snowshoes to inspect his trapline. He carries a rifle in case he might unexpectedly come across game, but he would be more dependent for his livelihood on small fur-bearing animals caught in his traps which would be traded to the Hudson's Bay Company. The spare trap he carries, as well as his blanket and rifle, are trade items he has purchased in exchange for furs. The fur trade dramatically altered the lives of the Cree, who turned almost exclusively to hunting for furs rather than for food.

was impossible at this latitude, and many groups faced a long period during which starvation was a constant possibility due to the depletion of local resources.

Slowly the tribes recovered, a number of them reverting to their old subsistence patterns and traditional lifestyles, which they continue to practice in a modified form today. Most people now purchase clothing rather than manufacture their own, and traditional beliefs and customs are sometimes blended with those of Christianity. To a large extent, however, the Athapascans of the

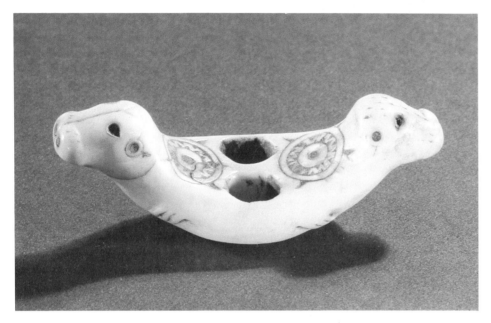

An ivory belt fastener from Western Alaska.

interior continue to live in a very similar way to that of their forefathers.

East of the Athapascans, in Manitoba, Ontario, Quebec and Newfoundland, are a number of other small groups speaking various Algonkin dialects. Unlike the Athapascans, these people originally resided in the prehistoric Woodlands areas and moved north in pursuit of game when the glaciers retreated and the forest cover expanded to the Great Lakes and beyond. Their early life must have been much like that of their western neighbours, with an emphasis on small communities dependent on hunting, fishing and gathering, but they were far more severely affected in the historic period by contacts with Europeans and the demand for furs. Their history is in large part the history of the northern fur trade.

In the northeastern part of the Algonkin territories lived small, widely scattered bands of Cree, Montagnais and Naskapi Indians. Some Cree and Ojibwa bands lived as far west as Manitoba, where they were in contact with Athapascan groups. To the south and east, the groupings were larger and more highly organized, forming distinct tribes. Prominent among them were the Beothuk and Micmac of Newfoundland, and the Ottawa and Algonquin – the tribe that gave its name to the language family – together with some Ojibwa, who lived closer to the Great Lakes in the southern parts of Ontario and Quebec.

All these peoples were dependent on hunting, trapping, fishing and gathering, with wild rice

becoming almost a staple food for those living on the edges of the Great Lakes. They generally lived in small, isolated settlements, consisting of a number of birchbark covered lodges called wigwams. Some of them used temporary skin – or brush – covered lodges when out hunting, those of the more westerly Cree being virtually indistinguishable from the lodges made by their Athapascan neighbours. All of them used birchbark for everything from canoes to boxes.

Tailored clothing of leggings and shirts was common throughout the area, and these were

usually supplemented in cold weather with mittens and fur caps, and sometimes with hooded fur-lined parkas. The tailored clothing of the Naskapi, however, is extraordinary. Their long coats, with tight-fitted sleeves and rear vents, were probably inspired by the frock coats worn by Europeans when they first came to the area, and the painted decorations on them often bear a recognizable similarity to braids and chevrons; yet at the same time they have an unmistakable quality that stems directly from the imagination and belief of the American Indian.

Among other manufactures are many items of bone and antler, beautifully softened, white elkskin moccasins, and netted bags with intricately woven patterns of mythological figures and animals. They are often decorated with a profusion of porcupine quillwork and moosehair embroidery, or with brightly coloured mallard feathers. Perhaps the most distinctive item, nevertheless, is the utilitarian babiche. This is made by cutting a stretched deerskin in a long spiral from the centre to form a continuous rope or cord, and was used for anything from bindings and carrying thongs to

The Chippewa or Ojibwa lived in the region just north and west of the Great Lakes, and had a lifestyle much like that of the Cree. Catlin painted this Chippewa band engaged in a Snowshoe Dance during the early 1830s.

setting traps and deadfalls. The accuracy and evenness with which it was cut, using a special knife with a curved blade known as a 'crooked knife', is astonishing. Babiche was probably the most important single item carried by the forest hunter.

Some of the coastal peoples, especially the Micmac and Beothuk, developed more specialized economies with a greater reliance on marine resources, and the Beothuk canoe, with a raised inverted V-shape in the centre, must be one of

Naskapi clothing was greatly influenced in its cut and decoration by the frock coats of the British, as shown in this tailored and painted mooseskin coat.

the most radical design concepts ever. The raised centre gave added strength to the vessel, but also decreased its stability, so that it was necessary to load it with a considerable quantity of stone ballast. Both the Micmac and Beothuk were aggressive peoples who fought each other bitterly, and when Norsemen from Greenland formed a settlement near the Beothuk about 1,000AD, it was quickly abandoned as a result of Indian harassment. The early histories of these peoples is little known, as whatever material artefacts they left behind have perished in the highly acidic soils of the region.

Some tribes were active in the French and Indian Wars, but none suffered as severely as the Beothuk. Their resistance to later White incursions was as strong as it had been to the Norsemen, but they were a small tribe who could not mount a concerted defence. They were forced away from the coasts and their essential marine resources, which seriously weakened their economy and changed them from a prosperous group into one that could barely survive. When the French incited their old tribal enemies the Micmac, and offered them bounty payments for scalps, they responded so efficiently that the Beothuk were extinct within a generation.

Other tribes of the east fared better, though for many of them, their lives were to be altered totally by the influences of the White newcomers. The Micmac, for instance, were consistently friendly to Europeans, though strongly favouring the French rather than the English, and soon found a ready tourist market for their exquisitely decorated birch bark boxes. Intricate geometric patterns in porcupine quillwork or moosehair embroidery had been traditionally used to cover the surfaces of these boxes, but they quickly adapted this technique to produce floral patterns that Europeans preferred, and started to apply them to such items as chairs and inlaid tables. Although they continued to follow their marine pattern of hunting, income from this new source has been a substantial part of the Micmac economy since the early period of European settlement.

Tribes, such as the Cree and Ojibwa, in the central parts of the north Canadian forests found themselves under increasing pressure to provide goods for the traders, both in the form of furs and in supplies for the trading posts. In return, they received European products. The most important of these was the gun, but the significance of other items should not be underestimated. Steel traps, knives, axes, kettles, cloth and European food products, such as flour, replaced many of the traditional manufactures, and enabled the tribes to hunt and trap almost exclusively for furs rather than for meat or for skins to make clothing.

In order to acquire large quantities of European goods, on which they were becoming rapidly dependent, they used their new-found firepower to subjugate other tribes. They exacted a tribute from these subject tribes in furs, which could then be traded back to the Hudson's Bay Company. Since many of the smaller tribes in this supply line were expected to pay tribute to specific Cree and Ojibwa bands, who were becoming wealthy while

The Montagnais were one of the most easterly of the Subarctic tribes, and lived in a manner that was closer to that of their Woodland neighbours than it was to that of other tribes to the north and west. Costume details shown in this drawing are characteristic of the northern Woodland Algonkins.

The modern State of Alaska derives its name from an Eskimo-Aleut word used to refer to the mainland portion of northwestern North America. This Oonalaska man, or mainland dweller, wears a characteristic Aleut bentwood sun visor, and has nose and lip plugs to indicate his high status.

Right: This antler and wood leister was used by the Eskimo for spearing fish. The fish would be caught on the central spike, while the barbed arms at the sides held it fast and prevented it from wriggling free.

others continued to struggle, factionalism arose and parts of the larger tribal groups moved into new areas. Both Cree and Ojibwa factions moved into the northern Plains, took over buffalo hunting, adopted the dress and customs of other Plains tribes, and forged completely new identities.

For those who remained in the forests and continued to struggle for survival, typical Woodland beliefs continued to be held. The power of the ancestors was the mainstay of their belief, since each person was considered to be the reincarnation of one of the deceased. Because of their system of totemism, where direct descent from an animal ancestor was thought to be a definite possibility, reincarnation applied to both the human and animal worlds. A hunter might be the reborn soul of a wolf as readily as a reborn warrior. Even gender could change in this transposition of souls. A new-born baby was carefully examined to see whether he or she bore any characteristic marks of an ancestor, and if a girl infant had, for instance, a birthmark similar to one borne by a deceased male relative, then she would be known by this man's name and her character would be deemed to be influenced by him.

Such souls or spirits dwelt in all the animals and flowers, in the birds and animals, and in the

sky and stars. The more powerful spirits among them – forces that a mere human would never dare assume – could change shape at will; a giant could be transformed into a dwarf, or a star could become human. Many of the myths deal with the battles between these major elements. In a land where only the fittest survived, the successful participants in these cosmic battles passed on to the people the knowledge they gained by defeating their opponents, thus enabling them to cope with severe circumstances by using rituals that were known to be successful.

This also enabled the people to call for assistance if their own limited resources should prove inadequate. Thus the Underwater Panther, a monstrous cat-like creature that dwelt beneath the waves and would drag people from the shores of lakes or overturn their canoes, could be defeated by Thunder, in the guise of the Thunderbird. This terrifying creature with a gigantic wing span, who caused thunderclaps when he flapped his wings and from whose eyes thunderbolts savaged the earth, came to the aid of the people and offered them his protection. All that was asked in return was that the proper observances should be made, and that the people should demonstrate their respect for the powers inherent in the other world.

As these beliefs became interwoven with Christian ideals, a curious mixture arose whereby a saint might exert power through a supernatural

Masks representing the spirit of the Moon were made by many of the Eskimo groups, reflecting the fact that over much of the area they occupied the moon did not set for almost half the year. Other elements symbolized by the flat board, the hooped rings, and the feathers, are air, the different levels of the cosmos, and stars.

189

Far right: Hunting became difficult for the Eskimo in winter, when the seas froze over and vast flat areas made it hard for hunters to approach game without being spotted. They were aided to some extent by the seals, which broke breathing holes through the ice and kept them open by continual use. The man shown here has placed a feather lure across the opening of one of these to entice fish to the surface, when he would spear them with the leister he is carrying. Such fishing methods were not uniformly successful, and usually entailed a long wait in sub-zero temperatures during which the fisherman had to remain virtually motionless.

Right: Mukluks, or fancy boots, were worn by Eskimo men on special occasions. The western Alaskan ones shown here are made from reindeer skin imported from Siberia, and are decorated with seal and caribou skin, seal intestine, dog hair, wolverine fur, and coloured thread.

animal spirit, such as the otter. For a member of a clan in which the otter was both supernatural animal and saint, the killing of an otter would be a violation of both his Native and Christian beliefs. This was particularly powerful among the Cree and Ojibwa, who had a very close association with the White trade communities. Marriages of White traders with Cree and Ojibwa women resulted in the births of a number of people with a mixture of Indian and White blood.

The Ojibwa accepted this in a very matter-of-fact manner: if someone of mixed blood felt he or she was more Ojibwa than White then they were accepted as full tribal members. If, however, they felt themselves more drawn to the White community, they were encouraged to seek marriage there. The Cree were apparently unable to draw such a

simple conclusion and felt that a mixed-blood was neither Indian nor White. They were 'inbetween people', who had allegiances to both races, but could never be fully participating members in the Cree societies.

Offspring of Cree/White marriages therefore created a group of people who were completely outside the normal frames of reference. They might be accepted into White society, although this rarely happened since racial prejudice was usually high. In this respect it is worth noting that the Ojibwa system of letting the individual choose resulted in virtually all mixed-bloods claiming Ojibwa nationality. Cree reluctance to grant these people tribal status resulted in the formation of a totally new phenomenon: that of the Métis.

Métis villages are composed entirely of people of

mixed Indian-White blood who now claim separate rights of their own. They form a powerful lobby, since their numbers are continually increasing, and have gained recognition from the Canadian government. Métis lands have been set aside, separate from those of the Native Americans and from the requirements of White expansion. As a group apart, the Métis make artefacts that are Indian in origin but European in application: moose hide pouches and mittens are decorated with floral patterns that are strikingly similar to those produced in Victorian England.

The Algonkin areas tend to show a blend of European and Indian influences, reaching a climax among the Métis, but by no means confined to this group alone. Indian bands that did not succumb to the lures of the fur trade simply moved out of the region altogether. Most Algonkin tribes today, with the exception of some in the inhospitable north, where they live much like the Athapascans of the west, have a lifestyle that amalgamates European and Native beliefs.

Further north, in the High Arctic, the prehistoric and historic sequences are totally different from those of the Subarctic. There is no evidence that people were living here even as recently as 5,000 years ago; but shortly after this the common ancestors of the Eskimo and Aleut crossed from Siberia. They parted company at an early date, possibly even before crossing the Bering Strait,

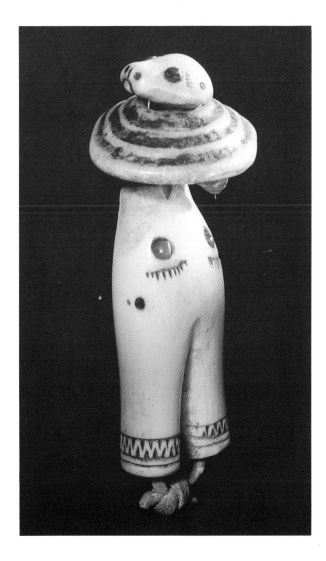

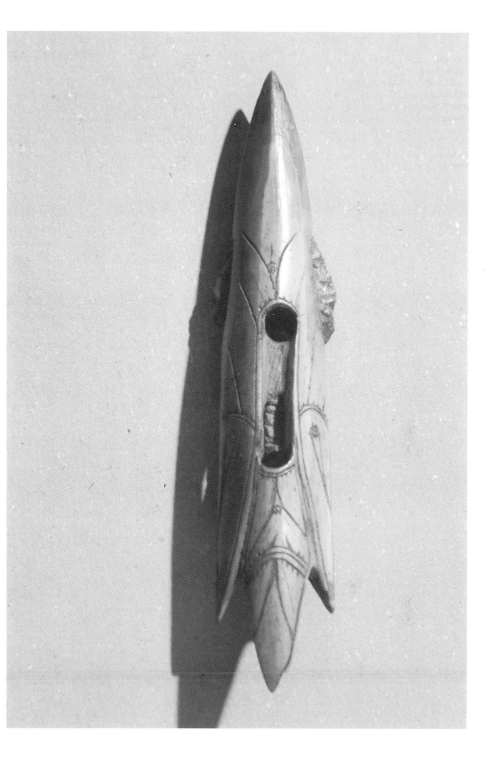

and the Aleut moved on to the chain of islands in Alaska that bears their name: the Aleutian Islands. The Eskimo moved to the north, gradually spreading eastwards along the shores of the Arctic Ocean and continuing as far as Greenland.

The Aleuts quickly established a specialized marine economy based on seal and walrus hunting, which involved the development of the toggle harpoon. This unique weapon, later taken up by the neighbouring western Eskimos, had a detachable head, with a spur that turned the point when it entered the quarry to form a 'toggle', preventing the point from being withdrawn. A tether line was attached to this, to which were fixed seal bladder floats designed to wear down the prey. Aleut culture shows influences from the Northwest Coast

Above: The ivory harpoon head shown in this photograph was made by the St. Lawrence Island Eskimo about 200AD, and has chipped chert blades inserted at the point.

Left: Drag handles were used by the Eskimo in manipulating the seal-bladder floats attached to harpoon lines. The one shown here represents a seal rising to the surface to breathe.

Far right: The Eskimo kayak was a very fast, streamlined hunting boat, used mainly in pursuing seals. Hunters strapped themselves into the boat, with a waterproof sealskin tied around their waists and fastened to the boat's superstructure. Should they capsize, the kayak could be quickly righted with a flip of the paddle and only the hunter's hands and face would become wet. A sealing harpoon with a detachable head attached to a long line is strapped to the deck of the kayak in this picture.

The seams of this Eskimo sealskin storage bag are ingeniously sewn and doubled to make them watertight for use during sea travel. The designs on it are appliquéd coloured sealskin.

in systems of rank and wealth used to validate prestige and status; but little is known about their social systems.

Russian dominance in the 18th century, when many Aleuts were enslaved, and the subsequent sale of Alaska to the United States meant that the indigenous culture was severely disrupted and soon suppressed. From the little we know, it is clear they were an innovative and original people who had the capacity for the independent invention of highly successful hunting systems, and we can only assume that their cultural institutions, their arts, and their social organization followed a similar pattern. The few Aleut artefacts in modern museum collections are distinguished by their sensitivity. Unfortunately, these peoples no longer exist as a tribal entity.

Eskimo culture has survived longer. The earliest settlements were relatively large tribal groupings showing clear Mongolian characteristics. All the evidence suggests that the Eskimos brought their culture with them and did not develop new traits in the Arctic; instead they elaborated existing institutions that had been developed elsewhere. The modern Eskimos of North America

and Greenland are culturally and physically closer to the tribes of Siberia than they are to the American Indians.

About 3,000 years ago the climate in the Arctic deteriorated, and the large tribal groupings broke up into the smaller bands of the historic period. Some of these people spent part of the year in snow houses called Igluviga, known to us as igloos, generally abandoning these in favour of driftwood houses, or karmats, in the summer months when warmer temperatures caused the snow igloos to melt. Others lived all year round in driftwood huts or in sealskin-covered lodges.

Their food supplies were almost entirely obtained from the sea. Fish were lured to holes cut through the ice, seal were speared at their breathing places. Open water fishing and hunting from kayaks, and later from the much bigger umiaks which could carry ten or fifteen people, secured larger sea mammals such as seals and walrus. Whales washed up on the beaches were a source of blubber, and provided bones from which many Eskimo artefacts were carved. Some groups even used whale ribs as the foundations for their driftwood houses, and among a few of the tribes, whale

This mask comes from southwestern Alaska and has the distorted eye and mouth shapes that indicate it represents a supernatural creature; but, since the spirit powers were personalized by the Eskimo and highly individual, it is not possible to identify the exact spirit being represented.

hunting was a regular economic activity. In the summer many Eskimos, particularly those located on the fringes of the area in tundra lands which they shared with the Athapascans, engaged in annual caribou hunts.

Perhaps the most fascinating thing about the Eskimo cultures is their ready adaptability to extremes. Arctic environments would not seem to attract people to live in them at any time of the year. Even summer does not release one from the essentially desperate condition of being surrounded by ice and snow. Vegetation is notable by its absence, animals are few and far between. The only thing the Arctic would appear to offer is unbounded space; but this is a space filled with nothing except frequent mists. The most characteristic aspect of the Arctic is icy winds, sweeping across snow flats and reducing visibility to a few hundred yards or less.

What, then, did the Eskimo find to attract him to this area? First, we must realize that the above description is a European one. It is the kind of comment we might expect from polar explorers, who carry their supplies with them and do not have to rely on the resources of the country. The Eskimo was well aware of the hazards he faced, yet he was also attuned to the riches of his land. Standing outside the igloo he could sniff the air and listen carefully, and know that a polar bear, the source of several days' food, prowled hungrily among the ice floes at some distance.

His husky team, given their heads, would quickly pick up the bear's scent and lead him unerringly to its presence. These same dogs could take him to the breathing holes that seals broke in the winter ice, but would baulk if he asked them to cross a frozen lake where the ice was beginning to melt and there was danger of breaking through. The rapport between the Eskimo and his dog team was perfect, although it was based on the need for survival rather than on any affection they may have shared. The lead dog, usually a female, had a fierce independence that matched the Eskimo's own. This mistress of the dog team kept the others in order, and where she led they followed.

For the Eskimo, the Arctic was a land whose resources only needed to be harvested, by those who were capable of finding them. Among the western groups, cold weather was a blessing, since at this time of year the sled runners moved swiftly over frozen ice and the tracks of animals were easy to follow. Many miles could be covered in a day at mid-winter, but this would be seriously reduced with the advent of warm weather when continual stops were necessary to carry the sledges over wet and thawing patches of tundra which impeded the progress of the dog team. The western Eskimo was a cold-weather person, looking forward to the freezing winter days rather than the onset of warmer conditions that made his life more difficult. Even the dance mask of Negafok, the Cold Weather Spirit, bears a sad expression because he must always leave the people when spring arrives.

To combat the extreme cold found along the edges of the Arctic Sea, the Eskimos manufactured sealskin and fur clothing designed to entrap maximum body heat. Double layers of thin clothing were worn, since these created air pockets and prevented body warmth from escaping. Boots, or mukluks, were made from the tough skin of the elk or caribou, and sewn so that stitches never penetrated the outer surface, where they would allow damp to enter. Their houses of ice blocks were relatively comfortable, constructed so that the cold from outside balanced the warmth of the seal oil lamps lit in the interior. As the ice on the inside melted, so the cold from outside froze it again into a solid barrier against the weather.

Entrances to these houses were below ground level, via a tunnel dug into the ice, and the doorways were protected by heavy curtains of sealskin or caribou which shut out the cold and freezing winds. Inside the igloo, sleeping platforms were arranged around the walls, generally about three feet above floor level, where damp could be avoided and the warmth of the seal oil lamp was most effective; but human body warmth was possibly the most immediate and natural way of alleviating cold. Eskimo peoples slept naked, the whole family gathered close together.

Hospitality demanded that a hunter who stayed as a guest in the igloo should remain warm and comfortable, and the logical consequence of this

During some Eskimo gatherings, women wore small finger masks such as those shown here, which would have been manipulated in accompaniment to dance performances. These ones are made from painted wood and caribou hair.

197

Long visored bentwood headgear can be immediately identified as Aleut. The example shown here was made in the 19th century, and carries long flowing streamers of sealion whisker.

was that he should share his bed with one of the women of the group. This custom has led to many early reports about the lack of morality in Eskimo life, since early White visitors and missionaries were usually offered a woman when it was time to retire. Their indignation was, however, an indication of their own moral viewpoint and their lack of understanding of Eskimo culture, since the invitation was not a sexual one, even though the Europeans may have interpreted it in this way.

On awakening, the first duty of the day was to rouse the huskies and throw them some frozen fish or seal blubber. Special attention might be paid to the team leader by giving her a little extra, but the idea of a more intimate relationship with the favourite dog by talking to her or patting her was completely alien. These dogs were wild, wolf-like creatures capable of chasing off a polar bear if it wandered too close to the encampment, and they served man of their own free will. If the human privilege of a secure food source was withdrawn, the husky was capable of surviving in the Arctic wilderness by means of its own resources.

Such toughness was a prerequisite for both man and animal. The Arctic is no place for weakness or for half-hearted measures; it is a country that

allows no compromise, where immediate decisions have to be made. This sometimes resulted in practices that seem particularly cruel to people accustomed to softer environments. Old people might be abandoned when they could no longer keep up with the movements of the group, since by slowing the majority down they forced everyone into a situation of potential starvation. Survival could only be assured if the people were able to travel rapidly and could exploit their resources to the full. Newborn children might be left behind and exposed on the ice if birth occurred while the group was in transit; there was simply no time to permit a leisurely birth or to slow the progress of the group. A weakened member of the community was a hazard to all.

Eskimo life was always lived on the very edge of survival, and there are many instances of entire groups being wiped out because the expected caribou or seal arrived a week or more later than the shamans had predicted. Although food could be stored, and underground caches of perishable meat were relatively easy in this frozen landscape – their presence was indicated by a marker so that any travellers could make use of them – the resources of the country were limited. It was

198

Dogs were of major importance to the Eskimos of the north, since they facilitated the movement of goods on sleds over ice or snow. They were also used in hunting and would protect a camp from intruders, whether human or animal. In extreme cases of hardship the dogs occasionally served as food; although this was resorted to reluctantly since it decreased the band's mobility. The sled being pulled by the dog team here is made from pieces of driftwood and bone, lashed together with sealskin ties, and has ivory runners that have been dipped in water to create a covering of ice to ensure they run smoothly. The driver of the team is wearing a pair of wooden snow goggles to reduce the glare of sunlight from snow as a precaution against snow blindness.

impossible to provide for extended periods during which the proceeds of the hunt were reduced. Even after European contact, it was not infrequent for delays in the arrival of supplies to result in the deaths of sizeable Eskimo communities which had planned their movements according to the predicted date when food would be available.

Yet in spite of these uncertainties, Eskimo culture flourished. When hunting had been successful and seal and walrus meat was abundant, or when a whale carcass washed up on the beach, the people would gather together for dancing and celebrations, and at such times the joy of the Eskimo was unequalled. They were a spontaneous people, much given to sudden outbursts either of happiness and laughter or of anger and sorrow. Like their environment, they vented their feelings fully, and their moods could shift dramatically in a short space of time.

A celebration might last for several weeks, until the supply of foodstuffs was nearly exhausted. After long periods of privation and desperation, they aimed to extract the maximum from a period of plenty. At this time, the men engaged in competitive sports – which continue today as the 'Eskimo Olympics' – where rivals would vie against each other to become the champion arm wrestler or ear puller.

These were spectator events, as much as competitions between individuals. In the ear pulling contests, which involved two contestants lashed together by a rawhide thong around the right ear, each attempting to pull the other off balance, the audience contributed the major part of the entertainment. Their shouts of encouragement, their songs and drumming, as well as the fact that people would suddenly jump up and give an exuberant and totally unselfconscious display of dancing, were far more impressive to European observers than the actual contest itself.

There were exhibitions of trampolining skills, when contestants attempted to jump higher than their rivals from a stretched platform of sealskin. This may have been a carry-over of an ancient hunting practice, where a team of hunters would throw one of their members high into the air in an attempt to spot distant game. There were also drumming contests in which teams from separate bands would attempt to out-drum their neighbours, and these had an almost magical effect. Drumming on tambourines, wooden hoops over which hide has been stretched, was very different from the kind of drumming experienced in the West. It had a high-pitched staccato note that has hypnotic, especially when performed in an enclosed space; listeners could be transported into a world that stemmed from the intangible control of the spirits rather than from the hands of the drummers.

Such sounds could only emanate from Thunder, Wind and Ice; they were harsh and discordant tones inspired by the mysterious forces that breathed life into them at the people's gatherings; yet at the same time they expressed the heartbeat of the Arctic. They contained an urgency that had to do with life and death, a message of survival emphasized by their own abruptness. They echoed the sudden changes that are a daily occurrence in this land of contrasts and extremes. Brought into the context of competitive social gatherings, these were factors the people could rationalize and come to terms with. The dances and competitions were, in a way, a means both of realizing the limitations and possibilities of human existence, and of finding methods whereby the spirit forces could be harnessed.

These forces were everywhere, yet they never formed a pantheon of gods, and the belief in specific powers varied widely from group to group and even between individuals. Many powers were connected with particular families, and would always care especially for their welfare; but there were also generalized spirits of the sky, stars, water, ice, and cold. Other figures are usually referred to as ghosts. These have no definite form or identity and would suddenly materialize out of the mist while hunters waited patiently at the seal breathing holes on the winter ice. All of them had animal equivalents and could be approached ritually through offerings and prayers. Small carvings might also be made in which the soul of the animal was released.

The Eskimo carver always felt that the ivory or driftwood he used contained an animal's soul as an inherent part of the material. He would study the unworked piece carefully, turning it over and looking for signs that told him which animal resided within it. Holding it to his ear, he listened carefully to the sounds it made as the wind passed across its contours. Hearing, perhaps more than sight, was an essential prerequisite for the Eskimo. Dense mists frequently blanketed his lands and the presence of animals or other people could often only be determined by listening. Whereas Europeans might say 'let's see if we can hear anything', the Eskimo would ask 'let's hear if we can see anything'.

If he could find no obvious animal power within the unworked material he held in his hands he would start to carve idly and without planning, until the animal source was unexpectedly disclosed. Then, by removing the absolute minimum of material, he would shape the piece to expose the likeness of the animal and thereby release its soul into the service of the people. Once this had been accomplished, the carving became valueless, since it was in the act of disclosure that its value lay. Archeologists and anthropologists working at Eskimo sites are frequently surprised to find numbers of intricately worked bone and wood carvings that appear to have been carelessly thrown away; but for the Eskimo these had already served their purpose. Having been carved, they were excess and unnecessary goods that did not need to be taken when the group moved to a new location.

Modern Eskimo carving, made purely for the tourist trade, lacks this spiritual quality. Much of it is very beautiful, and the carver's skill in cap-turing the sinuous movements of the seal in soapstone should certainly be admired and appreciated. They fully deserve their place in collections of modern artefacts, where they can compete very successfully with the artistic expressions of other peoples and where their high prices are fully

The lives of those people who inhabit the hostile environment of the far north of America are alleviated only a little by modern technological advances, such as motorized sleds and citizens' waveband radio.

justified; but they are not expressions of the release of spiritual power. If this had been the case, they would have been discarded when their function had been fulfilled in the carvings. For the majority of Eskimo people, the spirit forces were personalized. Perhaps the only power that came anywhere near being universal was Sedna, the Old-woman-who-lived-under-the-sea. She was immortal in her realm beneath the waves, where she controlled the movements and migrations of the sea mammals and fishes. If angered by the thoughtless act of a human being, she would whip the waves into a frenzy and send terrifying storms as a punishment.

Only a shaman, or angakok, had any influence over Sedna. He or she would go into a trance, when the soul left the body and travelled to Sedna's home for an audience with this Great Mother of all the sea creatures. They would speak together in the old languages of the Eskimo, which people no longer understood, and while the shaman's soul was in this underwater world, the house would fill with other spirits. People saw the ghosts of ancestors and of animals materialize in the half-light of the seal oil lamp. Some came to protect the shaman, others brought prophecies for the people. The ghosts of a family's ancestors advised them on domestic matters; those of the animals would tell them when the caribou herds would come or where shoals of fish might be found. All these powers spoke through the shaman in the old tongues, and their prophecies would be recited in songs when the angakok recovered from the trance.

Not all the prophecies were good ones, since the spirits could be both kind and cruel. They might warn of an impending disaster when starvation would stalk the camp and the people would die, but offer no hope or advice as to how this might be averted; yet at other times they would tell the people to move quickly to a new location where abundant food could be found. Their advice and warnings reflected life in the Arctic, since the possibility of an entire community dying if hunting had been poor was always high.

Some of these spiritual ancestors predicted the arrival of a strange race of people who would destroy the Eskimo with illnesses that ate at their bodies while they slept, as Sedna had gnawed at her parents' limbs to appease her prodigious appetite. Others said their children would be carried away to the spirit world, being returned to them later speaking strange languages and acting in a foolhardy manner.

These predictions came true with the arrival of Europeans. Their diseases had disastrous effects; entire communities died from influenza and the common cold. Even more serious was the European need to create administrative centres, where the welfare and education of the Eskimo could be coordinated. This prevented the groups from following their former nomadic life in which small

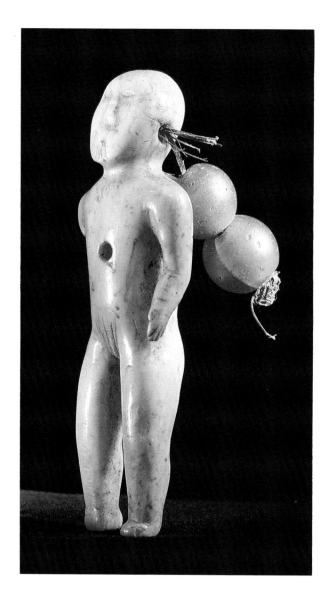

bands moved through areas of limited resources. If they did not pursue this wandering lifestyle, they were unable to obtain the provisions essential to survival, and many groups became totally dependent on imported foodstuffs almost overnight.

Modern Eskimo communities are larger than the traditional ones. They have schools and medical facilities, although these are fairly limited in some areas, and most families buy their food at supermarkets, live in well-insulated government issue frame houses, and travel on snowmobiles rather than on dog sledges. Hunting continues but does not constitute the major food source in any area, and the arts of the region are now almost all intended for the tourist market. Yet in spite of this, a very strong sense of national identity has evolved; replacing to a large extent the older family and band associations and creating a cohesive and unified political voice that speaks for all the Eskimo groups. Today the people of the Arctic think of themselves as the Inuit, an eastern Eskimo word meaning 'The People'.

MODERN INDIAN COMMUNITIES

By 'modern' Indian communities I refer to that period since control of their own affairs was taken out of Native hands up to the present day. Many comments have already been made about this in the various chapters on culture areas, since the dates at which outside interference in the politics and governments of the tribes began depend on their individual histories. Direct interference occurred earliest in the Southeast and on the border with Mexico, followed by California and the Southwest, under Spanish domination, and the Eastern Woodlands under the British and French. In the far north it has been relatively recent, except for Russian dominance in the Aleutians, and was again inspired principally by the British and French; while on the Plains under the Americans it goes back little more than 150 years.

All modern North American Indian communities now live under Canadian and American influences, but in general the Indians of Canada have been less affected by government legislation than those of the United States. This is not necessarily a reflection of more enlightened government policies, but is primarily the consequence of less competition for resources, the Canadian White population is about one-tenth of that of the United States, in a land mass that is greater. In both countries the Indians are very much a minority. They constitute about 5 per cent of Canada's total population and less than 1 per cent in the United States.

But they are a special minority, in that all these lands were originally theirs. Everyone else whether the descendant of a White settler who came voluntarily or of a Black slave who was forcibly shipped from Africa is a relative newcomer, whose roots lie outside the continent. Even the Eskimo, who are recent arrivals as far as the indigenous peoples are concerned, have been there for at least 5,000 years; while other groups can claim 30,000 years of habitation, and probably much more. When these time scales are considered, 500 years of European settlement since Columbus is very short indeed.

The wars prosecuted by the first Europeans were all directed by individuals rather than by

Old and new combine in contemporary North American Indian societies. The dancer shown here, photographed at a northern Plains Pow-Wow, wears an elaborate costume and traditional facepaint, but uses a portable cassette player to record drummers from a visiting tribe.

The old way of life of the Plains Indians was destroyed through the annihilation of the life-giving buffalo herds by White hunters and sportsmen. This engraving shows a train on the Kansas-Pacific Railroad, which has been brought to a halt so the passengers can enjoy a little diversion by shooting buffalo for fun. Instances like this were common occurrences. The carcasses of any animals they killed were simply left to rot, and wounded animals frequently escaped to suffer a long and painful death from the infection of their wounds.

ARCTIC OCEAN

• Western Inuit (Eskimo)

• Eskimo

• Athapascan

• Eastern Inuit (Eskimo)

• Tlingit

PACIFIC
OCEAN

• Haida
• Tsimshian

• Kwakiutl
• Nootka
• Coast Salish

• Blackfoot
• Nez Percé

• Cree

• Chippewa

• Crow • Sioux
• Arapaho
• Shoshone

• Klamath
• Modoc
Hupa •

• Sauk and Fox

• Iroquois
• Algonkin

INDIAN TERRITORY

Osage	Choctaw
Kaw	Pawnee
Oto	Kickapoo
Ponca	Iowa
Cheyenne	Modoc
Arapaho	Miami
Caddo	Ottawa
Delaware	Quapaw
Wichita	Peoria
Kiowa	Seneca
Comanche	Shawnee
Apache	Wyandot
Chickasaw	Sauk and Fox
Cherokee	Seminole
Creek	Potawatomi

• Ute
• Paiute

• Navajo

Mission •
• • Pima • Pueblo
Yuma • Papago
• Apache

INDIAN TERRITORY
(OKLAHOMA)

ATLANTIC
OCEAN

• Choctaw
• Creek

• Seminole

GULF OF MEXICO

Map showing the modern
locations of the major tribal
groups in North America.

governments. When the Spanish conquistadores claimed land in the name of the king, they were in reality claiming title for themselves. The French sought personal wealth in their territorial gains, as did the English colonists. Few of these people can be thought of as patriots; many were refugees from religious persecution in their own countries, or poor people who hoped to find success through a new beginning in the New World. In their

attempts to remove the Indians by paying scalp bounties, that encouraged wholesale slaughter, the colonies paid these monies from their own coffers and not from the resources of their distant homelands. They made their own laws, elected their own leaders, and usually ignored directives emanating from the countries they had left.

There was never any concerted Indian policy among these various groups. The Indians were

206

Navajo jewellers have gained an enviable, but well-justified, reputation for the fine quality of their silverwork. Although many now use modern production methods and tools, each item is still hand-crafted and bears the individual mark of its maker. Designs and patterns employed on the finished work have remained consistent since the Navajo first learned silverworking from the Spanish; but they have an even longer history than this, since they derive from ancient symbols that were formerly expressed using different media.

After tribes were placed on reservations there were increasing calls for them to be educated into the White system, and children were often forcibly removed from their families and made to attend schools that might be hundreds of miles from their homes. The first non-Reservation school was Carlisle Indian School, in Pennsylvania, which opened on 24 May, 1890. This illustration shows a group of Apache boys and girls after one year's attendance at Carlisle.

simply used when it was expedient, forced out when they were in the way, and killed if they refused to go or became a nuisance that hindered the progress of so-called civilization. Some enlightened individuals worked for the Indians' benefit and sought reforms on their behalf, but such people were few and their successes fewer still. Even when they were successful in their efforts, as the friar Las Casas was in persuading the Spanish government that the Indians had souls and could not be used as beasts of burden, local leaders and tyrants generally had their way. Las Casas' 'gentle Indians' were usually offered conversion as a means of saving their souls while the Spanish chopped off their hands and feet, and consigned any recalcitrant Indians to the bonfire.

The first formal documents concerning travel rights were treaty agreements made with sovereign Indian nations by the arriving colonists and then by the British government in Canada and the American government in the United States. An essential aspect of these treaties is that they were made between nations who considered themselves as equals. The Indians did not defer to superior force nor did the agreements require them to give up their lands or their hunting and fishing rights. They were simply a means whereby they allowed the use of part of their land, or guaranteed rights of travel across it, in return for various concessions made by the other party.

Fewer treaties were made in Canada than in the United States and many of the Canadian ones remain in force. Although the Canadian treaties are early ones, made with the British authorities, they are increasingly being called into question in the modern world. Mineral and timber rights are sought by large corporations, as other resources are exploited, and the energy companies are attempting to gain permission to flood large tribal areas, in order to generate hydro-electric power. In the far north, where no treaties were made, Canadian, U.S. and NATO military needs have claimed tribal lands. Low-level cold weather flight trials by the combined air forces have had a serious effect on the caribou migration routes, which

have also been disrupted by major projects like the Alaska pipeline.

Though the tourist industry provides employment for some Indians as guides, it has meant that certain Indian areas have been redesignated as National Parks and removed further from Native control. Sports hunters, too, are having a very damaging effect in wilderness areas that are still traditional hunting grounds. For many Canadian tribes, the absence of treaties has made it increasingly difficult for them to establish Native claims, since they must first prove they have an 'aboriginal occupancy' of the area. This is particularly difficult for nomadic tribes, who tend to move regularly within large areas, but it also affects village groups, and is complicated further by the need to define who is actually an Indian and entitled to make a claim.

Mixed marriages mean there are many people who have some Indian blood but who may not be registered on tribal rolls. There is also a complex law of Indian Status, which causes confusion even today. In this the children of an Indian father and White mother are Indian whereas those of a White father and Indian mother are White. This not only conflicts with the way descent is reckoned among tribes who have matriarchal systems, but creates an anomalous situation: children born to full-blood Indian parents who have divorced before they reached the age of majority, where the mother has then married a White man could be classed as White; whereas those of White parents where the mother has remarried an Indian could be registered as Indian.

Another complicating factor is that until the early 1980s most Canadian Indians considered themselves to be bound by agreements made with the British Crown. Canadian authorities were

believed to administer Indian affairs on behalf of the United Kingdom. The repatriation of the Canadian Constitution in 1981, however, absolved the British parliament from any further responsibility. This angered the Indian groups, who were not consulted and whose rights were not enshrined in the draft of the new Constitution. They have now been written in, yet many Indians feel this has been done merely as lip-service to their protests and that its provisions are hopelessly inadequate.

The situation in the United States is different, creating problems for tribes such as the Blackfeet, Coast Salish and Chippewa whose traditional lands cross the Canadian/U.S. border. For most

Modern artefacts often use traditional skills in new ways. The Eastern Woodland pouch at top is made as a small purse or wallet, and employs floral patterns that were already in use at least 200 years ago. The knitted sweater is Cowichan, a Coast Salish group on Vancouver Island, and depicts the killer whale in a manner that is strikingly similar to that on early Chilkat woven blankets. The knitting technique, however, was introduced by Scottish immigrants.

tribes in the United States, the early treaties were abrogated as European populations increased and expanded. New agreements were sought by the settlers that actually ceded land, and were less favourable to the indigenous groups. Many tribes did not accept the new treaties willingly, and a number were obtained by clearly fraudulent means. Even when agreements could be made that the Indians accepted, Congress often failed to ratify them, on the grounds that they contained too many concessions.

To deal with this situation, which was not only a difficult one to resolve but was also the direct cause of many armed conflicts, Congress passed

the Indian Removal Act in 1830. This authorized the states to remove tribes to Indian Territory (later to be incorporated as the state of Oklahoma), a vast land across the Mississippi that was beyond the permanent Indian frontier and reserved in perpetuity for the exclusive use of the Native populations. Here, in harsh lands that the settlers did not want, they were supposed to eke out a meagre living unmolested by Whites.

Indian Territory was originally reserved for the Creek, Cherokee, Choctaw, Chickasaw and Seminole, with a small portion of its northeastern corner set aside for groups such as the Quapaw. With time more tribes were removed beyond this Indian frontier, and the lands occupied by the original 'Five Civilized Tribes' dwindled to a fraction of their former extent. Over the next 35 years a series of treaties were made with various tribes in which the U.S. government gave guarantees that the Indians could reside permanently in Indian Territory, or which permitted them to occupy small portions of their homelands in return for ceding the rest.

These treaties were established by Acts of Congress and negotiated by a treaty commission appointed by central government. In return for ceding millions of acres of land to the United States, the Indians received assurances that the country they continued to occupy would be protected from White encroachment. They would be permitted to hunt and govern themselves, but at the same time would receive government aid in goods, tools, provisions, and annuities, together with schools and medical facilities if they required them.

A government body known as the Bureau of Indian Affairs, which was originally part of the War Department, was set up to represent Indian concerns in Washington, and to ensure that treaty commitments were met. They appointed agents who would act as local officers and reside on the reservations, where they were to oversee the education and welfare of the Indians and to distribute treaty goods and annuities. The system was corrupt, however, and many of the treaty provisions were simply ignored when it was convenient to do so. Agents were usually either religious fanatics who interpreted their duty as a crusade to convert and save the heathens, or rogues and scoundrels who appropriated funds intended for the tribes.

The few honest agents who made real efforts to improve conditions on the reservations soon found themselves up against protests from local White communities, who thought the Indians still had too much land that was not being used productively, and mounted campaigns to open the reserves to White farmers and stock-raisers. Protests to central government from powerful farmers and ranchers about the 'incompetence' of honest agents, expressing fears that the agents 'were inciting the Indians' and 'letting the Indians run the agency' usually led to their dismissal and replacement by agents whom the White communities felt were more satisfactory.

Conditions on the reservations were often intolerable. Promised supplies and annuities failed to get through on time, and when they finally arrived

Many modern Indians of the Southwest and Plains feel a natural affinity for animals, and use this actively in seeking employment as cowboys on the ranches of the area. The man shown here wears the contemporary cowboy garb of denim jacket, chaps and boots, but expresses his Indian identity through wearing his hair long, by the beaded pendant around his neck, and, most importantly, through the eagle feather attached to the headband of his hat.

The pick-up truck is the present-day equivalent of the old-time horse-drawn travois, and is commonly seen at modern Pow-Wows. It has been used here to transport this Blackfoot painted tipi, which bears symbolic designs that have been passed down through generations.

they were a fraction of what they should have been. 'Indian Rings' in Washington bought second-rate goods at premium prices through their own business contacts, so the Indians received half-starved cows instead of prime beef, or consignments of pork and flour that had been condemned. Health facilities were virtually non-existent. Sickness was never far away, and the death rate among reservation Indians was phenomenally high.

The policy of educating the Indians by sending their children away to schools provoked resentment and anger. Children were forcibly removed from their families and sent far away to a school at which they were forbidden to speak their own language, where their hair was cut short to make them more like White people, and at which severe punishments including chaining and forced labour were employed as discipline for minor infringements of the rules.

Under such circumstances the demoralized

tribes were unable to prevent illegal settlement of Indian lands. If they protested, they were 'trouble-makers', and in any case they had no recourse to legal jurisdiction since they were considered to be 'wards' of the government. The U.S. troops stationed locally for Indian protection were generally mobilized in response to Indian protests when the agents felt their lives were threatened, but there are few instances in which the troops forced illegal settlers off the reservation lands.

The reservations were further diminished by the Railroad Enabling Act of 1866, which gave a strip of land 40 miles wide on either side of the track to the railroad crews, as an incentive to obtain workers. When the tracks crossed Indian country, considered to be public lands, they received no compensation. Just two years later, in 1868, the Fourteenth Amendment granted equal rights and the freedom to practice their own religions to all citizens of the United States, but the original occupants of the country were denied these benefits since they were not citizens.

Railroads brought more White people into the tribal areas, and increased pressure for Indian lands to be further reduced. This proved difficult under existing treaty agreements, which generally required the consent of three-fourths of the adult male population before additional lands could be ceded. Treaty commissioners regularly 'invented' Indians to obtain the requisite numbers of signatories, and there are even incidents when Indian boys of four or five years old were asked to put their mark on the White man's papers in return for sticks of candy. Some muted cries of protest in Washington at this underhand use of the commissioners' powers resulted in the Indian Appropriations Act of 1871. Treaties were replaced by less formal agreements under which reservation lands could be increased or diminished by executive order of the President.

Presidential orders proved slow and cumbersome, and fears were expressed that the Indians could never become 'civilized' while they continued to occupy reservations that promoted tribal unity. The Dawes Act of 1887 was intended to bring the tribes into the mainstream of American life. Also known as the Allotment Act, this broke up the reservations and allotted homesteads to individual families. Any surplus lands were to be opened for White settlement. Of 150 million acres that were allotted, 90 million were deemed surplus to Indian requirements. The original family allotments extended from 10 to 140 acres, but these, especially for Indians who depended on a hunting economy, were far too small to provide sufficiently for their family needs. Many Indians were forced into a situation where they needed to realize immediate cash to prevent starvation. Others simply gave up and sold their allotments to

White settlers. Among some tribes the greater part of their reservation lands were signed away to White Settlers in this manner.

Indian Territory was seriously affected by the Dawes Act, and as the flood of westward expansion increased, so the permanent frontier receded until finally the Oklahoma land rush opened the area to any settler who could stake a claim. The land rush was a free-for-all. Would-be settlers raced into Oklahoma with their covered wagons and mule teams to set up wooden posts around the land they claimed for their own. In this headlong dash any rights granted to the Indians were ignored; most of the settlers did not even know they were entering country that had been assigned to the Indians 'forever'. These White settlers are

Above: Although this Northwest Coast silkscreen print by Robert Davidson uses a recently introduced medium, the forms employed in the depiction of the frog are identical to those of flat-surface paintings on house fronts seen by the earliest explorers.

Left: American Indian dances of today continue to feature elements that were familiar in the past. This modern dance hoop is made from red trade cloth, skin wrappings, and hawk feathers.

Pow-Wows, or modern dance gatherings, are great inter-tribal social events that attract people from a wide area. The Pawnee boy in this picture was photographed in Montana in 1984, many miles from his Oklahoma home. His beadwork costume depicts the American flag, but his facepaint is traditionally Pawnee.

known as Sooners, since in an attempt to claim the best lands for themselves many of them began the land rush 'sooner' than they should have done; before the lands were officially opened for homesteading. The Indian Reorganization Act of 1934 ended the allotting of tribal lands, and in 1947 an Indian Claims Commission was established to investigate fraudulent treaties and to settle any unpaid treaty claims. More than 800 claims were filed which the Commission started to deal with at the rate of roughly 10 per year, finding in the Indians' favour in about a fifth of the cases they considered. Reorganization did, however, bring some benefits to the tribes. Health and educational facilities were improved, tribal constitutions were adopted, and loan funds were made available for community purposes. The Indians began to recover their numbers and form stronger

economies, and there was a resurgence in Native arts for the tourist trade.

In 1924 all Indians had officially became citizens of the United States; in 1950 Senator Joseph McCarthy used this as justification for the removal of 'favoured status' for Native communities. The loan programme was terminated and new policies to reduce reservations and remove federal protection and services from the tribes were instituted. Indians were encouraged to leave the reservations and move into the cities, where they were promised better health care, better education, better salaries and better housing. Instead, they found themselves alienated from their own people and subject to discrimination in the towns. McCarthyism created ghettoes of urban Indians.

These policies were vigorously pursued

Both Indians and Eskimos have always accepted change, even though in some respects this has not been to their advantage. This Eskimo man is using a snowmobile to transport goods purchased from a store. His snowmobile makes travel easier and faster than with a dog team and sled, and he is able to carry far more weight than was previously possible. However, he is unable to use his modern machinery for hunting, since the noise of its engine will frighten game away before he even sights it. His snowmobile is also unable to follow an animal's scent or to stop instinctively if he attempts to cross thin ice. Perhaps most importantly, his dog team was never subject to mechanical failure. Although modern Eskimos in remote areas maintain contact via Citizen Band radios, a breakdown at any distance from the village is a matter for very serious concern; without immediate assistance, being stranded in the Arctic will soon result in frostbite or hypothermia.

Right: Many old beliefs are expressed in contemporary Indian work, as in these turtle earclips made by the Hopi Indians of the Southwest. The turtle is an ancient symbol of power, and has its origin in the attributes of the mythological twins.

Far right: The netted hoop is known as a Dream Catcher, and acts as a charm through which the web of life woven by Spider Woman can be turned to the advantage of the people. As long as this web remains unbroken, dreams and visions can be brought to bear on the problems and difficulties of survival in a modern world. This recent hoop has been tied with black horsehair, and has beadwork patterns that identifiy it as Comanche.

throughout the 1950s, until eventually, in 1960, the University of Chicago initiated a new policy-making body for Indian affairs: the National Congress of American Indians. For the first time, Indian people were asked to take part, and their views as to what was needed were actively canvassed. Other Pan-Indian movements were also making themselves felt, and forming pressure groups that demanded radical reforms. None of these groups was truly Pan-Indian, in that it ever represented all the tribes; they were, nevertheless, a powerful influence for change.

The main obstacle to creating a unified Pan-Indian movement came from the tribes themselves. They had always thought of themselves as autonomous and independent. Their languages, cultures, and economies were widely divergent, and the needs of any particular group might be totally different from those of another. Although they shared a common heritage, all Indians thought in terms of a tribal identity first: someone was a Haida, a Sioux, a Pawnee, or a Hopi before ever considering the problem of a national identity. Even so, Pan-Indian movements stirred a new awareness in Red Pride and Red Power, and provided the incentive for Indians to start thinking

of themselves collectively as Native Americans. Finally, in 1968, Indian rights were enshrined in the Civil Rights Bill.

With the resurgence in Indian pride, modern communities began to assert themselves more forcibly and started to establish their own education and welfare programmes, using tribal funds realized through such things as the leasing of mineral or timber rights. It was an uneven development, since some tribes had healthy incomes from leases for such things as oil drilling and from lead and zinc mining, whereas others lived on lands that yielded virtually no return. For most, however, the need to administer funds at a tribal level caused political reorganization, the establishment of elected councils, and the formation of constitutions and charters of incorporation.

Changes have been rapid, and Indian communities today are often struggling to hold on to what traditions are left. In some cases a great deal has been retained, as among the Pueblo people of the Southwest, but in others there are too few Indians who remember the old beliefs and ideals. Looking back at the recent past, the modern Native American experiences shock and sadness at what has occurred. More than 75 per cent of the original inhabitants of North America were killed, most by diseases introduced by Europeans sometimes accidentally, often deliberately. Of more than 500 languages and dialects spoken in aboriginal North America, perhaps 50 survive. Some are still widely used, Blackfoot and Apache for instance are spoken by about 95 per cent of the population, but others are on the verge of extinction. Many old rituals and ceremonies are forgotten or obsolete. Over half the modern Indians live in cities, returning to the reservations for major gatherings but no longer part of the day-to-day life of the community.

Yet, surprisingly, beneath all this there is a strength and pride that is undaunted and untainted. Young people are returning to the reserves and asking the Elders to teach them the ancient ways before they are completely lost. Tribal councils are putting aside funds for Museums and Resource Centres, through which the myths and stories can be preserved, and which will form a repository of knowledge for the future, even though the money is desperately needed elsewhere. Families are financing their children through law schools, so they can continue the fight to maintain their lands and beliefs by challenging the treaty provisions in the courts.

The old and the new coexist, but the Indian has always been open to change and does not see this as a threat. Modern poetry and literature are powerful forces that encompass the old ways in a new medium. Tourist artefacts, though made for commercial sale and adjusted to a White market, still possess colours and patterns that have their origin in a distant past. The pick-up trucks, blue jeans, and cowboy hats of contemporary Indians are merely surface differences. They do not change the people's way of thinking. Anger, even fury, is still there, directed against the wrongs of the past and the misguided policies of the present, and demanding just retribution; but to the White visitor who has any sympathy and understanding, who visits their reserves and homelands from a genuine desire to learn, the Indian is open, friendly and generous, and maintains a powerful hold on the values that have been handed down by the ancestors. Modern Indians are not a defeated people; they are proud survivors who look forward to building a stronger future.

Such attitudes are honest and dignified, worthy of respect; and this, really, is all that the Indian demands. Common courtesy dictates that when travelling on a reservation, one goes as a guest. The Indians own the land; it belongs to them, and they have a deep reverence for it. The tourist who drops litter and talks loudly is abusing the spirit inherent in the land; disturbing the ancient rhythms and harmonies it contains, which continue to exert their influence on those who are sensitive enough to hear them. Indian advice to the tourist is summed up by a notice on the Navajo reservation: 'Leave only footprints; take only photographs'.

This Kwakiutl trade canoe, photographed by Edward Curtis, is bearing visitors to a Northwest Coast potlatch. They will make a ceremonial approach to the village beach, during which the costumed dancer in the prow of the boat exhibits the privileges claimed by his clan group.

221